THE INDIVIDUAL AND SOCIETY

A MARXIST APPROACH TO HUMAN PSYCHOLOGY

John Robinson

Index Academic

London

Published by Index Academic Books (Indexreach) Ltd.
28 Charlotte Streeet, London W1P 1HJ

Typeset by Sumner Type, London
Printed by Trade Union Printing Services, Newcastle-on-Tyne

British Library Cataloguing in Publication Data

Robinison, John
Individual and Society: Marxist Approach
to Human Psychology
I. Title
155.9

ISBN 1-871518-06-7

CONTENTS

Once a London firefighter, **John Robinson** read psychology at Trinity College, Dublin, where he also obtained his master's degree and a doctorate. For sixteen years he lectured at the North East London Polytechnic, now the University of East London. Here he ran a course, in conjunction with the local Health Authority, for psychiatrists-in-training. He now practises psychotherapy in south London.

FOREWORD

**By John Radford, Emeritus Professor of Psychology,
University of East London**

John Robinson has done me the honour of asking me to write a foreword to this book, and I am glad to do so. First, of course, because he is an old friend and a former valued colleague at what was, during most of our time there, the North East London Polytechnic (previously West Ham College of Technology and now the University of East London).

Second, because I feel strongly that the book deserves to be published and read. My own small experience as an author suggests that anyone who publishes a book must expect to be both praised and blamed, both justly and unjustly. But perhaps any of these combinations is preferable to being ignored. John Robinson's book is written explicitly from a particular viewpoint, the Marxist one, and will certainly be of great interest to those who share this viewpoint. It would be a pity if it did not reach others also. There are several reasons why different groups might think, wrongly, that the book has nothing to offer them.

The most obvious, perhaps, is the collapse of the 'communist' powers — I use quotes advisedly. As John Robinson points out at the start, the political systems that have disintegrated had little to do with the ideas of Marx. In fact they must have obscured the general understanding of those ideas. But the political changes have probably, and almost paradoxically, made it yet more difficult to see Marx clearly.

Then there is the relative unwillingness of scientists, which psychologists I fear share to some extent, to question the bases of their science. I think it is reasonable to claim that psychologists are more aware of fundamental theoretical issues than some other scientists. At least, these issues routinely figure in examination syllabuses and general textbooks, which is not always true for other sciences. But at the same time psychology, as practised and taught, does tend at any one period to be cast in a particular mode. As John Robinson points out, the dominant (though not the only) mode for the past two or three decades has been the 'cognitive' one. I will not summarise his critique of it; but I am in no doubt that a critique of prevailing ideas is valuable in itself, if only to remind us not to accept fashion as though it were immutable.

A third reason is what appears to be a growing trend away from the scientific analysis of human behaviour, associated with the loose grouping of ideas known as 'New Age'. Studies I have made of student attitudes suggest that of those who choose psychology, relatively few are interested in it 'as a science', which is probably what their teachers regard as its greatest value. They also tend not to think it of very great relevance to their own lives. John Robinson's answer is that it should be, not if it were less of a science but if it were a science based on the right premises.

Thus I hope that potential readers, studying or interested in human behaviour, will not dismiss the book out of hand. No doubt more thoughtful critics will find much that can be legitimately questioned. I myself by no means agree with everything John Robinson says; but this is not the place to detail any contrary views I may have.

John Robinson is to a certain extent dismissive of the achievements of psychology. I am much less so, but I certainly do think that less has been accomplished than ought to be possible. And the progress of psychology has often seemed to resemble that of a yacht heading into the wind: it is done by tacking, each tack almost at right angles to the desired direction and followed by an about turn — the introspective tack, the behaviourist, the cognitive and so on. Nevertheless there is movement forward, if slow, uncertain and difficult. But of course psychology is not just one yacht but a whole flotilla. John Robinson sets a course rather different, as far as I know, to that of any other skipper afloat at present.

At the same time there are quite strong indications that others are turning in a similar, though not identical, direction. There has been for some time a growing interest in the rediscovered ideas of the pioneering Russian psychologist Lev Vygotsky, which has intermingled with the growth of a new kind of cultural psychology. As with tacking, to continue the metaphor, one repasses old landmarks; there are more than echoes of Frederick Bartlett and even Wilhelm Wundt. It may be remembered that the founder of the first psychological laboratory (traditionally dated to 1879) also asserted: 'All phenomena with which mental sciences deal are, indeed, creations of the social community.' John Robinson would surely agree. But there is, I believe, progress: Wundt's claim was supported mainly by descriptive and anecdotal anthropology, a much less firm basis than more recent and controlled studies.

It is extraordinary, to my mind, that there are still some writers who can blithely declare that social, cultural, historical factors are not the province of psychology. To begin with, territoriality of this kind is surely quite inappropriate for science, which cannot progress if it erects barriers between areas of investigation. Then I would argue (and have done so at length elsewhere) that all the sciences that seek to understand human behaviour — history, anthropology, psychology and so on — must in principle be co-extensive: there is no sense in which any aspect of behaviour or its context can be ruled out as irrelevant. An ideal psychology is impossible: no-one could know it all, not merely because there is already too much, but because it keeps on changing. Human society and human behaviour do not stand still, and they change partly because of the very fact that they are systematically investigated — by us human beings ourselves. I would go on to argue that although we can never achieve complete understanding, we are not likely to make very much progress at all if we do not start from the basis that the very concept of behaviour is relative, not absolute. By this I mean not only that what we recognise as human is self-created, culturally and historically; but that any description of it can only be in terms of human norms. I do not see, for example, in what sense one can describe a person as intelligent, or proud, or skilled, except in comparison with others. There is no absolute 'intelligence' that remains constant over time, independent of human beings.

Here, I think, I come quite close to John Robinson's position, and thus I am in a sense arguing for at least some aspects of Marx's theorising. John Robinson would claim, indeed does claim, that Marxism is not just one more, if superior, plan for making scientific progress, but the only one that offers any hope of success. No doubt time will tell, for if the claim is true then historical necessity will bring it about.

To end with a different sporting metaphor, when John and I were in the same Department of Psychology, one of the chores he kindly and ably carried out was organising what I christened 'The Hobby-Horse Derby'. The idea was to get individuals — staff, students or visitors — to talk about a pet enthusiasm, related in some way to psychology. It never quite worked out as I planned it, but we had some interesting sessions. I'm not quite sure that one or two of the early ideas for this book may not have originated there. The book we now have is entered in the real-life race of published work. It may not win, but there should be a fascinating contest.

London, June 1992

1

INTRODUCTION

This book has been written primarily for the large number of people who have looked to modern academic psychology for answers to basic questions about human behaviour and thinking but who have been unable to obtain any real satisfaction.

Why is it that every so often literally millions of human beings show themselves capable of killing and maiming others during wars? Can a scientific understanding of human beings lead to an eventual end to greed, cruelty, indifference to the welfare of others and other psychological characteristics which at least most of us would like to see eliminated? What is human nature and to what extent can it be changed? In attempts to obtain at least partial answers to these sort of questions many people have looked to academic psychology only to turn away disappointed.

The reason for their disappointment is not to be found in any lack of psychological publications. It is estimated that in Britain and the U.S.A. about 20,000 books and scientific papers are published annually.[1] Academic psychology has in fact undergone an unparalleled expansion since the second world war. There is no doubt that modern academic psychology has made positive advances in a number of fields. It has given us a certain amount of knowledge of perceptual processes. It has also given us techniques which can assist our memories. Extensive studies have been carried out on the psychological development of children. Psychological tests have been devised which can be used to detect brain damage. A number of other examples could be given. Yet in contrast to the development, during recent decades, of other aspects of science such as electronics and biotechnology, the positive results of modern academic psychology, despite an enormous output of publications, seem very meagre indeed.

It is clear that what is lacking today is a set of clear-cut principles by means of which adult and adolescent men and women can at least begin to understand the everyday behaviour and thinking both of themselves and others.

It is the aim of this book to challenge, from a Marxist standpoint, the basic theoretical assumptions, both explicit and implicit, of modern academic psychology. Furthermore, the view will be expressed that an understanding of the false nature of the assumptions now underlying psychology can lead to a significant development of knowledge of the fundamental principles underlying the behaviour and thinking of individuals.

The term 'academic psychology' used in this book refers primarily to Anglo-American academic psychology. It does not refer to the psychology studied in countries such as France, where it is often consciously associated with philosophical standpoints. Neither, of course, does it refer to the numerous and proliferating psychological 'cults' to be found especially on the American West Coast. However, since the trends just mentioned tend to share the same basic theoretical assumptions as do Anglo-American academics, criticisms of the latter are, ipso facto, essentially criticisms of the former.

Brief mention needs to be made of psychology in the former Soviet Union, which in recent years has tended to recover from the several decades of rigid Pavlovian orthodoxy imposed upon it by the Stalinist bureaucracy. It is difficult to give a brief and concise account of its present state, beyond noting that it contains a number of contradictory features. On the one hand there is considerable Western influence, manifested in a widespread interest in the computer simulation of cognitive processes. On the other there exists a definite Marxist-oriented trend, probably constituting a minority, whose work has been highlighted by the use of Marxist theoretical principles to train blind deaf-mutes.[2] The same criticisms that can be made of Anglo-American academic psychology can therefore be made of the majority of psychologists in the Soviet Union.

The term 'Marxist' used in this book requires explanation.[3]

It is used primarily to denote Marx's conception of what is commonly described as 'human nature'. Contrary to common belief, the most significant aspects of Marx's theoretical works, including his major work *Capital*, are concerned with the elaboration of a scientific analysis of human society and of humanity and are of great relevance to the question of the nature of individual human beings. To put it very briefly, Marx postulated that the human race was a part of nature that obtained its natural needs such as food and shelter from the rest of nature through the making and use of tools, that is through production. In the process of production, human individuals had to enter into definite, objective relations with one another. These are known as the relations of production, examples of which are slave/slaveowner, feudal lord/serf and wage worker/capitalist. Since human individuals cannot engage in religious, political, artistic, sporting or other cultural activities unless they are first of all fed, clothed and housed and since food, clothing and houses have to be created by the processes of production, it follows that the decisive social relationships of any form of human society must be the relations of production upon which, indirectly but ultimately, all other social relations such as those of the family, together with political, religious and other cultural institutions, must depend. Human beings, therefore, have to possess the ability to learn both to take part directly in the processes of production and to enter into historically developed relations of production.

Although a more extensive account of the Marxist view of humanity will be given in the next chapter, enough has been said in the past few lines to indicate that Marx had a definite and unambiguous view of 'human nature'. Humanity's survival as a species depends first and foremost on the development of the process of production and it is here, and in the social relations that ensue therefrom, that the secret of 'human nature' is to be found. Furthermore, without an understanding of this 'human nature' there can be no true understanding of human individuals, that is of the fundamental principles of human behaviour and thinking. This is a point that will be argued further in ensuing chapters.

The need for an understanding of 'human nature' which can lead to an understanding of human individuals is a need not only felt by Marxists. Indeed, one of the best known theorists of contemporary academic psychology, Ulrich Neisser, who has undoubtedly made a considerable contribution in his chosen field, writes unequivocally:

> Because psychology is about people, it cannot shirk the responsibility of dealing with *fundamental* questions about human nature.[4]

Unfortunately, Neisser's plea appears mainly to have fallen upon deaf ears. The great majority of academic psychologists, instead of striving to understand what the term 'human nature' implies, restrict their research to specialist topics such as memory, perception, attention and the acquisition of language. Their position is summed up by the authors of a popular textbook, who state with obvious approval that:

> We could with some justification characterise present-day psychology as a collection of specialisms united only in their (empirical) methods.[5]

There have of course been theories of human nature in psychology, psychoanalysis[6] and behaviourism[7] being the best known. However, the majority of academic psychologists would now reject the basic assumptions of these two theories. Other theories, often referred to as personality theories, have made little impact on academic psychology as a whole.[8]

It is clear that any personality theory must reflect, explicitly or implicitly, a definite viewpoint about human nature. In other words, every personality theorist, whether he or she is conscious of it or not, takes as a starting point a definite set of theoretical presuppositions about the human race as a whole. This must imply that, if a personality theorist's views of human nature are false then his or her theory of personality will not correctly reflect the thinking and behaviour of individuals, or at least will reflect them only one-sidedly.

This book is written on the basis of the premise that only a Marxist view of human nature and the human race can provide an adequate starting point for a genuinely scientific theory of personality embodying the basic principles of behaviour and thinking, that is principles which can at least begin to give us an understanding of what a French writer describes as: 'What a man makes of his life and what life makes of him.'[9]

Modern academic psychology takes as one of its basic premises that the psychology of individuals is a subject to be studied by the methods of the natural sciences. It is assumed that since the human individual is a biological organism psychologists should use methods of investigation analogous to those used, at least for many years, by biologists. Thus it is stated in a popular textbook that: 'psychology has its roots in biology.'[10] An analogous assumption of at least a substantial proportion of modern psychologists is that human individuals can be regarded as machines. In another textbook the statement is found that 'the methods and model building activities of . . . psychologists subscribe to the "man is a machine" view.'[11]

The 'mechanical' outlook of modern psychology can be said to originate in the development of natural science during and immediately following the Renaissance. The most important aspect of the new science was the development of mechanics. Machines were seen as objects which interacted with other aspects of the material world, the form of their interaction being determined by their internal structure. Owing to the influence of mechanics other branches of the natural sciences adopted a mechanical approach to their subject matter. In biology, for example, where the first task was that of classification, animals and plants were classified according to their internal structure, which was seen as being directly responsible for their function. According to the mechanical viewpoint, we breathe because of the structure of the lungs and see because of the structure of the eyes. It would be true to say that today the mechanical approach has to a large extent disappeared from natural science, especially in physics and biology. Biologists now study organisms both in terms of the evolutionary development of their species and as integral parts of ecological habitats. However, modern psychology still clings tenaciously to this outmoded outlook, with consequences that can only be described as disastrous. Under its influence, psychology can only be 'a collection of specialisms', unable to work out a genuinely scientific theory of personality or of human nature.

The 'biological machine' approach of modern psychology must lead to the conclusion that human society is no more than a collection of individuals, each interacting with other biological machines and changing themselves as a result of these interactions. The interactions themselves and the changes they can bring about are attributed to the structure of the individuals themselves, or rather to the structure of their brains. This viewpoint has been strengthened, rather than weakened, by the impact made by computer technology. Although some psychologists do have reservations about the computer analogy, many others view computer technology as the source of important clues regarding the nature of human behaviour and thinking. It is important to realise, however, that computers are no more than sophisticated machines, but machines none the less. Although they can be programmed to change their own programmes as a result of feedback, their operation must always be limited by their internal structure and that of their programmes.

Closely related to the assumption that human society is a collection of individuals all interacting with each other in a manner determined by the structure of their brains is another frequently expressed viewpoint. This is that human individuals (as biological machines) develop psychologically as a result of their 'adaptation' or 'adjustment' to what is termed the 'social environment'. In other words they acquire psychological characteristics through a mechanical interaction with this 'social environment', the form of interaction being determined by the structure of their brains and that of the 'social environment'.

It is here that psychology is confronted by a dilemma. The term 'social environment' can only refer to society. But society cannot exist without individuals. Furthermore, if society has brought the human race from the Stone Age to the Atomic Age this can only be because individuals have themselves, through their purposeful activity, changed society. According to the logic of modern psychology, society can only be a collection of biological machines, together with the social environments with which they interact mechanically. However, this logic carries within it a contradiction. For individuals cannot 'adjust' or 'adapt' to a society of which they themselves are an integral part. Faced with this contradiction, modern psychologists, instead of consciously re-examining their basic theoretical premises, retreat into a study of highly specialised fields such as those of perception and memory and thereby avoid confronting the problem. It would appear that many of them share the somewhat vain hope that separate pieces of knowledge of how individuals perceive, memorise or react to stimuli can somehow be glued together to form an integrated theory of the human individual.

It is clear from what has just been said that psychology as a whole cannot make substantial advances unless and until the question of the relationship between the individual and society is understood. This book is written in the belief that the Marxist view of humanity and of society provides the necessary clue as to where to begin.

A more extensive criticism of psychology's 'biological machine' approach will be made in ensuing chapters. Meanwhile, brief mention needs to be made of the fact that Marxists see human society in a totally different light from that of those who see it simply as an entity to whose structure individuals 'adjust' or 'adapt'.

For Marxists, society cannot exist without individuals, just as individuals cannot exist outside society. At the same time, however, society consists of much more than a collection of individuals who interact with each other. One of the basic principles of systems theory, namely that 'the whole consists of more than the sum of its parts', applies to human society and its history just as to any other 'system'. Further, since no 'element' of any 'system' can be understood unless and until the system itself is understood, it follows that there can be no real scientific understanding of individuals unless and until society and its history is also understood.

The Marxist view of human nature is that it is not to be found in the genes of individual men and women. Rather it is to be found in the objective relationships between individuals. This is because objective social relationships cause individuals to undertake definite forms of activity. And it is during and as a result of this activity that individuals become what they are psychologically. When individuals are compelled by their social relationships to undertake activity which cannot be carried out simply by overt actions, the processes of thinking develop in order that they may cope. Further, when individuals think, they think with categories of thought, concepts, values and so on, which have arisen in the course of history. They do not arise simply in their own brains. Rather, they assimilate them from the same human culture which causes them to undertake definite forms of activity.

Thus, for Marxists, any psychology which seeks to base itself simply on biology and mechanics, that is any psychology which bases itself on the methods of the natural sciences, must of necessity be woefully inadequate. The human individual is of course a biological organism and any genuinely scientific psychology must take this into account. But if, as Marxists assert, individuals become what they are in the course of and as a result of their own activity, then it is from the social relationships which cause them to undertake activity that it is necessary to start.

The key theoretical question facing psychology is that of the relationship between individuals on the one hand and society in its historical development on the other. This question cannot of course be answered in a satisfactory manner unless there is a clear and unambiguous understanding of human society itself, its origin and its history. This book is written on the basis of the assumption that a decisive contribution towards this understanding has been made by Karl Marx.

A few words about the structure of this book. Its really essential content is to be found in Chapters Five ('The Individual as a Part of Society and of History') and Six ('Why Humans are not Machines'). Any reader who wants a short overview of this Marxist critique of modern psychology can turn to these two chapters first. Chapters Ten ('A Marxist Approach to Personality Theory') and Eleven ('Some Applications') are really put in as 'extras' and are not crucial to the basic arguments. Nevertheless their contents will tend to reinforce the views expressed in previous chapters.

The reader will note that throughout the book several important themes are repeated and reiterated. This is deliberate. To the author their repetition seemed necessary since they will probably unfamiliar to most readers. Another reason for their repetition is that their content stands in stark contrast to the basic theoretical assumptions of both psychologists and lay persons.

It is now necessary, in the following chapter, to outline in more detail the Marxist conception of the human race.

NOTES TO CHAPTER ONE

1. See Wright et al. *Introducing Psychology: An Experimental Approach*. Penguin, 1970, p. 9.
2. See, for example: Mescheryakov, A. *Awakening to Life*. Progress Publishers, 1979.
3. It is one of the tragedies of the twentieth century that millions of people throughout the world have indentified Marxism with the outlook and policies of the privileged and parasitic Stalinist bureaucracy which ruled the U.S.S.R. for about six decades — also with the outlook and policies of the bureaucracy's counterparts in China and eastern Europe. Doubtless Marx himself would turn in his grave if he knew how his world outlook has been distorted and misrepresented by the

Soviet bureaucracy in order to justify its parasitic existence — with its attendant brutal repressions and lack of democratic rights for the majority of the population. Fortunately, within what used to be the U.S.S.R., immensely powerful social forces are challenging the bureaucracy, which is — at the time of writing — in an advanced stage of disintegration. This disintegration will no doubt give rise to a resurgence of genuine Marxism. This resurgence of genuine Marxism has in fact already begun. In recent years the increasingly weakened grip of the bureaucracy has found its expression in the publication of a number of serious and important works by modern Russian authors which collectively represent a genuine development and enrichment of the Marxist world outlook. Indeed, without this development of Marxism inside what was the U.S.S.R. the writing of this book would not have been possible. (Amongst these works are the following, all published by Progress Publishers: Ilyenkov, E.V. *Dialectical Logic* (1977), Ilyenkov, E.V. *The Dialectic of the Abstract and the Concrete in Marx's 'Capital'* (1982), Naletov, I. *Alternatives to Positivism* (1984), Lektorsky,V.A. *Subject. Object. Cognition.* (1980) and Mikhailov, F. *The Riddle of the Self* (1980). This latter work is of especial importance to the subject matter of this book.)

4. Neisser, U. *Cognition and Reality*. Freeman, 1976, p. 2. My emphasis.

5. Wright et al. *op. cit.* p. 25.

6. The term 'psychoanalysis' refers to the theory and practice of Sigmund Freud (1878-1939) and his followers. Essentially the theory postulates the existence of unconscious motives innate in all individuals. The most important of these come into conflict with the superego — the internalised morals and values of society which the child acquires primarily from the father. A brief outline of Freud's theory is given in Chapter Ten.

7. The outlook of behaviourism tended to dominate academic psychology for about three decades, from the 1920s onwards. From the standpoint of the subject matter of this book it is extremely important, since it exemplifies with great clarity the essentially mechanical approach of modern psychology.

The originator of the behaviouristic outlook was J.B. Watson (1878-1958). Watson was heavily influenced by the work of the Russian physiologist Pavlov. The latter had noticed that hungry dogs tended to salivate just before they were given food. This led him to carry out an experiment which became world-famous. He would ring a bell just before a dog was fed. After this had been done several times he noticed that the sound of the bell alone (that is without the food) would elicit salivation. If the bell was again rung a number of times without reinforcement (that is without food) the salivation would diminish and eventually cease. The response of salivation to the bell became known as a conditioned response, since it was conditional on its reinforcement by food. This form of 'conditioning' became known as 'classical' conditioning to distinguish it from 'operant' conditioning (see below). Watson expressed a firm belief that the most significant aspects of human behaviour could be explained in terms of conditioned responses. He also maintained firmly that the behaviour of children could to a very large extent be moulded, by parents and educators, simply through the practical application of the principles of conditioning. This viewpoint implied, of course, that the most significant aspects of human behaviour were determined by the same laws that caused Pavlov's dogs to salivate in a laboratory.

Since Watson first initiated the behaviourist approach a number of other leading figures contributed to its further development. The most important of these has been B.F. Skinner (1904-1990), who is probably best known for his studies of rats in boxes (known as 'Skinner boxes'). Skinner would put a hungry rat in a box in which there was a bar. When the rat, in the course of random activity, pressed the bar it was rewarded by food. This caused an increase in the probability that the rat would press the bar again in a similar situation. Eventually the rat learned to press the bar whenever it was hungry. The bar-pressing activity was said to have been 'reinforced' by food. In an analogous fashion Skinner showed that 'negative' reinforcement could occur. Thus a rat put into a box could be taught to press the bar again in order to avoid an electric shock. This Skinnerian form of conditioning became known as 'operant' conditioning (as opposed to 'classical') since the rat operated on its environment.

Skinner, in a manner analogous to that of Watson, made clear his conviction that human behaviour is essentially governed by the same laws as those that govern the behaviour of rats in cages. Although Skinner himself denied that he was a theoretician (he described himself as a 'technologist of behaviour'), his viewpoint — together with that of Watson — was essentially a theory of human nature. From the behaviourist standpoint human individuals can be no more than the reflection and manifestation of environmental pressures.

Although the influence of behaviourism has waned in recent years its influence still finds expression in what is known as 'behaviour therapy' (See Chapter Eleven).

8. In Chapter Ten a critical examination of a number of such theories will be made.

9. Sève, L. *Man in Marxist Theory and the Psychology of Personality*. Harvester, 1978, p. 217.

10. Wright, et al. *op. cit.* p. 26.

11. Radford, J. and Govier, E. (Eds.) *A Textbook of Psychology*. Sheldon, 1980, p. 43.

2

THE MARXIST VIEW OF HUMANITY

In this chapter will be put forward a number of basic Marxist premises concerning the nature of the human race. These are as follows: Humanity constitutes a part of nature which survives through the making and use of tools (labour). It was in and through their own labour that the self-origin of the first humans took place. Human history represents an extension of natural history. The relationships into which people enter in the course of the making and use of tools form the ultimate basis of any socio-economic system (Marx's materialist conception of history). Humans are natural, social beings (to be human is to be social). 'Human nature' resides not as an abstraction inherent in individuals but in objective social relationships.

Marxists start from the premise that the human race is a part of nature. As a part of nature we have needs such as those of food and protection from the elements. We satisfy these through the making and use of tools. Further, it is this making and use of tools that decisively differentiates humanity from all other biological species.

It might of course be argued that other species also use tools. Monkeys, for example, use sticks to knock down fruit from trees. But the important point here is that the use of sticks by monkeys does not constitute a decisive element of their survival as a species. Also important is the fact that, unlike monkeys, humans purposefully make tools in order to perform tasks which may not have to be carried out immediately. Thus members of a primitive hunting tribe may make spears some time before embarking on a hunt, while in modern industry many of those engaged in the making of computers may never use one themselves.

Furthermore, in making tools we rely on knowledge which has been *historically developed*. The manufacture of computers, for example, involves a knowledge of physics and mathematics. Both these branches of science have been developed historically, their basic principles being passed from generation to generation primarily through the medium of language, itself the product of history.

The ability to make and use tools purposefully with historically developed knowledge enables us to *master* our environment rather than just change it. Animals other than *Homo sapiens* do of course change their environments. Goats, for example, in satisfying their hunger, sometimes destroy virtually all plant life in given areas. Humanity, however, not only changes its environment purely by its physical presence. Armed with the knowledge and skills accumulated by past generations, we think what changes we can make in our environment, choose a definite goal and purposely subordinate our activity to its attainment.

It needs to be emphasised most strongly that the mastering of our environment is essentially a *social* process. Thus the building of a house involves the co-operation of carpenters, bricklayers, plumbers and so forth. Even when people build their own houses, they have to rely on skills and techniques learned from others.

To put what has been said above in another way, humanity represents an unique part of nature. In contrast to all other aspects of the world, including other animal species, we exist by consciously and purposefully creating the conditions of our own material existence. It follows, therefore, that the *ultimate* basis of human history, from the Stone Age to the Atomic Age, can only be the development of our ability to create and re-create the conditions of our own lives.

A related belief of Marxists is that, in the course of mastering its environment through the making and use of tools, humanity changes itself. Every development in the making of tools must lead — actually or potentially — to their further development, and hence to individuals possessing new skills and knowledge. Moreover, the development of tools and techniques must lead to new forms of everyday existence. Thus with the first development of agriculture our ancestors tended to adopt a settled habitat rather than the nomadic existence characteristic of many of the earlier hunter-gatherer tribes. Similarly, the development of machinery, including the steam engine, led to vast social upheavals in Britain, the first major country to become industrialised, characterised by the transfer of a large proportion of the rural population into what were to become large industrial cities. It seems almost superfluous to mention the enormous social changes brought about by modern computer technology. This central Marxist belief that humanity has the ability to change itself in the course of its own activity will be reflected in the following chapters.

The term 'the making and use of tools' is virtually synonymous with the terms 'labour' and 'production'[1]. Henceforth, the three terms will be used interchangeably.

The key role of labour in the life of humanity is stressed by Marx in his major work *Capital*:

Labour is, in the first place, a process in which man of his own accord starts, regulates, and controls the material reactions between himself and nature. He opposes himself to nature as one of her own forces, setting in motion arms and legs, head and hands, the natural forces of his body, in order to appropriate nature's productions in a form adapted to his own wants. By thus acting on the external world and thus changing it, he at the same time changes his own nature.[2]

Further:

The labour process, resolved . . . into its simple elementary factors, is human action with a view to the production of use-values, appropriation of natural substances to human requirements; it is a necessary condition for effecting exchange of matter between man and nature; it is the everlasting condition of human existence, and therefore is independent of every social phase of that existence, or rather, is common to every such phase.[3]

Of great importance to the subject matter of this book is the insistence by Marxists that not only is labour 'the everlasting condition of human existence'. For it was also the very means by which humanity emerged from the animal kingdom. In other words, it was the labour of emerging humans that created, not only the necessities of life, but humans themselves. In his well-known essay *The Part Played by Labour in the Transition from Ape to Man*, Marx's co-worker Frederick Engels writes:

Labour is the source of all wealth, the political economists assert. But it is infinitely more than this. It is the prime basic condition for all human existence, and this is to such an extent that, in a sense, we have to say that man created himself.[4]

It is obvious that there must have been considerable interaction between the many aspects of the development of the human race, cause becoming transformed into effect and vice versa. The use of tools helped to develop the hand. The development of the hand stimulated the growth of the brain. The growth of the brain led to increased potential for abstract thought and language. More complex forms of social organisation became both necessary and possible. These factors in turn led to the further development of tools. The final product of all these interacting factors was the fully developed human being existing as a part of human society.

Some of the factors involved in the origin of the human race are outlined in the diagram below.

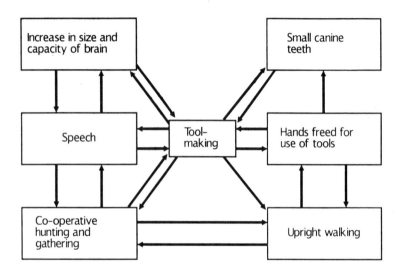

Diagram of the interconnected process of hominisation through labour (adapted from R.E. Leakey and R. Lewin, *Origins***). Reproduced from C. Woolfson** *The Labour Theory of Culture.* **Routledge and Kegan Paul. 1982. With kind permission.**

Much work of contemporary anthropologists tends to confirm the role of tools in the development of humans from non-human primates. The anthropologists Washburn and Howells assert:

Man was often defined on the basis of brain size. . . . It would now appear, however, that the large size of the brain of certain hominids was a relatively late development and that the brain evolved due to new selection pressures after bipedalism and consequent upon the use of tools. The tool-using, ground-living, hunting way of life created the human brain rather than a large-brained man discovering new ways of life. . . . The important point is that the size of the brain . . . has increased threefold subsequent to the use and manufacture of tools.[5]

Perhaps a more succinct summary of the modern view is given in a later paper by Washburn:

It is now clear that tools antedate man and that their use by non-human primates gave rise to *Homo sapiens*. . . . Man began when populations of apes, about a million years ago, started a bi-pedal, tool-using way of life that gave rise to the man apes of genus Australopithecus. Most of the obvious differences that distinguish man from apes came *after* the use of tools.[6]

It is thus clear that a whole number of features that distinguish humans from other animals — large brains, sensitive and supple hands, developed vocal cords, the capacity for abstract thought, a developed language and relatively complex forms of social organisation — evolved in constant interaction with the development of tools.

It is important to realise that the first elementary form of human society, that is the objective relationships between individuals, arose simultaneously with the prototype male and female individuals. It is *not* the case that individuals were produced by some evolutionary process which caused them to possess some innate 'human nature' upon which society had to be imposed, or of which society was a manifestation. The process of labour by means of which the human race created itself out of the rest of nature was by its very being a *social* process.

The labour process by means of which humanity emerged must have been from the very beginning an *historical* as well as a social one. Not only did individuals have to co-operate in the use and manufacture of tools. The skills, techniques and knowledge that were acquired had to be handed down from generation to generation.

In the same way, since the basis of human society is production, all human beings are not only the product of society, but also of *history*. For the skills and techniques of production at any given stage of historical development must rest on the technical and scientific achievements of previous generations.

It is a common assumption that human history is in some way opposed to natural history. Marxists, however, would dispute that this is so. Humanity is a definite part of nature, but by virtue of the fact that we developed ourselves from the rest of the animal kingdom through labour, exists as a highly unique natural species. It is an important aspect of our uniqueness that we survive as a species through historically developed culture rather than through changes in our anatomy and physiology. Thus we cope with the cold not by growing fur or by developing extra layers of fat but by building houses and making clothes. To obtain food we do not develop longer arms to enable us better to reach food on trees. Instead we develop all the tools and techniques of modern agriculture.

Humanity's survival as a species therefore depends, not primarily on the adaptation of individuals to the environment, but on our mastery of the environment through historically developed culture. Marxists thus see history primarily as the development of culture (based on production) by means of which the survival of the human species is ensured. It follows that human history must be regarded as a *process of nature ensuring the survival of the human race.* Marx himself writes:

History itself is a real part of natural history — of man's coming to be man. Natural science will in time subsume itself under the science of man, just as the science of man will subsume under itself natural science.[7]

Further, Marx makes reference to: 'My standpoint, from which the evolution of the economic formation of society is viewed as a process of natural history.'[8]

As has already been stated at the beginning of this chapter, from the Marxist standpoint the ultimate basis of history is the development of our ability to create the material conditions of our own lives through production. However, since production is a *social* process, it follows that individuals have to enter into definite relationships with others in order that production can take place. These are referred to by Marxists as the *relations of production.* It is these relations of production, such as primitive communal(see below), slave/slave owner, feudal serf/feudal lord and worker/capitalist, that form the real basis for any given historical form of society (referred to above by Marx as 'the economic formation of society').

It is in this context that the development of the various historical forms which human society has taken have to be considered.

The first form of human society, termed by Marx and Engels 'primitive tribal communism', must have been characterised by a very high level of co-operation. The tools of these first hunter-gatherers were of necessity of a very primitive nature. In order to survive, therefore, the primitive nature of their tools had to be compensated for by solidarity and co-operation. A contemporary author writes that:

> [Anthropologists] suggest that aggression, if not entirely absent in hunter-gatherer society, has a very secondary role in their affairs. Indeed, it could be argued that early humans, living within the 'primitive herd', an essentially primordial form of social organisation, would have been unable to build enduring human collectives unless unbridled 'zoological egoism' began to be subordinated to that type of sustained social co-operation required for successful labour.[9]

It is evident that before the advent of the first form of class society — slavery — perhaps 5,000 years ago, the human race had previously existed for a far longer period in a form of society characterised by co-operation rather than oppression.[10]

The many thousands of years of primitive tribal communism were necessarily characterised by a slow development of the means of production (that is, of tools). However, over several tens of thousands of years significant developments were made, including those of the lever, the wheel, pottery, iron-working and agriculture. Eventually a point was reached at which individuals and groups of individuals could produce enough for their own upkeep together with a relatively significant surplus. In other words a point had been reached at which slavery could become profitable.

There can be no doubt that the first source of slaves came from the rivalry that existed between different tribes. It should be noted that, as the name implies, under the system of primitive tribal communism the economic unit was the tribe. As has been pointed out above, economic necessity must have dictated a very high level of co-operation and tribal solidarity. However, there was no economic necessity for one tribe to co-operate with another, except perhaps when a mutually advantageous barter of products could be arranged. On the other hand, there were undoubtedly clashes between different tribes over economic interests. Hunting rights must have been a frequent source of conflict. Once agriculture had become well established serious conflicts became inevitable. If the soil from which an agricultural tribe made a living became exhausted, the tribe had no alternative but to move on. But if alternative suitable land was already occupied by other tribes, the first tribe also had no alternative but to embark upon a war of conquest in which the members of the defeated tribe were put to death and their land and other possessions stolen. However, once the productivity of labour had reached a certain level it became profitable to turn members of defeated tribes into slaves rather than simply killing them. Engels writes:

> Production had developed so far that the labour-power of a man could now produce more than was necessary for its mere maintenance; the means of maintaining additional labour forces existed . . . such forces were provided by war. . . . Up to that time one had not known what to do with prisoners and had therefore simply killed them. . . . But at the stage of the 'economic situation' which had now been attained the prisoners acquired a value; one therefore let them live and made use of their labour. . . . *Slavery* has been invented.[11]

Thus slavery — the first form of society based upon economic classes whose interests were mutually antagonistic — arose not from any inherently anti-social tendencies in 'human nature' but from economic contradictions inherent in primitive tribal communism. There were two basic contradictions: first, the inability of certain tribes to survive unless they could conquer other tribes; second, the inability of human culture to develop further unless a minority of the population — slaveowners and their representatives — had the leisure time available to engage in pursuits not *directly* connected with labour, the bulk of which was of course performed by slaves.

Class society has existed throughout its history — at least until modern industry had been created — on the basis of the productivity of labour being relatively low. It was only through class society that the productivity of agriculture and industry could be raised to a level at which abundance became a practical possibility for all. Once this practical possibility existed, class society became historically unnecessary and obsolete.[12] Thus from the time that this possibility existed, some time during the late nineteenth century, the greatest need of humanity has become that of returning to the co-operation characteristic of primitive tribal communism, only this time on the basis of a high and developing productivity of labour.

Generally speaking, history has produced three successive forms of class society — slave, feudal and capitalist.[13]

While revulsion might be felt at the horrible way in which slaves were treated in ancient times, it nevertheless has to be recognised that slave society was an historical necessity. For without the slave societies of Greece and Rome the foundations of many essential aspects of human culture — natural science, philosophy, art and literature — would not have been laid.

It is no accident that following the collapse of the slave societies of Greece and Rome the next form of class society — feudalism — should emerge. The most important aspect of production remained agriculture. Yet over the centuries the productivity of agriculture had increased due to improved techniques. The important point here is that slaves had no incentives to learn these new techniques. As slaves, they were fed, clothed and housed anyway, while anything they produced belonged automatically to their masters rather than to themselves. A new system of production relations became historically necessary — a system which provided the producers with an incentive to learn the new agricultural techniques.

The historical contradiction between the need for the producers to learn the new agricultural technology and the unwillingness and inability of slaves to learn these techniques was resolved through the emergence of a new form of class society — feudalism. Under feudal class relationships the feudal lords owned the land while the serfs created the wealth. The lord allowed the serf to work a piece of his land in exchange either for a portion of what the serf produced or for spending part of his time working directly for the lord. Thus both the serf himself and his lord benefited from an agricultural productivity which had arisen on the basis of techniques which were more advanced than those of slave society.

The real and decisive basis of the final stage of class society, capitalism, came with the development of machinery and manufacture. For different historical reasons, discussion of which is outside the scope of this book, there was a considerable interval of time between the break-up of feudal lord/serf relations in the Middle Ages and the beginnings of the Industrial Revolution which made England the world's first major capitalist country. However, capitalism and feudalism were clearly incompatible. Unlike today, when the microchip and other inventions mean industry can be run, at least in principle, by very few people, early manufacturing industry required large numbers of proletarians. But these proletarians had to come from somewhere. By definition, proletarians are people whose only possession is their ability to work or their labour-power. In order to live they had to sell their labour-power to a capitalist who was the owner of a manufacturing concern. However, in a feudal society, in which the bulk of the population is tied to the land, manufacturing industry cannot develop since it is deprived of proletarians. Hence the two forms of class society were historically incompatible.

As it happened, the disintegration of feudal relations in the Middle Ages had left England with a large number of independent and tenant farmers. In order that they might become transformed into proletarians the Enclosure Acts and similar legislation were passed by Parliament. This had the effect of driving the small farmers off the land and thus forcing them into manufacturing industry.[14] The Industrial Revolution which first transformed Britain and then the world could then proceed in earnest.

Once capitalism had created modern industry and had developed into a world-wide system of production, its usefulness to humanity came to an end. Class society, it should be recalled, came into being when labour productivity had developed to a point at which the producers of wealth — in the first place slaves — could produce enough for their own subsistence plus a relatively small surplus which was appropriated by their owners. It was historically necessary for class society to continue as long as labour productivity was such that abundance was impossible. However, once modern industry had been developed and once capitalism had become a world-wide economic system, that is by the latter part of the nineteenth century, the relations of production under capitalism had become a barrier to human progress. For the first time in history, a developed industry and agriculture made it technically possible to provide the human race with an adequate and continually improving standard of living. However, the very nature of capitalism contained within itself a fundamental weakness. This was the anarchical nature of the market within which the commodities produced by industry were sold. Each industrial capitalist concern flung its commodities on to the market in the hope that buyers would prefer its commodities rather than those of its competitors.

The relations between people are, under capitalism, dominated by the laws of the market. Thus today the lives of millions of people are determined by the relationship between gold and oil, over which no one has any control. Similarly, not even the most powerful politicians can decide the relationship between the pound and the dollar or that between commodities such as cars, computers or candy floss on the one hand and the special commodity that constitutes money on the other.

The domination of humanity by the blind laws of the market is accompanied by another fetter on human development. This is the continuation of historically obsolete national boundaries. The world economy became an integrated whole many years ago. Yet national boundaries are still maintained by vested interests which represent an integral part of capitalism.

At the present time capitalism threatens us with a cataclysmic collapse of the world banking system, thermo-nuclear war and the increasing pollution of the planet. A prodigious amount of humanity's resources is devoted to armaments while millions throughout the world lack adequate nourishment. It is clear that capitalist relations of production have outlived their historical usefulness and have to be replaced by the social ownership of industry and the abolition of national boundaries.

The fundamental law of history can now be made explicit. As humanity's ability to create its own conditions of life through production increases, so new relations of production become both necessary and possible. Yet in turn, with the development of new knowledge, techniques and skills, these new relations of production themselves become obsolete and need to be replaced. To put what has just been said in another way, each historical set of relations of production becomes necessary if humanity's ability to create the conditions of its own life is to develop. Yet at a certain point — due to the continued development of knowledge, skills and techniques within its framework — each set of relations of production becomes a fetter upon the further development of human abilities and potentialities. Thus capitalist relations of production, which were historically necessary if modern industry was to develop, now prevent the mass of the world's population from utilising our capacity and ability to provide the abundance of the necessities of life which industrial technology now makes possible.

The fundamental law to which reference has just been made is, by itself, inadequate to explain the relationship between the relations of production on the one hand and other aspects of human social life on the other. This relationship is in fact explained by a further important contribution by Marx to human knowledge, namely his materialist conception of history, often referred to as historical materialism. Here Marx starts from the basic premise that before humans can engage in ideological, legal, religious, literary, sporting or artistic pursuits we have first of all to be fed and protected from the elements. Therefore the relations of production into which we have to enter in order to produce the fundamental necessities of life must, in the final analysis, determine the legal, religious, educational and political institutions of any given form of society, together with its ideological and theoretical assumptions and beliefs and indeed the form of the family. Marx himself sums up the materialist conception of history as follows:

> In the social production which men carry on they enter into definite relations that are indispensible and independent of their will; these relations of production correspond to a definite stage of the development of their material forces of production [i.e., of humanity's ability to create purposefully the conditions of our material existence]. The sum total of these relations of production constitute the economic structure of society — the real foundation, on which rises a legal and political superstructure and to which correspond definite forms of social consciousness. The mode of production of material life determines the social, political and spiritual life processes in general. It is not the consciousness of men

that determines their being, but, on the contrary, their social being that determines their consciousness.[15]

Marx here challenges the common and entrenched belief that social relations — including the relations of production — are determined by ideas. Rather, he insists, ideas arise out of concrete material activity. And since all forms of human activity are ultimately dependent on the activity involved in production, the active relationships into which people enter in the course of production (the relations of production) must ultimately give rise to the ideological and theoretical concepts and ideas of any given form of society. At each stage of history certain ideas were necessary to keep intact the existing relations of production. Thus slave owners believed that slaves were not really human and could be killed off when not needed, much as manufacturers now send obsolete machinery to the scrapheap. Feudal lords believed that their ancestry made them morally superior to the serfs. Those who profit from the capitalist system believe that it is the best possible system because it accords with some form of 'human nature' inherent in all individuals. Without the predominance of these sorts of beliefs and ideas at the various stages of history, the processes of production could not have functioned effectively. Here it is worth noting the way in which the most important aspects of law represent a reflection and a manifestation of the ongoing relations of production. Thus Roman law centred on the ownership of slaves. Feudal law centred on the ownership of land. Capitalist law centres on the ownership of property generally.

In the course of human history there have of course been ideas which challenge — directly or indirectly — the existing relations of production. These ideas are to be explained by the fact that advances in technology have made obsolete — or are about to make obsolete — the existing relations of production. Hence the idea of overthrowing 'the divine right of kings' which inspired Cromwell's New Model Army and the slogan of 'Liberty, Equality, Fraternity' which accompanied the French revolution of 1789 were but ideological reflections of the fact that the objective conditions for the development of capitalism had matured in the respective countries and that it was necessary to overthrow the remnants of feudalism in order that capitalism could developed unhindered.

Thus when the relations of production (the basis of any given form of society) are such that our ability to create the conditions of material existence can develop relatively unhindered the ideological and political superstructure keeps them intact. However, when our skills, techniques and knowledge have grown to such an extent that the existing relations of production become a fetter on their further development, the superstructure of society reacts on the base, causing it to be changed to a form more appropriate to the level of development which has been reached by human abilities.

At this point it is necessary to warn against a widespread error. It is often supposed that Marx maintained that all thought was a direct reflection of the economic relations of production. This is in fact absurd. When Marx writes that: 'The mode of production (that is, the relations of production) in material life determines the general character of the social, ideological and spiritual processes of life', the words 'general character' need to be emphasised. For there is a definite *relative* independence of the political, ideological, artistic and religious aspects of society from the relations of production. Thus if in the second world war Hitler decided to ignore the advice of his generals and fought on two fronts simultaneously, thereby losing the war, his decision cannot be explained simply in terms of the relations of production of capitalism. However, the war itself remained a definite manifestation of the historically outmoded social system of capitalism together with its equally outmoded national boundaries. Similarly Shakespeare's plays, Beethoven's symphonies and Darwin's theory of evolution were all manifestations of definite historical periods. Yet the creative genius of these outstanding men has to be seen as the product of the many factors which contributed to their biographies. It is necessary to recall, however, that the various concepts used by individuals like these are all historically developed and that the basis of history is production. Engels writes on this question as follows:

> According to the materialist conception of history the determining element in history is *ultimately* the production and reproduction in real life. More than this neither Marx nor I have ever asserted. If therefore someone twists this into the statement that the economic element is the *only* determining one, he transforms it into a meaningless, abstract and absurd phrase.[16]

It becomes obvious that Marx's materialist conception of history enables us to see more clearly that human history cannot be regarded as an haphazard jumble of the whims and wishes of kings, emperors and statesmen. Rather, human history represents an extension of natural history. It is an extension of natural history because the survival of the species *Homo sapiens* is ensured through the relatively continual development of the human ability to create, consciously and purposefully, the material conditions of our own lives. The term '*relatively* continual' is used here because the development of technology and scientific knowledge has by no means always proceeded, as it were, in a straight line. Witness the stagnation of human culture in Europe which occurred following the collapse of the Roman Empire. However, the passage of the human race through the successive socio-economic formations of primitive tribal communism, slavery, feudalism and capitalism can only reflect — however indirectly — the transition of humanity from the Stone Age to the Atomic Age.

One further aspect of the Marxist view of the human race needs to be mentioned. This is that there is no innate 'human nature' with which individuals are born. No human individual can exist without society, and the basis of any form of society, as has been stressed before, is the relations of production into which individuals have to enter in order to produce the necessities of life. In other words, the basis of society does not exist inside the genes of new-born babies. Neither does it exist as a result of the spontaneous maturation of their brains. What causes individuals to develop in such a way that when adults they can — actually or potentially — enter into relations of production is the historically developed social relationships into which they have to enter, relationships such as those of parent/child, teacher/pupil and so on. It is in the course of these active relationships that children develop the knowledge and abilities enabling them to play an active role in society in later life. With great foresight Marx himself wrote:

> The human essence is no abstraction inherent in each single individual. . . . In its reality it is the ensemble of the social relations.[17]

This is a point of great importance, for there exists today a widespread belief that there exists some 'human nature' embedded in the genes of every individual. Indeed, a fierce battle has to be fought out between Marxists on the one hand and the many contemporary writers who believe that there is some innate 'human nature' residing in the genes, on the other. This is a point which will be developed in subsequent chapters.

To summarise this chapter, Marxists believe that the human race came into being through the process of labour, involving the making and use of tools. Throughout history humanity has existed — and can only exist — as a part of nature which, through production, obtains its needs from the rest of nature. Production is essentially a social and historical process since individuals have to enter into definite historically developed relationships in order that production can take place.

The basis of any given form of society is the relations of production which ultimately, and usually relatively indirectly, determine the ideological, legal and social superstructure. It is the function of this superstructure to maintain intact the existing relations of production whenever production (and hence the ability to create the conditions of our own lives) can develop relatively unhindered within their framework. When production has developed to a point at which the existing relations of production hinder its development, then the function of the superstructure is to bring about a transition to more appropriate relations.

Humanity is an animal species. However, due to our emergence from the rest of the animal kingdom through *social* labour, we constitute a very unique species. We are the product of human history as well as of natural history. Humans are natural, social beings. *To be human is to be social.* The human race is also a unique animal species in that the survival of the species does not primarily depend on the adaptation of individuals to their respective environments. Our survival as a part of nature depends first and foremost on our own conscious mastery over nature itself. In turn this depends on the historical development of culture based on social production.

The fundamental law of history — that the relations of production must correspond to the level of our abilities to create the conditions of our own lives — thus constitutes a definite natural law. As a natural law it exists independently of the will and consciousness of individuals.

The 'human essence' or 'human nature' does not reside in the genes of individual men and women. Rather it exists in historically developed social relationships.

The relevance of all these points to the development of a genuinely scientific psychology will constitute a central theme of this book.

NOTES TO CHAPTER TWO

1. It should be noted that some forms of labour do not *directly* involve the making and use of tools. There must, however, be some connection, however indirect. An example is that of the purely intellectual labour of a mathematician. Here it is important to realise first, that the science of mathematics could only have developed when the making of tools had reached a certain level and second that — especially in the age of modern technology — the making of at least the more complex forms of tools requires the use of mathematics.
2. *Capital*, Vol.1. FLPH, Moscow, 1959, p.177.
3. *Ibid*. p.183-184.
4. *Dialectics of Nature*. Progress Publishers, Moscow, 1964, p.172.
5. *Evolution after Darwin*, Edited by Tax, S. University of Chicago Press, p.186.
6. Washburn, S. 'Tools and Human Evolution', *Scientific American*, Sept. 1960. Washburn's emphasis.
7. *Economic and Philosophical Manuscripts*. International Publishers, p.143.
8. *Capital*, Vol. 1. Lawrence and Wishart, 1949, p.10.

9. Woolfson, C. *The Labour Theory of Culture*. Routledge and Kegan Paul, 1982, p.33.

10. It is hard to estimate the period of humanity's history characterised by 'primitive tribal communism' since it is difficult to estimate the precise point in time at which an ape-like creature became finally transformed into the species *Homo sapiens*. However, it can be said with confidence that 'primitive tribal communism' existed for several tens of thousands of years.

11. *Anti-Duhring*. FLPH, Moscow, 1954, p.250.

12. In capitalist society, of course, it is economic necessity that forces working people to sell their labour-power or ability to work for wages. Their wages bear little relationship to the value of whatever they produce. See, for example, Marx's *Capital* Vol.1. Chapter 7.

13. The qualification 'generally speaking' is made because although slave society was the first form of class society and capitalism is the final one, the transition from one form to the next has not always been clear cut. Elements of capitalist society developed within the old feudal framework. The boundary line between primitive tribal communism and slavery was blurred by the emergence of the Oriental despotisms such as those of Egypt and Mesopotamia. In this form of society — at least in its initial stages — the most important aspect of the means of production, the land, was communally owned but nevertheless administered by a highly privileged priesthood. In the USA forms of slavery existed until the Civil War.

14. See, for example, Marx's *Capital* Vol. 1. Chapters 26-32.

15. *Contribution to a Critique of Political Economy*. Lawrence and Wishart, 1971, pp.20-21.

16. Engels, F. *Letter to Bloch*, Sept. 20-21 1890. *Selected Correspondence*. Progress Publishers, 1965, pp. 417-419.

17. Theses on Feuerbach. In Engels, F. *Feuerbach. Opposition of the Materialist and Idealist Outlooks*. Progress Publishers, 1976.

3

MARX, DARWIN AND HUMAN SURVIVAL

The Marxist view of the human race represents an essential and effective challenge to one of the basic assumptions of modern psychology. This is the latter's uncritical acceptance of the Darwinian approach to humanity.

Darwin's view was that there was no *qualitative* difference between humans on the one hand and other animal species on the other. He wrote: 'The difference in mind between man and the higher mammals, great as it is, certainly is one of degree and not of kind.'[1]

It is thus clear that Darwin did not understand the significance of the use of tools by an ape-like creature to transform itself into humanity by labour. He did not, of course, have the benefit of the knowledge now given to us by anthropologists and archaeologists. Likewise it is unlikely that he had read Engels' famous essay *The Part Played by Labour in the Transition from Ape to Man.* Marx, however, although he saw an evolutionary continuity between humans and non-human animals, also saw that within this continuity there simultaneously existed a discontinuity. As has been stressed in the previous chapter, the human race constitutes a unique animal species. Our survival as a species depends, not primarily on the adaptation of humans to the environment, but on our conscious mastery of nature through historically developed culture based on production.

Marx, of course, recognised the significance of Darwin's theory of evolution. He saw in Darwin's belief that new species develop on the basis of older ones a confirmation of his own view that new forms of society, that is of social relationships, arose out of previous forms. Likewise Darwin's prediction that the future would see the emergence of entirely new species strengthened Marx's belief in the emergence of a world society based on socialist relations of production. Historically, Darwin's theory of evolution made a profound impact on the developing discipline of psychology. It helped to give rise to the important school known as 'functionalism', one of the principal exponents of which was William James (1842-1910), a very influential figure, who proposed that human consciousness represented a biological adaptation. The basic tenet of functionalism is that the most essential aspects of the thinking and behaviour of individuals have the 'function' of enabling them to survive as individuals. A contemporary American texbook explains that 'in functionalism we have an "is for" psychology . . . behaviour is adaptive in the sense that the individual's responses result in a better adjustment to the environment.'[2] A British textbook makes the point that 'the functionalist argument [was] that there was no point in regarding behaviour as an object of study unless it was the context of understanding the organism's adaptation to the environment.'[3]

The school of functionalism arose and developed in a sometimes fierce battle with a rival school known as 'structuralism'. The latter school eventually became historically outdated and is really of little interest today. After its victory over structuralism, functionalism ceased to be a school of thought as such since its basic tenets became almost universally accepted:

> As a systematic point of view functionalism was an overwhelming success, but largely because of this success it is no longer a distinct 'school' of psychology. It was, so to speak, absorbed into contemporary psychology. No happier fate could await any point of view.[4]

The two best-known psychological theories of 'human nature', psychoanalysis and behaviourism, both imply functionalist assumptions. Brief mention has to be made of these.

In Freud's theory, the development of the 'ego', operating the 'reality principle', clearly has the 'function' of adapting the organism to the real world, thus ensuring survival. The leading contemporary exponent of behaviourism, B.F. Skinner, has demonstrated that rats in cages will learn to carry out certain actions both to obtain food and to avoid electric shocks. This ability to learn can of course be regarded as adaptive since it leads to survival. Skinner makes plain his conviction that the most important aspects of the behaviour of humans in social situations are basically determined by the same natural adaptive laws that underlie the behaviour of rats in cages.

The influence of functionalism is further demonstrated by the influential theorist Allport, who defines human personality thus: 'Personality is the dynamic organisation within the individual of those psychophysical systems that determine his unique adjustments to his environment.'[5] It should be noted that Allport's definition of 'personality' is well-known and often quoted. A similar widely used definition has been given by Eysenck, undoubtedly the best known of contemporary British psychologists: 'Personality is the more or less stable and enduring organisation of a person's character, temperament, intellect and physique which determines his unique adjustments to the environment.'[6] It is clear here that, in both definitions, the term 'adjustment' is used synonymously with the term 'adaptation'. Finally, an American textbook states categorically that: 'American psychology today *is* functionalist.'[7]

Since many of our psychological processes tend to enhance the chances of individual survival they can of course be regarded as adaptive. Perceptual abilities are an example. Blind people develop acute senses of hearing, smell and touch in a manner which is clearly adaptive. The drivers of motor cars involved in accidents will tend to drive with more caution than they did before. An infinite number of other examples could be given, all of which would give credence to the theoretical premise underlying the outlook of functionalism.

At the same time, however, it has to be recognised that, despite the adaptive nature of many aspects of behaviour and thinking, numerous individuals today engage in activities which, far from enhancing their chances of survival, in fact cause them to decrease considerably. People smoke, overeat, consciously fail to eat a balanced diet and otherwise behave in a manner likely to lead to ill health and/or premature death. During major wars, literally millions of individuals volunteer to risk death or mutilation — a form of behaviour which no one could possibly describe as adaptive. Another example of behaviour which is maladaptive is neurotic behaviour. Although a precise definition of the term 'neurotic' is difficult, most psychologists would agree that a common feature of the large number of people who acquire the label of 'neurotic' is that the individuals concerned engage in behaviour patterns which in the long run do not contribute to their chances of survival. An extreme example of this is suicide.

It is clear that the discipline of psychology faces a dilemma of major proportions: If the functionalist hypothesis is correct and human behaviour and thinking enhance the chance of survival, how is it that so much of human behaviour is so obviously maladaptive?

For Marxists, the above dilemma is based on the acceptance of a false premise, namely that the survival of the species *Homo sapiens* depends *primarily* on the survival of individuals. As stated previously, Marxists believe that the survival of the species depends not on the survival of individuals as such, but on the development of culture based on production. It will be argued in the next chapter that, especially in capitalist society, the objective social and historical circumstances that create individuals capable of carrying out positive tasks in the development of culture are of necessity the same as those that cause so many individuals to engage in maladaptive behaviour.

It would be true to say that contemporary psychology tries hard to avoid confronting this dilemma. The attempted avoidance takes two main forms.

The first form of avoidance is that of focusing undue and excessive attention on what has become known as 'cognitive' psychology. This term implies the investigation of such psychological processes as memory, perception, attention and concept formation. It is held that such processes help the 'biological machine' that is a human individual to adapt to his or her environment. Thus the authors of an influential book on concept formation state: 'The learning and utilisation of categories (concepts) represents one of the most elementary and general forms of cognition by which man adjusts to his environment.'[8]

It is undoubtedly true that efficient memories and perceptual processes, together with the ability to form concepts, do contribute to the survival of individuals. But if the discipline of psychology is to become a genuine science, other aspects of behaviour and thinking need to receive just as much attention as do the topics just mentioned. Yet today it would be true to say that, in terms of books and scientific papers published, the study of memory receives more attention than any other topic. The study of visual perception comes a close second. Attention given to such topics as why people believe in God, why some people are homosexual rather than heterosexual, why so many marriages break up or why people are able to kill each other in wars is negligible when compared to that given to 'cognitive' psychology. It would indeed be true to say that although newly-qualified psychology graduates might possess an extensive and thorough knowledge of the various theories about how memory functions, they possess no more knowledge about their own personal psychological problems — or those of others — than they did when they first entered the degree course.

The excessive concentration of attention on 'cognitive' psychology to the relative exclusion of other important topics of course reflects the fact that the discipline of psychology has become a 'collection of specialisms'. Within such a framework it is possible both to ignore fundamental questions of 'human nature' and to select for attention, in a quite arbitrary fashion, areas of study in which the functionalist hypothesis appears to be confirmed rather than areas in which it might be questioned.

The second form of the avoidance of the dilemma by contemporary psychology is a refusal to make a serious analysis of the objective relationship between individuals on the one hand and society on the other. Society is usually held to be no more than a 'social environment' to which individuals have to adapt. Individuals are often said to 'adapt' to the pressures of the 'social environment' by carrying out behaviour which in the long run does not lead to survival. The pressures to conform to social standards are an example. Thus the felt need to conform may lead children and young people to smoke and young men to volunteer to fight in wars.[9]

However, Marxists would reject the outlook which regards society simply as a 'social environment' to which individuals have to 'adapt' or 'adjust'. This is for the very simple reason that society cannot exist without individuals. And individuals do not adapt to society but, in the course of their life-activity, actively change it. History is made, not by any *impersonal* social or historical forces or by 'social environments', but only by individuals. Furthermore, one cannot logically 'adapt' to an entity of which one is an integral part. In terms of systems theory, the elements of which a system is composed cannot adapt to themselves.

It is clear that what is needed for the development of a genuinely scientific psychology is a correct understanding of the objective relationship between the individual and society. This will form the subject matter of Chapter Five.

To summarise this chapter, it is clear that contemporary psychology faces the dilemma: If behaviour and thought are biological adaptations, how is it that so much behaviour is obviously maladaptive? Those psychologists who adopt the Darwinian, functionalist approach cannot give a satisfactory answer. The discipline of psychology therefore faces a choice:

EITHER: The human race is no qualitatively different from other animal species and survives as a species primarily through the successful adaptation of human individuals to their respective environments.

OR: We are qualitatively different from other species in that we survive as a species primarily through our mastery of nature through historically developed culture based on production.

This theme will be developed further in subsequent chapters.

NOTES TO CHAPTER THREE.

1. Darwin, C. *The Descent of Man.* John Murray, 1912, p. 193.
2. Chaplin, J.P. and Krawiec, T.S. *Systems and Theories of Psychology.* Holt, Rinehart and Winston, 1968, p. 49.
3. Radford, J. and Govier, E. (Eds.) *A Textbook of Psychology.* Sheldon Press, 1980, p. 13.
4. Chaplin and Krawiec, *op. cit.* p. 50.
5. Allport, G. *Personality: A Psychological Interpretation.* Holt, 1937, p. 48.
6. Eysenck, H.J. *The Structure of Personality.* Methuen, 1953, p. 2.
7. Chaplin and Krawiec *op. cit.* p. 47.
8. Bruner, J.S., Goodnow, J.J. and Austin, G.A. *A Study of Thinking.* Wiley, 1956, p. 2.
9. Freudian theory provides an excellent example of such a view. Here the individual, while operating on both the 'pleasure' and the 'reality' principles, has to adapt to a relatively unchanging 'social environment' by internalising society's social codes and values to form the 'superego'.

4

WHAT QUALITIES MUST INDIVIDUALS POSSESS FOR HUMAN CULTURE TO EXIST AND DEVELOP?

In the previous chapter the inadequacy of the Darwinian, functionalist approach to psychology was demonstrated. It is now necessary to show why the Marxist approach is superior to that of the functionalists. This is best done by raising the question of what psychological qualities and characteristics individuals must possess if human culture is to exist and develop. This is of course basically the same question as that of what qualities and characteristics individuals must have possessed for humanity to have developed from primitive tribal communism through both slave and feudal societies to capitalism.

From the Marxist standpoint, there are three principal qualities which human individuals must possess if human society and culture are to exist. Firstly, the ability to change themselves during and as a result of their own activity. This implies the ability to learn the various skills and techniques which are necessary for society to function. Secondly, the absence of any genetically determined behaviour which might interfere with this ability to learn. The third quality is that of human consciousness. The term 'consciousness' is used in this book in a specifically Marxist sense, which will be explained later.

It is necessary to comment on these three qualities in turn.

The first quality, that of changing oneself in the course of, and as a result of, one's own activity, may be inferred from the basic Marxist premise, outlined in Chapter Two, namely that the human race emerged from the rest of the animal kingdom as a result of its own labour. It was through the making and use of tools that humans, in striving to obtain their basic needs through their struggle to master the forces of nature, became truly human, social beings.

Since human individuals are, by definition, a part of the human race, the emergence of a truly human society must have presupposed the ability of individuals to change themselves through their own actions.

The premise that individuals change themselves by and through their own actions has in fact been accepted by a number of non-Marxist psychologists. For example, the well-known Swiss psychologist Jean Piaget who, although many of his views approached that of Marxism, was not a Marxist. Indeed, Piaget wholeheartedly accepted this basic principle as his own. He insisted that children developed their knowledge of the world through their own activity in it. Writing from what he saw as the standpoint of the young child, he stated: 'I only know an object to the extent to which I act upon it.'[1]

So important is the above principle that more needs to be said. It is interesting to note that Piaget himself started his career as a biologist. It was undoubtedly his grounding in the basic principles of biology that led him to use biological concepts to describe the development of thinking and knowledge in children. He saw that living matter could exist only by carrying out interchanges with the environment. He also saw that living matter possessed a fundamental tendency to change itself during and as a result of such active interchanges.

This takes place at all levels of activity. The digestive system of a newborn baby is such that he or she can only digest liquids. Yet the very activity of the digestive system in digesting liquids is such that in due course the child becomes able to digest mushy foods. This new digestive activity in turn strengthens the system so that eventually solid food can be eaten.

Many examples can be given of physical activity changing the organism. A weakling who undertakes vigorous exercise such as weight-lifting will become muscular and strong. As his or her muscles lift the weights so they develop and harden. At the behavioural level precisely the same principle applies. The learning of skills is an excellent example. We learn to drive a car by sitting behind the steering wheel and driving it. Surgeons and dentists acquire their skills by performing operations and drilling teeth. We acquire the ability to cope with awkward social situations by the experience of trying to cope with such situations. At the purely mental level, we learn mathematics by solving mathematical problems. An infinite number of examples could be given. It would indeed by true to say that human individuals become what they do, that is, an individual's activity becomes embodied in his or her subjective life or personality. As Hegel wrote: 'The true being of man is . . . his act.'[2] For if it is true that all living matter is, by definition, in a constant state of activity and if it changes itself in the course of and as a result of its own activity, then it must also be true that human individuals cannot exist without engaging in activity and thereby changing themselves.

Although an understanding of the above fact is fundamental for the discipline of psychology, a further important point needs to be stressed. This is that an individual's activity takes place in objective situations which exist independently of his or her consciousness or will. These situations are such that individuals are frequently forced into forms of activity that they otherwise would not undertake. Indeed, it would be true to say that those forms of activity which are forced on individuals are by far the most significant from the standpoint of their psychological development. The toilet training which is forced on children by their parents is an example. Another is that of the objective situation faced by nearly all adults who are compelled, in order to live, to engage in activity that will cause them to obtain money, or at least obtain the support of those who either possess it or can obtain it. It would in fact be true to say that the real basis for the development of thought lies in the young child having to undertake activity for which actions not guided by thought are inadequate. As the well-known Russian psychologist Luria put it: 'the origin of thought is always the presence of a task.'[3] It would also be true to say that the basis for the development of new forms of thought, in both children and adults, lies in the overcoming of the contradiction between, on the one hand, objective situations which force individuals to undertake new forms of activity and, on the other, the inadequacy of the individual's existing forms of thought to cope with the task at hand.

What has just been said becomes clearer when it is realised that all social situations necessarily involve objective social relationships. To put it another way, the basis of an individual's activity is the social relationships into which, as a part of a society, he or she is forced to enter. Children are born into definite active relationships with their parents. They are forced by these relationships to carry out definite forms of activity which are determined by the parents. Parents who are cruel to their children and who reject them will, generally speaking, cause them to undertake different forms of activity than those forms of activity undertaken by children whose parents are kind to them and who attempt to give them genuine love and guidance. Every child — at least in most countries — has to go to school. This is not a matter of his or her own choice. Here the activity of those children who are bullied by older children and treated with contempt by teachers will differ substantially from that of those who are treated with kindness and concern both by other children and by teachers. On leaving school each young person has to confront an objective situation involving social relationships in which he or she has to obtain a livelihood. In most cases this involves getting a job — if indeed he or she is lucky enough to get one. The activity involved in a job will of course be determined by the nature of the job itself — it might be interesting and congenial or it might be boring and irksome.

In the above examples, the activity engaged in will give rise to definite psychological characteristics. Thus children who are treated kindly by parents and at school will grow up feeling emotionally secure and self-confident. On the other hand children who are rejected by their parents and treated unkindly at school will tend to feel insecure and be lacking in self-confidence. Similarly, people who enjoy their jobs will, generally speaking, tend to behave more pleasantly towards others than those with less congenial occupations.

Thus far, then, individuals become what they are psychologically through their own activity. The most significant aspects of their activity are those forced on them by social situations and relationships which exist independently of their consciousness or will.[4] It is now necessary to emphasise the historical nature of social situations and relationships. The most significant situations for the young child are of course those occurring within the framework of the nuclear family. Yet the nuclear family has existed only for about the last 5,000 years. This compares with the many tens of thousands of years of humanity's existence.[5] Similarly the situations involving the need to obtain money are of relatively recent historical origin. For the period of time during which money in various forms has existed constitutes only a small fraction of the total time that humanity has been on the earth.[6] Furthermore, the most significant aspects of an individual's activity are carried out by means of relationships with others, and these relationships are of necessity mediated by various aspects of human culture such as concepts, knowledge, language, tools, clothing, buildings and so on, all of which are the products of history. All psychologically significant human activity is therefore historical activity. This historical nature of human activity will form part of the subject matter of the following chapter.

What has just been said helps to provide an understanding of how it is that each generation brings up children destined to grow up to play definite roles in society, thus ensuring the continuity of human culture. For every engineer, miner, dustman, teacher or doctor who dies or retires, other individuals from the next generation capable of carrying out their tasks will take their place. To put it another way, at each stage of historical development, human society has created social situations and relationships capable of producing sufficient individuals able to ensure the maintenance and development of social and cultural institutions.[7]

It is now possible to raise the question of why it is that so much of human behaviour is maladaptive rather than adaptive, a question that contemporary psychology, with its premise that the human race survives primarily through the adaptation of individuals to their environment, cannot answer.

As has been stated, objective social situations (family, school, employment etc.) create individuals capable of playing the various roles that maintain the historical continuity of society. However, not every individual created by objective social situations plays such a role. Thus there exist today in Britain and in other countries such people as the inmates of prisons and mental hospitals, tramps, petty thieves, playboys and professional gamblers, all of whom make no positive contribution to the development of culture at all. Also included in this category at the moment are those millions of unemployed who would be quite willing to work if they had the chance to do so. In addition to creating these sorts of people, objective, historically developed social situations also create large numbers of individuals who, whilst being able to play necessary social roles — at least to some extent — may also engage in neurotic behaviour or else smoke, overeat, volunteer to fight in wars or otherwise behave in a manner likely to decrease their chances of survival. In other words, the social situations and institutions of capitalism are such that they cannot create people capable of playing necessary social roles unless they simultaneously create people who are either parasites or who behave in such a way that their chances of individual survival are reduced. It is only by starting from this premise that the maladaptive behaviour of individuals can be understood.

What determines the future of young children is, of course, their own particular biography. Whether they become parasites or people playing a necessary social role and the extent to which they engage in some form of maladaptive behaviour depends upon their specific individual circumstances. What must be clearly understood, however, is that the biographies of all people take place within an historically developed social framework.

The maladaptive behaviour of large numbers of human individuals can perhaps be better understood when other animal species are considered. Generally speaking, all non-human behaviour is adaptive, if not from the standpoint of the individual than at least from the standpoint of the species as a whole. Domestic dogs and cats will learn to show affection to their owners, thereby ensuring a continued supply of food. Farmyard chickens will rush to meet the person who is coming to feed them. Numerous further examples of adaptive behaviour can be given from the non-human animal kingdom. Some adaptive behaviour is, of course, of an innate, reflex nature. Other forms, especially in higher animal species, are learned. However, whatever form adaptive behaviour takes in non-human animals, virtually all non-human species are prone to what may be termed 'biological wastage'. This implies that many individuals of the different animal species perish before reaching the age at which they can procreate. Many fledgling birds, for example, either fall from the nest or become the victim of predators. Many young fish are eaten by larger fish before they are able to reach maturity. It may well be, of course, that the 'biological wastage' of individual members of some species enhances the chances of survival of the species as a whole. If too many members of a species survived the existing food supply might prove to be inadequate. Thus the very environmental conditions which permit individual members of a given species to adapt successfully are those that at the same time cause other members of the species to perish before they can procreate. It is as if some species have to sacrifice a certain number of their individual members to the rest of nature if they are to survive as biological species.

A certain analogy can be made between the maladaptive behaviour of individual humans and the 'biological wastage' that occurs in other animal species. It has of course already been stressed that the human race survives primarily through the conscious mastery of nature through culture rather than through the adaptation of individual humans to their respective environments. It has also been stressed that it has been necessary for the human race to go through an historical period of class society in order for our skills and abilities to develop to a point at which abundance for all is technically possible. One of the inevitable concomitants of class society is that large numbers of individuals are forced by objective situations to carry out behaviour which is maladaptive, such as becoming neurotic or getting themselves killed in the wars which class society makes inevitable.

Thus humanity has to share in common with other animal species the inevitability of a certain proportion of its individual members being unable to survive until the end of the potential life span is reached. However, this analogy should not be pushed too far. Marxists believe that, in the future world socialist society, individuals will not be regarded as expendable and that each individual will be able to play a useful role — directly or indirectly — in the maintenance and development of our struggle to master nature through production and through culture generally. Thus the 'biological wastage' which is associated with at least most non-human animal species can be regarded as a more or less permanent aspect of nature. In contrast to this, the 'biological wastage' represented by the maladaptive behaviour of human individuals is a manifestation of class society and will disappear when the latter disappears.

To conclude this section of the present chapter, the relationship between the ability of individuals to adapt to their environments and their ability to play objective social roles needs to be made clearer.

It is obvious that many psychological processes have the effect of enabling the individual to survive as a biological organism. Our perceptual processes are clearly adaptive in that they enable us to cope better with the external world. The learning processes which enable us to acquire various social and motor skills are likewise adaptive. It would in fact be true to say that most of the behaviour of young children is adaptive, ranging from their ability to respond positively to their parents' affection to learning to avoid things that hurt them and situations that frighten them.

It would also be true to say, however, that the significance of the adaptive behaviour of children — and indeed of adults — is that it enables individuals to survive until, through their own activity, they learn to play a direct or indirect role in the development of historical culture. Of course, the activity involved in actually playing this role may itself be maladaptive from the standpoint of the long-term survival of the individuals themselves.

To sum up what has just been said, the significance of adaptive behaviour and adaptive mental processes in humans is not that it leads to individual survival as such, but that it leads to the historical development of culture. The maladaptive behaviour of so many individuals in class society represents a necessary sacrifice from the standpoint of the survival of the species.

Although the ability of human individuals to change themselves through their own activity is undoubtedly a precondition for the development of culture, it is not the only one. Just as important is the absence of any genetically determined behaviour which might interfere with the ability of individuals to learn, through their own activity, to play the roles necessary for society to function and to develop. It is necessary to develop this point further, especially as it is contradicted by the views of a number of influential theorists.

Most of the views to which reference has just been made concern aggression towards others. In its simplest form the argument runs something like this: Man is descended from non-human animals. Some of these carry out acts of aggression directed against others of the same species. The human race must therefore have inherited innate tendencies to commit acts of aggression against fellow humans. Despite cultural influences, each one of us possesses savage animal-like 'instincts'.

One of the best known of those who postulate innate aggressive tendencies is the ethologist Lorenz, a highly respected and influential Nobel prize winner. Lorenz does not himself attribute human aggressive behaviour to our evolutionary relatives. Instead he maintains that it became innate during a period in our early history. He writes: 'Aggression . . . is an instinct like any other . . . In man . . . the aggressive impulse often has destructive results.'[8] Further:

> A state of affairs must have prevailed in which the counter-pressures of the hostile neighbouring hordes had become the chief selecting factor determining the next steps of human evolution. Small wonder indeed if it produced a dangerous excess of what has been termed the 'warrior virtues' of man. . . . I believe . . . that present day civilised man suffers from insufficient discharge of his aggressive drive. It is more than probable that the evil effects of the human aggressive drives . . . simply derive from the fact that in prehistoric times intra-specific selection bred into man a measure of aggressive drive for which in the social order of today he finds no adequate outlet.[9]

Intelligent people, Lorenz suggests, should come to terms with the fact that humans possess an aggressive 'instinct' and arrange for our innate aggression to be dissipated through the medium of such activities as football matches rather than through wars.

An assumption somewhat similar to that of Lorenz is made by the writer Robert Ardrey. In his widely read *The Territorial Imperative* he draws attention to the fact that some non-humans animals possess innate tendencies to fight over territorial rights. He draws the conclusion that, since the human race is part of the animal kingdom, human beings must also possess similar tendencies. He further suggests that, when there was overcrowding of humans beyond a certain limit, aggression towards others would naturally result.[10]

The non-Marxist belief that there is no fundamental evolutionary discontinuity between man and other animal species is also revealed in the works of other writers such as Desmond Morris, author of *The Naked Ape*[11] and *The Human Zoo*[12] Essentially the message is the same: We are all basically animals covered over by a thin veneer of 'civilisation'. We all need to recognise this fact and adjust our lives accordingly.[13]

The assumptions just referred to are in effect shared by the psychoanalysts. In Freudian theory each individual is born with an innate disposition to be sexually attracted to the parent of the opposite sex. These feelings of attraction are of course socially reprehensible and are usually repressed from consciousness. Neuroses are held to result from the incomplete repression of these feelings. On top of this, each individual is alleged to be born with an innate desire for self-destruction. This desire is deflected or 'displaced' into feelings of aggression directed toward others. It is this which is held to be responsible for wars and similar upheavals. Freud was deeply pessimistic about the future of the human race. He in fact likened the conscious mind to a man riding a horse (by analogy the subconscious mind containing aggressive tendencies). The man usually had the horse under control but every so often it would rear up and throw him off.[14]

Jung, who led a breakaway movement from Freud and his followers, believed that each individual inherited from his ancestors — both human and non-human — predetermined ways of thinking and behaving. These were termed 'archetypes'. One archetype, named the 'shadow', embodied the non-human animal ancestry of the human race and propelled individuals along a course of aggression and war. The Jungian-oriented psychiatrist Anthony Storr writes:

> The sombre fact is that we are the cruellest and most ruthless species that has ever walked the earth . . . we know in our hearts that each one of us harbours within himself those same savage impulses that lead to murder, to torture and to war.[15]

Last but by no means least come the sociobiologists, represented by such writers as Dawkins[16] and E.O. Wilson.[17] Their view is that the driving force in evolution is the need for genes to survive. The bodies of individual members of a given species exist solely to propagate the genes within them. This implies that the behaviour of every animal — human and non-human — is ultimately determined by the struggle of each individual's genes to survive in order to reproduce. Each set of genes contained within the individual is thus seen as being engaged in a battle the outcome of which is determined by the laws of natural selection. The strongest genes survive and reproduce, the weakest perish in the struggle for survival.

The sociobiological viewpoint therefore necessarily implies that the most significant aspects of human behaviour are determined by genetic factors rather than by the social activity by means of which individuals become able to carry out goal-directed behaviour. The significance of the development of culture based on production by means of which the human race is able to survive is not understood. Culture is simply seen as an incidental manifestation of the survival needs of sets of genes belonging to certain individuals.

The social and political implications of the sociobiological outlook are numerous. It is held, for example, that bonds of affection between parents and their children are attributable to the fact that parental genes are reproduced in their offspring. The primary function of parental affection is therefore to ensure the survival of those genes which have, so to speak, taken up residence in the bodies of their children. Similarly the affection between members of an extended family is to be explained by the fact that they share more genes amongst themselves than they do with others outside the family. Conversely, in the battle for survival, the laws of natural selection ensure that individuals with widely differing genes will exhibit at least a certain amount of hostility to one another. Although sociobiologists may not state so explicitly, the logic of their views must inevitably lead to the conclusion that the greater difference there is between sets of genes, the greater the hostility. This in turn could lead to the justification of racialism and indeed of wars.

It will be noted that the sociobiologists share with the functionalists the belief that there exists no evolutionary discontinuity between humanity and our evolutionary ancestors. In other words, both approaches to the question of humanity's origins share in common a total ignorance concerning the way in which the human race created itself through its own labour in the making and use of tools.

It is also clear that both sociobiologists and psychoanalysts, together with writers such as Lorenz, Ardrey and Morris, postulate innate biological tendencies, existing in all human individuals, causing them to engage in significant forms of goal-directed behaviour in relation to others.

It would probably be true to say that, although the lay public has been considerably influenced by the views of those referred to above, the majority of contemporary psychologists do not believe in the existence of innate aggressive tendencies directed towards others. Indeed, no little effort has been made to provide adequate explanations of aggression. For example, Dollard and his co-workers have postulated that aggression stems from the frustration of individuals in objective situations.[18] Bandura has demonstrated the role of imitation in promoting aggression.[19] However, despite such efforts, no adequate explanation has been forthcoming of why it is that throughout history millions of people have been willing to kill and maim each other in periodic wars. It is as if the 'social environment' contains within itself the cause of wars and similar upheavals to which individuals 'adapt'. But any such explanation must be false. For wars can be fought only if individuals allow themselves to fight them.

Brief mention needs to be made of the fact that aggression is not the only complex behavioural tendency alleged to be innate. Some psychologists assert that I.Q. score, or the ability to perform well on what are known as 'intelligence tests' resides, at least in good measure, in the genes. Thus Jensen, quoted with approval by Eysenck, states categorically: 'Individual differences in intelligence

— that is I.Q. — are predominantly attributable to genetic differences . . .'[20] Marxists would insist that the knowledge required to take an intelligence test is developed, not in the genes of individuals, but in history. Furthermore, quite apart from anything else, the ability to take an intelligence test requires language, which is definitely the product of history rather than of genes.

As in the case of alleged innate aggression, many contemporary psychologists would reject the views of Eysenck and his co-thinkers and correctly argue that the I.Q. score of an individual results from the complex interpenetration of many variables. On top of this, the methods used by those who claim to possess evidence for 'genetic I.Q. scores' have been subjected to severe criticism.[21]

What has to be discussed, of course, is the need for individuals to be able to change themselves in the course of their own activity so that they become able to play objective roles in the historical development of production and of culture generally. A moment's consideration will show the enormous variety of social roles that have had to be played during the history of the human race. The tools, techniques, skills, language, values and customs of those living in the Stone Age differed considerably from those of the present day. Yet, generally speaking, individuals living in those far off times possessed the same sort of anatomical and physiological features as we do today. In today's capitalist society, based on a high level of technology, there are to be found a huge number of social roles that have to be played if the socio-economic system is to function. There are miners, computer operators, dockers, solicitors, housewives, teachers, scientists, clerks, busmen, policemen, dustmen, doctors and dentists. Every newborn individual must possess inherent characteristics that will — at least potentially — enable him or her to play one of the many social roles which need to be played if capitalist society is to function. It is quite evident, therefore, that any innate biological tendency to carry out complex forms of goal-directed behaviour in relation to others would impede the ability of individuals to become able to carry out any of the different social roles which society in its historical development has made necessary. In other words, the ability to learn specific social roles must be such that significant innate tendencies to engage in complex goal-directed behaviour are precluded. As a French psychologist states: 'If the organism were capable of fixing such systems [i.e., innate tendencies to carry out complex behaviour patterns] would not the biological stability of the fixed systems be an obstacle to the rapid development of the techniques without which human history would have been impossible?'[22] This is very well put!

It is in fact now recognised by many psychologists that humanity as a species relies for its survival on complex behaviour which is learned rather than innate. It is stated in a contemporary British textbook that:

> In the most complex of all organisms — namely man — psychologists have tended to see most behaviour as learned. Roughly speaking, if we compare the balance of innately 'wired in' behaviour and learned behaviour, the balance shifts in favour of learning as we ascend from the lower to the higher animals.[23]

An American textbook, drawing heavily on empirical evidence, makes the important point that:

> The newborn begins life with very few specific emotional or motivational responses to other people. He has no innate tendencies to love, fear, approach or avoid people.[24]

Additional evidence for the absence of complex innate behaviour patterns is afforded by the fact that the gestation period for human beings constitutes a relatively small proportion of the total life span. The young human infant is expelled from the safety of the womb to face all sorts of dangers such as extremes of temperature, infections and physical trauma. In contrast to humans, our nearest evolutionary relatives spend a much longer period in the womb relative to life span. As compared with the helplessness of human babies, young apes and monkeys can move about and cling to their mothers soon after birth, thanks to the fact that they have had a relatively longer time to develop their bodies within the safety of the womb. From these facts must arise the question of why young humans are expelled from the safety of the womb so early in life as compared to other animals. Surely the answer can only be that the evolution of the human race demanded an early exposure of the young to social situations in which they could learn elementary social responses leading to their increasing integration into human culture.

The absence of similar gestation periods between humans and our evolutionary relatives is accompanied by another important difference. This is the relative difference in the length of time during which the young remain dependent on adults.

> The human infant is helpless for a longer time than any other mammal. If we consider only man's nearest relatives in the animal world, a scale of dependency can be made from the comparatively primitive lemur through the more highly evolved primates to man. The newborn lemur can move about by himself within

a few hours; the monkey is dependent for a few days or weeks; the infant chimpanzee remains with his mother three to six months. The human infant is dependent for a number of years. Despite (or because of) this slow start a human being has had a highly diversified background by the time he becomes an adult. He is subjected to a long period of learning and interaction with other before he is fully 'on his own'.[25]

It is clear that this relatively long period of dependence is necessary for the child to learn patterns of behaviour which will equip him or her to play an objective historically determined social role in later life.

Finally, there is an important theoretical reason for rejecting beliefs in significant unlearned social behavioural patterns. It is necessary to recall the statement made by the anthropologists Howells and Washburn and quoted in Chapter Two that: 'the size of the brain . . . has increased threefold subsequent to the use and manufacture of tools.' What has been implied here is that about two thirds of the human brain has been developed through labour. This in turn must imply that there are very few aspects of human behaviour — at least above the level of certain innate reflexes — that have not been created by and in the course of the struggle of developing humanity to raise itself above the rest of the animal kingdom through the making and use of tools.

An analogy would be useful here. The prototype humans created by labour possessed physical characteristics perfectly suited to the labour process: Erect gait, sensitive and supple hands, opposable thumb and forefinger, stereoscopic vision, developed vocal cords and so on. Conversely, they did not possess — and we do not possess now — any physiological or anatomical characteristics which would make them or us unsuitable to participate either directly in the process of production or in other social activities which indirectly assist in its continuity and development. Of course, we do possess some useless physical vestiges of our evolutionary past. Examples are the appendix and toenails. But these do not hinder our participation in humanity's mastery of nature through production in the least. In a similar fashion we also possess some behaviours inherited from our evolutionary ancestors: We sometimes howl with pain and become paralysed with fear.[26] However, behaviour such as this certainly does not interfere with the development of production, any more than does the possession of toenails.

To conclude this section of the present chapter, it may be stated with confidence that humanity, having developed through its own labour, is in all respects perfectly suited for the continual historical development of culture based on production. There are no innate behaviour patterns that could put limits to our mastery over nature. Wars and similar upheavals which cause millions of people to kill each other are not to be explained by savage animal-like tendencies innate in individuals. Rather they are to be explained by historically produced objective social situations, existing independently of the will and consciousness of individuals. It is these objective situations, of course, which cause individuals to undertake definite forms of activity which in turn cause them to develop psychological tendencies such as feelings of hostility towards other human beings.

The third quality necessary for individuals to possess if human culture is to exist and develop, namely consciousness, has now to be discussed. The term 'consciousness' has been much abused in contemporary psychology. It is often used very loosely, often synonymously with other terms such as 'attention' or 'wakefulness'. However, consciousness is a definite and important philosophical category, which it is necessary to understand if human individuals are to be understood.

From the Marxist standpoint, there are two essential and closely related aspects of human consciousness. The first of these is the ability to perceive the various component parts of the world in terms of what they can become with human intervention. Thus carpenters can look at their tools and some wood and perceive in them the table they want to make. Similarly a farmer can perceive a field in terms of the crops that could be grown on it. An infinite number of such examples could be given. The second aspect of consciousness is the ability to be the subject of one's own activity, that is to view one's own activity objectively. This implies looking, in one's imagination, at one's own past, present and future activity from the side, as it were, as if it were perceived by someone else. This ability enables us to examine critically our own past and thereby learn from our own mistakes, not in a mechanical fashion like a rat in a Skinner box, but consciously. In our imagination we can ask ourselves such questions as: 'Could I have done better?' or 'Should I have done it the other way?' and in this way prepare ourselves to accomplish more effectively present and future tasks. Similarly, activity in contemporary situations can be undertaken self-critically. Thus in driving a car, we can always remind ourselves not to overtake unless it is safe to do so and to observe other elementary precautions. Importantly, in planning a future task, we can think of a number of alternative ways of achieving it, sum up the 'pros and cons' and come to a decision as to precisely what course of action to undertake.

A little consideration will show how the two aspects of consciousness to which reference has just been made are inter-related. They are inter-related because of to the historical nature of human knowledge. The ability to perceive the world in terms of what can be done to it with human intervention presupposes historically developed knowledge and skills. To return to the two examples given above, carpenters could not imagine the transformation of the wood into a table unless previous generations had developed saws, hammers, chisels and so on, just as no farmer could perceive a field in terms of growing crops on it without the previous historical development of agriculture. This must imply, however, that when individuals regard their own activity objectively, as if from the side, they must perceive it in terms of historically developed knowledge of what human beings are able to do, their skills, abilities, knowledge, capacities and so on.

It is necessary to emphasise that human consciousness is the product of social activity, especially since without an understanding of this fact it would be difficult to comprehend the precise relationship between the individual on the one hand and society on the other. (This will form the subject matter of the next chapter.)

The social nature of our ability to perceive the world in terms of what it could become with human intervention is quite evident, since it clearly depends directly on historically developed knowledge. Less obvious, however, is the social nature of the ability of individuals to view their own activity objectively. It is therefore necessary to comment on this particular ability further.

Of direct relevance to this question is an extremely interesting and significant contribution made by psychologists in the former USSR. This is the training of a relatively large number of blind deaf-mutes up to a reasonably high educational level. There are in fact a number of individuals who were either born blind and deaf-mute or who became so soon after birth engaged in postgraduate research in universities. This of course represents an outstanding scientific achievement on the part of Russian psychology. It can be stated without fear of contradiction that contemporary psychologists in the West, with their view of individuals as biological machines interacting with the environment, could not possibly undertake successfully such a challenging task.[27] Briefly, the training of blind deaf-mutes involved, not a mechanical system of rewards and punishments such as behaviourists would undoubtedly attempt, but rather continual joint activity carried out by the individuals and their teachers. For example, in a feeding situation the teachers would help the children to hold a spoon and then guide their hands and spoons to their mouths. Similar joint activity involving the guiding, by the teacher, of the children's various actions with different objects, together with the constant correction of mistakes, would also — over a long period of time — be undertaken. Eventually the children's imagination would develop in such a way that they could mentally put themselves in the place of the teacher, thereby attempting to correct their own mistakes. Thus they would come to possess the ability to 'view' their own activity 'from the side', that is to become the subjects of their own activity.[28]

Some of the Russian psychologists engaged in this work maintain that the psychological development of these blind deaf-mutes provides a model, a sort of slow motion film, of how consciousness develops in normal children. It would perhaps be wise to treat this view with a little caution. Psychological variables such as sight, speech and hearing undoubtedly influence the way consciousness develops in normal children. This having been said, however, the fact remains that the immense contribution to psychological science just described does show the essentially social nature of the acquisition of human consciousness.

From the Marxist standpoint, consciousness represents an essential and fundamental aspect of human existence. For the basis of human society is production and this cannot take place without individuals who possess consciousness as defined above. Marx writes:

> A spider conducts operations that resemble those of a weaver, and a bee puts to shame many an architect in the construction of her cells. But what distinguishes the worst architect from the best of bees is this, that the architect raises his structure in the imagination before he erects it in reality. At the end of every labour process, we get a result that already existed in the imagination of the labourer at its commencement. He not only effects a change of form in the material on which he works, but he also realises a purpose of his own that gives the law to his *modus operandi*, and to which he must subordinate his will.[29]

It is clear that in the example given by Marx the architect performs his task with consciousness. He perceives a plot of land, building materials and so on in terms of what they can become as a result of human activity. Further, he can think of his own future activity which will take place when he supervises the various stages of construction. The same is true of every labour process, even though this may not be immediately apparent. The repetitive movements of a worker on a motor car assembly line may not at first seem to conform to Marx's 'model' of the labourer, but production is a social process involving co-operation, and the production manager who superintends the assembly line certainly carries the finished product in his imagination. Furthermore, every assembly line worker has to perform his given task, however repetitive it is and however limited its aim might be, with consciousness.

From a Marxist standpoint, consciousness as defined above represents an essential feature of all genuinely human individuals — as distinct from members of the biological species *Homo sapiens*. Newborn babies, whilst being members of the biological species, are not strictly speaking truly human. They only become so to the extent that they acquire the ability to view their own activity objectively and perceive the world with historically developed knowledge of what it could become with human intervention. Thus for Marxists humans are essentially historical individuals. This point will be developed further in the following chapter.

This chapter has outlined those characteristics of individuals necessary for human culture to exist and develop — the ability to change during and as a result of one's activity, an absence of complex innate behaviour patterns that would prevent individuals from learning to play specific social roles, together with the possession of consciousness. A knowledge of these characteristics is essential for an understanding of the relationship between the individual and society, which can now be considered.

NOTES TO CHAPTER FOUR

1. Inhelder, B. *Some Aspects of Piaget's Genetic Approach to Cognition*. Quoted in Furth, H. *Piaget and Knowledge*. Prentice Hall, 1969, p. 24.

2. Hegel, G.W.F. *The Phenomenology of Mind*. Allen and Unwin, 1931, p. 338.

3. Luria, A.R. *The Working Brain*. Penguin, 1973, p. 327.

4. It should not be thought that, because the need for action is forced on individuals, they do not possess free will. The question of choice and free will is discussed in Chapter Six.

5. See, for example, Engels, F. *The Origin of the Family, Private Property and the State*. Lawrence and Wishart, 1972.

6. The historical development of money is discussed thoroughly in Marx's *Capital*, Vol.1. Chapter 3.

7. Here it is worth repeating a point already made in Chapter Two. Human history has not proceeded smoothly and uninterruptedly, in a straight line, as it were. Witness the collapse of the Roman Empire and the decline of civilisations such as that of ancient Egypt. However, the fact remains that, despite perturbations, humanity has been able to evolve historically from the Stone Age to the Atomic Age.

8. Lorenz, K. *On Aggression*. Methuen, 1967, p. x.

9. *Ibid*. p. 209.

10. Ardrey, R. *The Territorial Imperative*. Fontana, 1977.

11. Morris, D. *The Naked Ape*. Cape, 1967.

12. Morris, D. *The Human Zoo*. Cape, 1969.

13. Genuine Marxists cannot regard Marx or his co-thinker Frederick Engels as infallible popes. It is therefore necessary to recognise that Engels made the same sort of mistake as those writers just mentioned. Thus in one of his major works Engels writes: 'It is . . . inherent in the descent of man from the animal world that he can never entirely rid himself from the beast, so that it can always be only a question of more or less, of a difference in the degree of bestiality or of humanity.' *(Anti-Duhring*. FLPH, Moscow, 1954, p. 251.) It is obvious here that Engels could

not have realised the significance of his own well-known essay *The Part Played by Labour in the Transition from Ape to Man*. (See Chapter 2, Note 4)

14. See for example Freud, S. *New Introductory Lectures on Psychoanalysis*. Norton, 1933.

15. Storr, A. *Human Aggression*. Allen Lane, The Penguin Press, 1968.

16. Dawkins, R. *The Selfish Gene*. O.U.P., 1978.

17. Wilson, E.O. *Sociobiology: The New Synthesis*. Harvard University Press, 1975.

18. Dollard, J. et al. *Frustration and Aggression*. Yale University Press, 1939.

19. Bandura, A. *Social Learning Through Imitation*. In Jones, M.R. (Ed) *Nebraska Symposium on Motivation*. University of Nebraska Press, 1962.

20. Jensen, A. *Bulletin of the Atomic Scientists*, March 1970. Quoted in Eysenck, H.J. *Race, Intelligence and Education*. Maurice Temple Smith Ltd., 1971, p. 25.

21. See for example Kamin, L. *The Science and Politics of I.Q.* Penguin, 1977. The question of intelligence is discussed further in Chapter Eleven.

22. Wallon, H. *L'evolution psychologique de l'enfant*. Librairie Armand Colin, Paris, 1968, pp. 63-64. Quoted in Mikhailov, F. *The Riddle of the Self*. Progress Publishers, 1980, pp. 189-190.

23. Radford, J. and Govier, E.A. *Textbook of Psychology*. Sheldon Press, 1980, p. 216.

24. Mussen, P., Conger, J. and Kagan, J. *Child Development and Personality*. Fourth Edition, 1974, p. 193.

25. Hilgard, E., Atkinson, R. and Atkinson, R. *Introduction to Psychology*. Fifth Edition. Harcourt Brace Jovanovitch, 1953, p. 54.

26. Doubtless the tendency to become paralysed with fear assisted our evolutionary ancestors to survive in situations in which they suddenly found themselves close to predators. Instant immobility would cause them to be less likely to be perceived.

27. For an account of this scientific achievement see Meshcheryakov, A. *Awakening to Life*. Progress Publishers, 1979.

28. See Mikhailov,F. *op. cit.* pp. 260-263.

29. Marx, *Capital* Vol.1. FLPH, 1959, p. 178.

5

THE INDIVIDUAL AS A PART OF SOCIETY AND OF HISTORY

The title of this chapter is self-explanatory. In it the following questions will be discussed: The basic contradiction facing the human race (the need to transmit skills and knowledge from generation to generation and the inability to fix these genetically). The false nature of the 'adaptation', 'adjustment' and 'interaction' approaches. The dialectical nature of the relationship of individuals to society and to history. Consciousness and creativity (the terms being used in a Marxist sense). Why human society is able to change. The relevance of the categories 'universal', 'individual' and 'particular' to an understanding of individuals. How individuals can be changed. Finally, why it is that modern psychologists fail to understand the true relationship between individuals and society.

The question of the relationship between the individual and society is one that is generally characterised by enormous confusion. This is especially true of contemporary psychology.

Generally speaking, there are two poles of thought. On the one hand, as has been pointed out in the previous chapter, there are those who, like the sociobiologists, together with some ethologists, maintain that most complex behaviour patterns directed toward others are determined by the make up of the genes of individuals. This conception of course resembles that of many lay people, who postulate the existence of what is vaguely termed 'human nature' with which each individual is allegedly born. From this standpoint, society is simply a manifestation of the content of our genes. On the other hand, there is another viewpoint which is probably that of the majority of contemporary psychologists. These believe that 'society' is something to which individuals have to learn to 'adjust' or 'adapt'. This latter view reflects the 'functionalist' approach discussed in Chapter Three. Thus a comparatively recent American textbook refers with obvious approval to 'a biological survival model . . . which borrows much from Darwin . . . individuals must adapt to the world around them.'[1] Further: 'The structure of a society and its cultural traditions exert powerful influences on the personalities of individuals born into it.'[2] The Skinnerian 'reinforcement' model referred to previously is relevant here. Rats in a 'Skinner box' will learn to behave in certain ways, for example pressing a bar, if the behaviour is 'reinforced' by food. Many contemporary psychologists believe that, in an analogous way, 'society' reinforces individuals in various ways. The individual is held to 'adjust' or 'adapt' to society by responding to society's 'reinforcers'. It is stated that:

> For ages man has attributed the social conditions in which he finds himself to various sources of motivation within himself. Society is the way it is because man's nature is the way it is, and we may despair of trying to change it. Reinforcement theory suggests at the outset that man is the way he is because of the conditions prevailing in his social situation. The sources of social reinforcement are to be found in the structure of society, and we may have some hope of being able to find them and perhaps some day of changing them.[3]

The clash of viewpoints just referred to — on the one hand that which sees society as the manifestation of behaviour patterns innate in individuals, on the other that which sees it as something to which each individual has to adapt — does not always reflect a clear-cut division. Freudians, for example, see the individual as possessing innate unconscious sexual and aggressive urges (contained in the 'id'). It is these urges which are alleged to be responsible both for human culture and for wars. Since the individual is brought up in society, however, he or she has to *adapt* to society by internalising society's moral codes and values. This 'internalisation' of social morals and values form the basis of the 'superego', which contains the individual's conscience. The individual's 'personality' is thus held to be in large measure determined by a continual conflict between innate anti-social urges on the one hand the internalised demands of social morality on the other.

There is, of course, a relatively large section of modern academic psychology which is referred to as 'social psychology'. It constitutes a definite part of most university psychology degree courses. Lay people may well be led to think that social psychologists (as opposed to those studying, for example, 'information processing') would take as one of their starting points the need to elucidate the precise nature of society and of the relationship of individuals to it. But this is far from being so. The basic assumption of social psychologists is still that of individuals adjusting to or being influenced by various aspects of the environment, in this case those of other individuals or of groups of individuals. Thus the author of a textbook of social psychology states:

> The key phrase . . . is 'social influence'. And this becomes our working definition of social psychology: the influence that people have upon the beliefs or behaviour of others.[4]

This outlook of course represents no more than the previously quoted functionalist belief that the 'structure of society . . . exert(s) powerful influences on the personalities born into it.'

The relationship between the individual and society is a question that cannot be understood unless the precise nature of human society is made clear. For this it is necessary to return to the Marxist conception of humanity outlined earlier. The human race raised itself from the animal kingdom — and exists to this day — through the making and use of tools. In this basic activity individuals enter into definite relationships with each other. It is on these relations of production that all other social relationships ultimately depend. The making and use of tools (production) of course involves historically developed knowledge and skills. It is this knowledge and these skills that have to be handed on from generation to generation if we are to survive as a species. However, as has been pointed out in Chapter Four, the many historically developed production techniques and skills are so varied and complex that the learning of them by individuals would be impossible if we were born with fixed and rigid patterns of behaviour. Similarly, the learning of other skills and knowledge not directly linked with production but entirely necessary if production is to continue and to develop — skills and knowledge associated with child-rearing, art, literature, natural science, civil administration and so on — would also be impossible. The human race, therefore, during our whole historical development, *faces a contradiction unlike that facing any other animal species*. On the one hand, skills and knowledge associated directly or indirectly with production have to be transmitted from generation to generation. Yet on the other hand the very nature of our skills and knowledge precludes the possibility that they be passed on through genetic fixation, that is through fixed, unlearned and rigid behaviour patterns. It is the way in which this contradiction is resolved that determines the nature of human society.[5]

It was also argued in Chapter Four that individuals develop psychologically as true human beings during and as a result of their own practical activity. It needs to be repeated that this activity takes place in situations involving definite social relationships (those of family, school and so on)[6] which exist independently of the individual's consciousness or will and are the product of historical development. In other words, activity is forced on individuals by objective social relationships and it is through this activity — carried out directly or indirectly with others — that the consciousness, goals and knowledge of individuals develop. The basis of the conscious life-activity[7] of individuals, therefore, is the objective social relationships which force them to undertake definite forms of activity, together with the means and media of these relationships such as language, concepts, values and knowledge plus more tangible products of historical culture such as money, buildings, tools and clothes.[8]

It therefore follows that the contradiction referred to above is continuously resolved by the passing on, from one generation to the next, of historically developed social relationships and their means and media. It is only within this context that it is possible to arrive at a satisfactory definition of human society. *Human society is the sum total of social relationships, together with the means and media of these relationships.* It exists and develops as a resolution of this fundamental contradiction. The transmission of social relationships and of their means and media from generation to generation must therefore constitute *the very essence of human history.* To illustrate this point, it could be said that although very few people in Britain were alive one hundred years ago, many objective social relationships, together with their means and media, remain relatively unchanged. Men still have to get coal out of the ground, build houses and empty dustbins. The upbringing of children is still the legal responsibility of the biological parents. Parliament still makes laws, which are enforced by the police and the judiciary. Clergymen still take services, bookmakers still take bets and parents still take their children to the zoo. This relative continuity is only possible because each member of each new generation carries out his or her life-activity on the basis of the social relationships and their means and media created and brought about by the life-activity of previous generations. In turn, the life-activity of every new generation re-creates the relationships and their means and media which will determine the life-activity of the following generation. Of course, during the past hundred years numerous changes have taken place in British life. Coal miners now use complex machinery rather than picks and shovels to extract coal, while the number of one-parent families has increased. However, a discussion of the reasons for the continual changes that take place in society, that is in history, will be deferred until later in this chapter.

It needs to be made absolutely clear that human life-activity cannot take place outside the framework of social relationships and the means and media of these relationships. It is impossible for individuals to carry out purposeful activity without the relatively continual co-ordination of that activity with the purposeful activity of others.[9] Buyers must co-ordinate their activity with that of sellers, employers with employees, husbands with wives, parents with children, pupils with teachers, goalkeepers with centre forwards, car drivers with other drivers, conductors with others in the orchestra. The list is endless. Similarly, the co-ordination of the purposeful life-activity of individuals with that of others involves at all times and at all stages the means and media of social relationships. Such co-ordination would be impossible without means and media such as language, concepts, knowledge, money, houses, cars, clothing and so on. All products of human culture, including art, literature and music, represent — directly or indirectly — means and media of the coordination of the life-activity of individuals with that of others. It is worth re-emphasising that, since all purposive behaviour involves thought, and since thought involves historically developed language, concepts, values and so on, such behaviour cannot take place outside these means and media. Marx writes:

> When I am active *scientifically*, etc. — when I am engaged in activity which I can seldom perform in direct community with others — then I am *social*, because I am active as a *man*. Not only is the material of my activity given to me as a social product (as is even the language in which the thinker is active): my *own* existence *is* social activity, and therefore that which I make of myself, I make of myself for society and with the consciousness of myself as a social being.[10]

Even hermits who retreat into the wilderness cannot survive on their own unless they use social means and media such as skills and knowledge. An analogy would be of use here. The basis of the physical development of children developing in their mothers' womb is the life-activity of the mothers. If the mothers should die the developing children would also die. After birth, the basis of their development is the *social* 'womb' of relationships entered into with the mother and with others, using means and media such as food, bottles, cots, blankets, nappies, rattles and so on. Eventually, of course, the child's life-activity, carried out in co-ordination with that of others, leads to the development of truly human consciousness, and then he or she will become a fully-fledged human being as distinct from being simply a member of the species *Homo sapiens*.

The basic premise of academic psychology — that we develop psychologically as individuals by adapting or adjusting to our respective environments —

is so deeply entrenched that it is necessary to state clearly and precisely why it is false. Of course, lay persons can use the term 'adapt' and 'adjust' to describe behaviour in a meaningful manner. They can say that a child has adapted or adjusted to a new school situation. They can also say that members of a family have adapted or adjusted to the loss of a loved one. However, from the standpoint of a genuinely scientific psychology, which must of necessity start from a clear understanding of the relationship between individuals and society, the use of these terms to describe the very basis of the life-activity of individuals is totally inadmissible. For the following reason: Individuals become what they are psychologically through and as a result of their life-activity, the basis of which is their social relationships together with their means and media. (If the term 'social environment' is used it can only refer meaningfully to social relationships.) What is of crucial importance here is that individuals themselves, that is their needs, skills, abilities, values and so on, must constitute essential elements of any relationships into which they enter. Examples are necessary to make this clearer. Factory workers enter into social relationships with their respective employers. They are paid wages in return for their ability to enter into the process of production, that is their ability to work. It is necessary to understand that this ability to work is an organic part of the individual workers themselves. It does not exist outside them. Similarly it is their need for money, reflecting in turn a need for the satisfaction of internal, organic needs such as those for food and shelter, which constitutes a definite aspect of the social relationship. Also, of course, individual employers have organic needs which they have to satisfy by means of the money obtained from employing people to work in their factories. Thus the social relationship between factory workers and their employers cannot take place apart from the internal, organic needs and abilities of both. The social relationship between patients and doctors cannot exist apart from each patient's respective illness or injury on the one hand and the doctors' *internal*, individual medical skills and knowledge on the other. The social relationship of marriage, of course, involves all sorts of internal needs and abilities. Sexual relations between marriage partners, which cannot take place without individual anatomical and physiological features, provide just one example. Virtually all social relationships, especially those between adults, are mediated by means of language. But language can never exist apart from the individuals who speak it and who understand it. It can never be something which stands above and apart from individuals.

To put what has been said in another way, no social relationships can take place without their respective means and media. Although of course there are means and media which are not intrinsic components of individuals — such as money, tools, cars, houses, clothes and works of art — social relationships as a whole (i.e., society) cannot exist outside internal, individual means and media such as organic needs for food and shelter, also knowledge, values, abilities and skills. Furthermore, the felt need for houses, cars, clothes and so on which cause individuals to enter into social relationships in order to obtain or use these represent the *internal* needs of definite concrete individuals. Thus it is meaningless to talk — as modern psychologists do — of individuals existing by means of their adaptation or adjustment to any 'social environment', just as it is meaningless to write of 'the structure of society' (i.e., social relationships) exerting 'powerful influences on the personalities born into it'. For — it must be re-emphasised — it is individuals themselves (with their internal needs, abilities, etc.) who constitute a definite and integral part of any social relationships into which they enter.

It is thus clear that individuals cannot adapt or adjust to social relationships (society) of which they themselves constitute a definite part. One cannot adjust to oneself. Individuals can never adapt or adjust to 'powerful influences' exerted by 'the structure of society' precisely because they themselves — their own internal needs, values and abilities — constitute an integral part of social relationships and hence of 'the structure of society'. The false nature of the basic premise of functionalism lies precisely in this fact. The premise of functionalism needs to be contrasted to the insight of Marx who, in one of this earliest works, wrote that: 'Above all we must avoid postulating "society" as an abstraction vis-à-vis the individual.'[11] Here Marx undoubtedly was thinking of his basic premise that humanity exists by mastering the environment (rather than by adapting to it) and changing itself in the process.

The conception of human individuals existing as biological organisms adapting or adjusting to their respective 'social environments' is closely linked with the view that we develop psychologically as a result of our interactions with other individuals (or with the 'social environment', which really means the same thing.) Thus what is referred to as 'personality' is defined in the *Encyclopedia of Psychology* (edited by Eysenck) as follows: 'Personality is the relatively stable organisation of a person's motivational dispositions, arising from the interaction between biological drives and the social and physical environment.'[12]

As with the term 'adaptation', the term 'interaction' can be used meaningfully by lay people. Marriage partners can be said to interact with each other, as can the opponents in a game of chess. However, the term becomes meaningless when used by psychologists intent on elucidating the basis of human thought and behaviour. The word 'interaction' used in the context of the above definition has to be rejected on the same grounds as the terms 'adaptation' and 'adjustment'. Society (the 'social environment') consists of relationships and, as has been shown above, individuals constitute a definite part of all social relationships. Therefore, just as one cannot 'adapt' or 'adjust' to oneself, so one cannot interact with oneself. The concept of 'interaction' used by modern psychologists is closely linked to the current *mechanistic* view of human individuals. This will be discussed in the following chapter.

The failure to understand that individuals themselves constitute definite aspects of their own relationships has given rise to the very misleading concept of 'socialisation'. The implicit assumption underlying this conception is that the environment of a young child can be divided into two. Thus:

> Learning comes about through the contact the child is constantly making with the world around him. It is a world inhabited by other people who influence his development in a number of different ways. It is also a world of things and natural forces and elements like gravity, wind and rain. Thus the child's environment has a social and a physical aspect . . . The term 'socialisation' [is] used to refer to the effects of the social aspect of the environment on the young child.[13]

What the author of these lines fails to understand is that the needs to combat 'gravity, wind and rain' constitute definite aspects of objective social relationships. The need to combat gravity involves learning to walk on two feet. This in turn involves the co-ordination of the activity of the young child on the one hand and the activity of other members of the family on the other. Similarly the need to combat the effects of wind and rain involves dressing up in a raincoat and stout shoes, which the young child cannot do unaided. The need of each individual to combat physical aspects of the environment represents an aspect of his or her own life-activity. Moreover, it needs to be stressed again that human life-activity can take place only in the context of direct or indirect relationships with others. To look at the matter in another way, the activity involved in satisfying an individual's basic bodily needs such as those of food and shelter must at all times involve, directly or indirectly, active relationships with others. And relationships *are* society. What occurs in the life of the young child is not a process of 'socialisation' but rather one of *individualisation*. The child acquires his or her own mental life through the *specific* relationships into which he or she enters, together with their specific means and media, including his or her own bodily needs.

For this reason, therefore, society is not and can never be something that stands above the individual. It is not — let it be repeated — something to which individuals have to adapt or adjust. It is not something designated by the term 'social environment' (or 'the social aspect of the environment' which has 'effects' on 'the young child'). Rather, *society is the very content of the lives of individuals.* There can be no human life-activity outside relationships with others and outside the means and media of such social relationships. Likewise there can be no mature human thought without historically developed language and concepts. Similarly, since human history is essentially society in its movement and development, history must also be regarded as the content of people's lives. History is not, as is widely supposed, simply a backdrop against which people enact their individual lives. Rather, it constitutes the very *biographies* of all individuals.

At this point it might be objected that the content of a person's life might include features which are not directly historical. This is indeed true. A man living today might fall down and break his leg just as one of his ancestors did 20,000 years ago. The important point, however, is this: Although their actual fractures may be very similar, the former would go to the hospital, have an X-ray and get his leg set in a plaster in a manner which would have been impossible for the latter. This would also involve differences in historically developed human consciousness. The former would think in terms of getting to hospital to obtain help. The latter would probably accept that he would soon die or at least remain a life-long cripple.

The essentially *historical* nature of the human individual can be seen more clearly through a consideration of formal education. When children go to school, they do not have to discover for themselves the techniques of simple algebra, which were developed by the Arabs. All they have to do is to assimilate and understand what has been discovered by previous generations. Similarly when learning chemistry they do not have to discover for themselves the relationships between the elements that are expressed in the Periodic Table of the Elements. This was done by Mendeleyev, and all anyone learning this particular aspect of chemistry has to do is to absorb Mendeleyev's discovery. Medical students absorb the discoveries of past generations such as those of anaesthetics, X-rays and antibiotics. Of course, having absorbed such knowledge, they become able to go on to make fresh discoveries themselves. Science can go forward precisely because each young scientist has absorbed and assimilated the achievements, inventions and techniques of past generations.

What has just been said is, of course, clearly understood by most people. What is not generally understood, however, is that virtually *all* aspects of life rest on the life-activity of past generations. For what has just been said about mathematics, medicine and science generally is also true of art, religious institutions, child-rearing practices, law, morality, civil administration and so on. Importantly, it is also true of *all* social relationships and their means and media which, Marxists insist, are all ultimately derived from the relations of production. It is this aspect of the historical development of individuals which is not clearly understood, especially by the majority of contemporary psychologists. For example, the institution of the monogamous nuclear family is not seen by most people as the product of a long historical development, but as the result of some innate motivation in individuals. Likewise, the cut-throat morality of modern capitalism, summed up by the old saying: 'Every man for himself and the devil take the hindmost' is often held to result from some innate 'human nature'.

In one of their earlier works, *The German Ideology*, Marx and Engels outline the historical nature of individuals as follows:

> Individuals have always and in all circumstances 'proceeded *from* themselves', but since they were not *unique* in the sense of not needing any connections with one another, and since their *needs*, consequently their nature, and the method of satisfying their needs, connected them with one another (relations between the sexes, exchange, division of labour), they *had to* enter into relations with one another. Moreover, since they entered into intercourse with one another not as pure egos, but as individuals at a definite stage of development of the productive forces [i.e., abilities, skills, etc.] and requirements, and since this intercourse, in its turn, determined production and needs, it was, therefore, precisely the personal, individual behaviour of individuals, their behaviour to one another as individuals, that created the existing relations and daily reproduces them anew. . . . Hence it certainly follows that the development of an individual is determined by the development of all the others with whom he is directly or indirectly associated, and that the different generations of individuals entering into relation with one another are connected with one another, that the physical existence of later generations is determined by that of their predecessors, and that these later generations inherit the productive forces and forms of intercourse accumulated by their predecessors, their own mutual relations being determined thereby. In short, it is clear that development takes place and that the history of a single individual cannot possibly be separated from the history of preceding or contemporary individuals, but is determined by this history.[14]

This quotation shows that, well over 100 years ago, the developing Marxist world outlook included a conception of a definite relation of individuals to society and its history. However, it should also be pointed out that at least a few psychologists have come close to recognising the basically historical nature of individuals. Thus J.A.C. Brown, writing of the Marxist-influenced personality theorist Erich Fromm and of the analyst Erik Erikson, states that:

> Character is moulded by the family, which is described as the 'psychic agency of society'. The family is a factory which produces characters, but it produces them according to definite specifications supplied by the society within which it is functioning. While a certain degree of latitude may be allowed in character-formation, it is generally the case that if a society is to function well its members must acquire the kind of character which makes them *want* to act appropriately as members of the society or of a special class within it. They have to *desire* what objectively is necessary to do. *Outer force* is replaced by *inner compulsion*, and by the particular kind of human energy which is channelled into character traits. (Fromm, 'Individual and Social Origins of Neurosis. *American Sociological Review*, LX, 1944). Another analyst, Erik Erikson, notes that in primitive societies: '. . . systems of child training . . . represent unconscious attempts at creating out of human raw material that configuration of attitudes which is (or once was) the optimum under the tribe's particular natural conditions and economic-historical necessities. (Quoted in David Riesman's *The Lonely Crowd*). Thus each society develops in its members a "social character" common to all and derived from its dominant social and cultural patterns, and upon this are imposed the variations of the individualised character permitted in that society'.[15]

Although both Fromm and Erikson do not break from the premise that the individual 'adapts' to society, they do at least indicate the social and historical nature of what Fromm terms 'character'. It is indeed a pity that so few psychologists have followed up this promising approach!

It is now possible to consider in another way the question of the relationship that exists between the individual and society. This relationship has to be understood *dialectically* rather than mechanically. This statement requires some explanation, especially as the term 'dialectical' is little understood by non-Marxists. The term denotes the essential unity, conflict and interpenetration of opposites. Thus both the individual and society are opposites in the sense that one is not the other. A human individual is a biological organism, obeying the laws of human biology, who has been born and who will die. On the other hand society is the sum total of social relationships — parent/child, husband/wife, employer/worker and so on which change in the course of history in a manner determined by historical laws which have objective existence independently of the will and consciousness of individuals (see Chapter Two). To put it another way, an individual's life span is finite, determined by the laws of human biology, while the history of human society, determined by historical laws is — at least in the foreseeable future — an unending process. However, although the individual and society are opposites they are at the same time *united in conflict*. Despite the fact that many contemporary psychologists see society as something to which individuals have to 'adjust' or 'adapt', what has to be faced is the obvious truth that without individuals there would be no society. Individuals, and only individuals, make history and thus cause society to be what it is. Some more than others, of course. We have only to consider the impact of a few outstanding individuals to illustrate the point. Einstein, Darwin, Shakespeare and Marx come to mind. And without the individual personalities of Lenin and Trotsky there would have been no Russian Revolution of 1917. Thus while history constitutes the sum total of the biographies of all past and present individuals, the individual mind represents the individual's unique way of understanding and treating the world, determined by his or her unique biography.

On the other hand, however, individuals become what they are only because their life-activity takes place in historically developed social situations which confront them with the need for action. Simultaneously individuals make history while history makes individuals. This is the dialectical conflict of opposites referred to above. To look at the matter in another way, *the individual is the social and the social is the individual*. Further, since human thought is impossible without historically developed language and concepts, and since the thought of no two individuals can be alike, thought is *simultaneously* both unique and individual on the one hand and social and historical on the other.[16]

A word of warning is necessary here. While it is true that individuals make history and history makes individuals, a qualification is essential. Individuals become humans as such — as distinct from being members of the species *Homo sapiens* — only to the extent to which they acquire human *consciousness*. As has been outlined in the previous chapter, this implies viewing the world with *historical* knowledge of what the world could become with human intervention. Only this knowledge, together with the ability to be the subject of one's own activity, makes it possible for the individual to master his or her environment consciously rather than simply change it as a non-human animal would do. Since children acquire consciousness only as a result of their activity in objective historically developed social situations which exist independently of their will, it can be said that before individuals can make history, history has to make them. To put it another way, individuals can make history only because they themselves are the *products* of history. It is therefore obvious that without a clear understanding of the true nature and role of consciousness the relationship between individuals and society cannot be understood.

In view of what has been said in preceding paragraphs it becomes clear that each individual is the product of history. However, it remains to be shown that *all* human individuals — rather than just outstanding ones — are in fact the makers of history as well as its products. History (the movement of society) can take place only to the extent that social relationships and their means and media are transmitted (and developed) from generation to generation. Every worker who obtains employment in a factory thereby plays the role of helping to lay the basis for future worker/employer relationships. Every man or woman who marries thereby maintains intact the historically developed institution of marriage. Every child who goes to school helps to maintain intact educational establishments. Everyone who speaks a language helps to maintain it. (It has been remarked previously that language, an essential aspect of the means and media of relationships, can exist only because individuals speak and understand it). Even those certified as insane make history, as they have to enter into social relationships with the sane and thus help to preserve institutions such as mental hospitals. Thus there can be no human individual who is not both a product and a maker of history.

The question of the role of consciousness in the relationship between the individual and society needs to be taken further. Consciousness is closely linked with *creativity*. Creativity is an aspect of human psychology which has been much neglected by contemporary psychologists. Just as they tend to limit the term 'consciousness' to a state of wakefulness or attention, so the term 'creativity' tends to be limited to such aspects of psychological functioning as the ability to solve problems in an unorthodox manner. For Marxists, however, the term implies the ability to see the world in terms of what it could become with conscious intervention. In other words the term 'consciousness', used in a Marxist sense, must necessarily imply creativity as defined above. What is important here is that, since the life-activity of each individual is unique and since thought is a manifestation of life-activity, it must follow that every individual must — at least potentially — possess the ability to think of new and original ways of changing the world. Unique and original works of art, music and literature as well as advances in science have to be understood in this light. To look at the question in another way, the term 'creativity' must imply, for example, the ability to perceive a selection of paints in terms of a landscape to be painted or to perceive various notes in terms of a symphony to be composed. Of course, such abilities could not exist without the *historical* development of painting and composing. Creativity therefore cannot be understood outside the context of history. It certainly cannot be understood in terms of the current 'information processing' approach, which carries with it the implication that the structure of the brain is such that it can 'process information' in a creative manner.

From a Marxist standpoint, the question of creative thought is a central one whenever the nature of the human race is considered. Recall Marx's words, quoted in Chapter Four:

> What distinguishes the worst architect from the best of bees is this, that the architect raises his structure in his imagination before he erects it in reality. At the end of every labour process we get a result that already existed in the imagination of the labourer at its commencement.

In other words, individuals create, in their imagination, mental goals to which their life-activity is consciously subordinated. Furthermore, since the labour process is ultimately the basis of all human existence, the creation of goals in the imagination is an essential aspect of humanity's ability to survive as a biological species. The dialectical relationship between the individual and society is clearly manifested in this process. On the one hand the historically developed knowledge, values, goals and ideas of past generations are transmitted to the individual by parents, education and so on, primarily through the medium of language. On the other the individual, in his or her imagination, analyses, rearranges and synthesises these ideas, values and so on in a unique and creative way.[17] This is most clearly revealed in nocturnal dreams, when all sorts of imaginary situations are created. But every individuals is a dreamer, even in waking life. We all create, in our imaginations, unique situations some of which become goals to which we consciously subordinate our practical activity to attain.[18]

There are, of course, numerous examples of historically significant creative thought taking place both in nocturnal dreams and in daydreams. Einstein began to develop his ideas of relativity when he was seated in a tram observing the Town Hall clock receding into the distance. He tried to imagine what would happen to his perception of the clock if the train began to approach the speed of light. The chemist Kekulé, while trying to discover the structure of the benzine molecule, gazed into a fire and imagined a snake with its tail in its mouth. This gave him the idea that the molecule took the form of a ring. The basic idea of the Periodic Table of the Elements came to Mendeleyev in a dream. It is thus clear that, since consciousness implies the ability to perceive the world in terms of what it could become, there must be a close connection between consciousness on the one hand and creativity on the other. The individual helps to create the world, first in thought and then in action, but only because he or she has acquired consciousness and creativity from objective and historically created relationships and situations.

A correct understanding of the nature of human creativity makes it possible to answer an interesting theoretical question. This is why human society is constantly changing. To be more precise, why is it that human abilities to create and re-create our own conditions of life continually develop? It should be recalled that bees build hives, birds build nests and beavers build dams. However, these and other animals construct nests and so on in ways that, relatively speaking, do not change. In contrast to other animal species, the human race constantly develops its knowledge, techniques and skills. Generally speaking, human history has been characterised by a continual — if sometimes erratic — development of our ability to master nature, primarily through production. In view of what has been said above about creativity, an understanding of human progress becomes possible. Two principal factors have to be considered.

Since the thought of all individuals is social and historical as well as unique and individual, their thought is not limited by their direct experience as a biological organism. Through historically developed means and media, in the first place language, they are able to assimilate many of the achievements of past and present generations and to utilise these in a creative way.

The second factor which differentiates humans from non-humans is the ability to think about what they are going to do long before they actually do it. This contrasts with the action of a monkey who picks up a stick in order to knock down fruit and whose action is dominated by the presence of the fruit. Recall the words of Marx, quoted previously, that 'the architect raises his structure in imagination before he erects in reality.' Not being dominated by the immediate situation in which he is confronted by the task of superintending the actual building of his structure, he thereby has time to think creatively, taking into account social and historical experience. Indeed, human beings have the unique ability to think about what other people can do. Thus a playwright does not have to act in his or her own plays and the designer of a bus does not have to drive it. Of course, these two mental abilities together constitute the human faculty of consciousness, discussed in Chapter Four.

One additional factor has to be taken into account in any consideration of human creativity or of the continual development of the human ability to create the conditions of our own lives. This is the basically social and historical nature of many human needs. There exists a dialectical relationship between the development of production and of the needs of individuals. For the process of production not only makes possible the supply of goods, services and so on which are needed by individuals. At the same time it *creates new needs*. This is shown by a consideration of what is termed the 'standard of living'. This is something the *historical* nature of which can be clearly demonstrated. Thus in at least the most advanced countries, the average home is considered to be incomplete without a television set. Yet 50 or so years ago they were possessed by only a very few people. Many homes are also equipped with telephones, washing machines, vacuum cleaners and so on. Yet a few decades ago such articles of use were not to be found in the majority of homes. They were not even considered to be necessary and their absence not noticed, even though housewives must undoubtedly have longed for something to take some of the drudgery out of their work. But the very production of these created a need for them. Similarly a few years ago few people would consider having a computer in the home. Yet owing to the prospect of industry producing relatively cheap computers it is not difficult to foresee a situation in which home computers become as widespread as television sets are now. Yesterday's luxuries are today's necessities while today's luxuries are the necessities of tomorrow. All that has just been said is relevant to the question of creativity. For what is created — especially in the field of production — will give rise to new needs and these new needs will in turn place new demands on humanity's creative powers.

A correct understanding of the role of creativity in the development of human culture — in the first place of production — provides an opportunity to re-examine the basic 'functionalist' view that the individual has somehow to 'adapt' or 'adjust' to society. This view has been expressed succinctly by those 'reinforcement' theorists who assert that an individual's behaviour is determined by what aspects of it are 'reinforced' by society. It is necesssary to return to the statement by the theorist Bolles quoted earlier in this chapter. In this statement he asserts that:

Reinforcement theory suggests . . . that man is the way he is because of the conditions prevailing in his social situation. The sources of social reinforcement are to be found in the structure of society, and we may have some hope of being able to find them and, perhaps one day, of changing them.

The functionalist 'reinforcement' point of view is also described succinctly by an American textbook which characterises the Skinnerian approach thus:

Science raises the possibility of realising George Orwell's fictional *1984* - a terrifying new world wherein the methods of the behavioural sciences become the weapons of control. Skinner offers neither a counsel of retreat nor despair in face of such frightening questions, but instead dispassionately examines the alternative — free men in the traditional sense, or *man controlled by science.*' [i.e., by society. My emphasis. J.R.][19]

The 'reinforcement' approach of course represents a modern version of the old belief that 'better conditions create better people'. It is thoroughly misleading. For while it may in principle not be untrue, it avoids the central question. This is that it is human individuals who, daily and hourly, create and re-create their own conditions of life. Further, in the course of their own creative life-activity they become what they are psychologically. To look at the matter in another way, the approach which suggests that 'better conditions create better people' is *one-sided* and hence false. For it is *only* individual people who create social conditions. Once again it needs to be repeated: The individual is the social and social is the individual.

The relation between the individual and society is made easier to understand by the use of the Hegelian categories of the Universal, the Individual and the Particular. Since these terms will be unfamiliar to most readers a brief explanation is required together with an example.

The 'universal' refers to an entity which is composed of discrete individual parts. The relation between the universal and its discrete individual parts is one of mutual and dialectical interdependence and interpenetration. Thus the universal 'domestic cats' is made up of individual domestic cats. In other words the biological species *Felis domestica*, which evolved from its ancestors to form a new species, can exist only in and through *individual* cats. There can be no 'cattiness' without individuals of the species. Similarly there can be no individual cats which do not express the qualities of the species in a unique and *particular* way. There are no abstract individual cats, but only *particular* cats such as Fluffy, Felix, Ginger and Twinkle. Every *universal,* therefore, can exist only in and through *individuals* while individuals can exist only by expressing the universal in unique and *particular* ways.

The relevance of the categories Universal, Individual and Particular to an understanding of human beings now becomes obvious. The human 'universal' is of course society and its history.[20] It is necessary to recall that society and its history represents a resolution of the contradiction between the need to transmit skills, knowledge and values from generation to generation and the inability to fix these genetically. The contradiction is resolved through the physical and psychological development of human individuals (with creativity and consciousness) who carry out practical activity which will — directly or indirectly — lead to the maintenance and development of production. In other words the universal (society) creates (particular) individuals whose life-activity in turn re-creates and develops the universal.

The content of the lives of individuals (their practical activity — what they do) of *past* generations has created the social relationships and situations together with the means and media of social relations of the *present* generation. It needs to be repeated that *individuals* are born and die whereas the historical development of society (the *universal*) is a continual process. Therefore the universal is not the same as the individual yet it can only exist in and through the life-activity of individuals. Similarly there can be no individuals without their own life-activity, the content of which *is* society and history (the universal).

Every human being is an expression, an embodiment and a manifestation of the universal of society and history. But each individual is a unique, particular expression. This is because he or she embodies and manifests certain aspects or shades of the universal. The nuclear family (part of the universal) which carries within it the principle that the upbringing of children is the responsibility of the biological parents, creates a wide variety of social situations which children have to confront. To return to a previous example, some children may confront parental situations in which their parents give them adequate love and guidance. These will tend to grow up feeling emotionally secure. Others may have to confront parental situations in which parents reject them. These will tend to grow up feeling insecure and lacking in self confidence.

Alfred Adler (1870-1939), who led the first breakaway from Freudian psychoanalysis, postulated an interesting connection between a child's position in the family and the development of many of his or her psychological characteristics. Thus as a general rule, children born into a large family would grow up to be markedly different from only children. The first to be born in a family, who were once the sole beneficiary of the parents' attention, often became disillusioned and insecure when the parents' attention had, at least partly, to be switched to the second child. The second child, never having been the sole centre of the parents' attention, faced a world in which it seemed natural to compete in life with someone (the firstborn) who was already well ahead in the race. However, since the second born could not compete directly with the first, he or she usually chose some field of endeavour outside the family tradition. Hence there tended to be a marked difference between first and second born children. The firstborn tended to be conservative in attitude, looking back with regret to the time when he or she was the sole focus of attention. The second born, however, learned to view the world as a place of natural competition and innovation. It should be noted that other studies of birth-order in families do not necessarily agree with the conclusions of Adler. It should also be noted that Adler's views can only reflect general trends which may be counteracted by other factors. However, his findings are mentioned here as they illustrate, with great clarity how the (universal) nuclear family may find different expression in (particular) individuals.[21] It is of course well known that parental influence has an important effect on the development of language in children. Those brought up in middle-class homes tend to acquire a larger vocabulary than those brought up in working-class families.

Further examples of the relations between the Universal, the Individual and the Particular are afforded by the *particular* ways in which *individuals* acquire money (a significant aspect of the *universal* of society). No adult human individual can exist without money — or at least without relying on someone who has it. Individuals acquire money in particular ways. Large numbers of individuals obtain it by working in factories, offices and so on. Others become burglars, confidence tricksters or professional gamblers. There are plenty of people who marry members of the opposite sex primarily or at least partly for a share in their marriage partner's money. Each particular way of acquiring the universal of money causes individuals to engage in particular forms of life-activity which contribute to the development of their psychological characteristics.

Here it might be objected that the *physical* characteristics of individuals affect their psychological development and that such social universals as the nuclear family and money are not responsible for at least most physical characteristics. This is of course quite true. A child is born either a boy or a girl. However, a child's gender will determine the demands placed upon him or her in family, school and other situations. The psychological significance of physical differences between individuals is a question that will be deferred until Chapter Seven. It needs to be recalled, though, that the development of human consciousness depends on reciprocal and joint activity with others rather than on any physical factors.

It thus becomes clear that (particular) individuals cannot be understood unless the universal of society and its history is understood. The framework of each individual's life-activity consists of particular shades and aspects of the universal as a whole. The enormous diversity of the life-activity of different individuals, especially in contemporary capitalist society, is apparent for all to see. There are to be found beggars and millionaires, pacifists and mercenaries, dustmen and academics, surgeons and mortuary attendants, bishops and burglars, publishers of pornography and the supporters of Mrs Mary Whitehouse. The list is almost endless. Differences in life-activity are not due, as is sometimes supposed, to the unfolding of some innate 'personality characteristics' of individuals. Rather they are due to differences in historically developed social situations — all representing various aspects of the universal — which individuals are forced to confront. Differences in the life-activity of individuals must be seen as representing a *unity in diversity*. They are united in having one historical root. Each individual's life-activity represents a particular manifestation and embodiment of the resolution of the basic contradiction of the human race: the need to transmit the skills and knowledge of production and other activities from generation to generation and the inability to fix these genetically.

A further question of which mention has to be made is that of how the thinking and behaviour of individuals can be consciously changed. If the assumption is made that individuals develop psychologically through their 'adjustment' or 'adaptation' to the 'social environment', then logically it must follow that to change them it is necessary to carry out one of two types of procedure. Either individuals must be changed directly, without the 'social environment' changing, or alternatively the 'social environment' must be changed. From a Marxist standpoint, however, the really decisive way to change the thought and behaviour of individuals is to effect a change in their life-activity. This is a point which will be developed further in Chapter Eleven.

Finally, it is necessary to raise a further important question. This is that of why modern psychologists are unable to see clearly the true relationship between individuals and society.

From a Marxist standpoint, the answer lies in the nature of capitalist society. The objective nature of social relationships under capitalism is such that individuals — including psychologists — feel themselves isolated and somehow separate from society as a whole. It will be recalled from Chapter Two that the anarchical nature of the market, into which each industrial concern flings its commodities, dominates the social relations between people. Thus today the lives of millions of individuals are dominated by the relationship between gold and oil. Whether or not a factory — or indeed a whole branch of industry — is able to continue production or not is determined by the relationship between whatever it produces on the one hand and the particular commodity that is money on the other. Marx writes that the producers 'own social action takes the form of the action of objects, which rule the producers instead of being ruled by them.'[22]

What has just been said can be put in another way. Under capitalism —
quite unlike any previous form of society such as feudalism or slave society
— the lives of individuals are dominated by laws of the market which most
of them are unable to comprehend and over which no one has any control.
Few people can understand why it is that millions are thrown out of work,
why there is widespread poverty or why it is that every so often wars break
out. Indeed, few psychologists can really understand why their own jobs or
those of their colleagues may be threatened by cuts in government or local
authority expenditure. Thus the social forces which the vast majority of
individuals are unable to comprehend — let alone control — are the same
objective forces that create the illusion that our lives are dominated by a
'society' standing separately and apart from us. Thus society is seen, not as
the sum total of social relationships of which individuals themselves constitute
a part, rather, society is seen as an entity to which individuals have to adapt
or adjust or with which they have to interact.

It may be concluded that modern psychologists fail to comprehend the true
relationships between individuals and society not because they are in any way
stupid. Rather their lack of comprehension represents a reflection of the
objective nature of social relations under capitalism.

To conclude this chapter, it would be useful to summarise the differences
between the Marxist and the non-Marxist approaches to the question of the
relation of the individual to society and to history.

The non-Marxist approach is really one of three:

1.   That which views society as the manifestation and creation of thought,
values, motives and so on innate in all individuals.

2.   That which sees society as something to which individuals have to
'adapt' or 'adjust' and which exerts 'powerful influences on the personalities
of the individuals born into it'. This is of course the 'functionalist' approach,
discussed earlier, to which the great majority of modern psychologists
subscribe.

3.   That which represents a fusion — as it were — of the first and second
approaches and which may be termed a neo-Kantian view.[23] It is believed that,
although the individual has to 'adjust' or 'adapt' to the 'social environment',
he or she also possesses some innate mental tendencies often referred to by
lay persons as 'human nature' or 'common sense'. In other words this approach
starts from the premise of a mechanical interaction of the subjective and
objective rather than their dialectical unity (a point to be discussed in Chapter
Six).

In contrast to the above three approaches, Marxists start from the dialectical unity of the individual and society. The individual and society are *opposites*. They are opposites since individuals are born and die while society has existed since the origin of the human race through labour and — if it is not terminated by a thermo-nuclear war or by the pollution of the planet — promises to continue indefinitely. At the same time the two opposites mutually interpenetrate. There are no individuals without society and no society without individuals. This is expressed in the fact that the individual is the social and the social is the individual. Society is the sum total of historically developed social relationships together with their means and media. It is thus neither a projection of any innate thought, values and motives of individuals. Nor is it something standing outside individuals to which individuals have to 'adjust' or 'adapt'. It needs to be emphasised once again, however, that before individuals become really human, that is before they acquire human consciousness, they must enter into historically developed social relationships which have objective existence independently of their thought or will.

The failure of most contemporary psychologists to appreciate the true nature of society and hence of the relationship between the individual and society is closely linked to their belief that the individual interacts in a *mechanical* fashion with the 'social environment'. This point will be taken up in the following chapter.

NOTES TO CHAPTER FIVE

1. Fesbach, S. and Weiner, B. *Personality*. D. C. Heath and Co., 1982, p. 77.
2. *Ibid.* p. 62.
3. Bolles, R. *Theory of Motivation*. Harper Row, 1967, p. 451.
4. Aronson, E. *The Social Animal*. Freeman, 1976, p. 5.
5. It is of course true that social skills and knowledge are transmitted from generation to generation in animal species other than man, for example apes and monkeys. But since these skills and knowledge are not derived directly or indirectly from the purposeful making of tools any analogy here between humans and non-humans would not be useful.
6. The term 'social relationships' used in this book refers to the co-ordination of the activities of individuals with those of other individuals. Parents co-ordinate their activities with those of their children, teachers with pupils, employers with employees and so on.
7. The term 'life-activity' is used throughout this book to refer to everything individuals actually do. From the standpoint of the development of the most significant aspects of the subjective life of individuals — their goals, aspirations, values, knowledge and so on — the most important features of life-activity are those that are purposeful, that is, which are carried out with consciousness as previously defined.
8. It should be noted that the term 'means and media' refers both to those that are internal to the individual (language, values, concepts, knowledge) and those that are external (money, buildings, tools, clothes). It is also important to note that without means and media such as these the co-ordination of activities that constitute social relationships could not take place.
9. In the context of the subject-matter of this book, the term 'purposeful activity' implies activity

subordinated to the achievement of a goal which exists in the imagination. For Marxists, the labour process upon which all human life ultimately depends would be impossible without activity that was purposeful.

10. Marx *The Economic and Philosophic Manuscripts of 1844*. International Publishers, 1964, p. 137.

11. Marx *Ibid*. pp. 137-8.

12. *Encyclopedia of Psychology*, Edited by Eysenck, H.J. Search Press, 1972, p. 383.

13. Radford, J. and Govier, E. (Eds.) *A Textbook of Psychology*, Sheldon Press, 1980, p. 420.

14. Marx and Engels, *Collected Works* Vol.5. Lawrence and Wishart, 1976, pp. 437-8.

15. Brown, J.A.C. *Freud and the Post-Freudians*. Cassell, 1961, p. 161.

16. The simultaneous nature of social and individual thought is demonstrated by the fact that, for each individual, objects, people, situations and so on have both personal and social *meanings*. Thus if a boy is a staunch supporter of a certain football team and his team wins a match, the result of the match has personal meaning for him as a victory about which he feels jubilant. Simultaneously it also has social meaning for him in that football is an historically developed game the result of which is determined not only by the activity of the players but also by a socially defined set of rules. This reflects the fact that the game 'football' would have no meaning for individuals if there were no socially defined rules like scoring a goal by kicking the ball into the space between the posts. Yet the game itself could not take place if individuals did not take any personal interest in it. Similarly, students who take examinations give personal meanings to the results. For each individual student a 'pass' has personal meaning in that it gives rise to feelings of pleasure while a 'fail' has personal meaning in that it gives rise to feelings of disappointment. Simultaneously, for every student, examination results have social meaning in that they represent a socially determined method of assessment. This reflects the fact that students would not take examinations if the latter had no social significance, while examinations would not take place if no one was interested in taking them.

17. One of the achievements of contemporary psychology and of neurology has been to show that, just as the heart cannot exist without beating, so the brain cannot exist without being in a constant state of activity. It is certainly not the case that, as was once believed, the brain becomes active only when stimulated by sensory input. The constant activity of the brain represents the biological prerequisite for creative thought. However, since human consciousness and creativity are simultaneously social and individual, the brain's constant activity cannot by itself serve as an explanatory principle. A life-activity which is a part of ongoing history is also absolutely necessary.

18. The ability to subordinate one's activity to the attainment of goals is of course learned only in social situations. A child learns to get to school by getting ready, leaving the house, waiting for a bus and so on. Children learn to get fully dressed by postponing the putting on of coats and shoes until they are wearing underwear and socks. The ability to subordinate short-term to long-term goals is one of the criteria for the attainment of psychological maturity.

19. Chaplin, J.P and Krawiec, T.S. *Systems and Theories in Psychology*. Holt Rinehart and Winston, 1968, p. 271.

20. It might be said that particular human individuals would represent the universal of the species *Homo sapiens*. However, it is necessary to recall that although babies are members of the species from birth onwards, it is not until they acquire consciousness (in the Marxist sense) that they become truly human.

21. See, for example: Brown *op. cit.*

22. *Capital*, Vol. 1. FLPH, 1959, p. 75.

23. Immanuel Kant (1742-1804), the first of the school of German classical philosophy, which culminated in Hegel, postulated that each individual possessed unlearned mental abilities which enabled him or her to understand and interpret sensory input received from the external, objective world. All science could discover was limited by these unlearned abilities and by the superficial appearance of things.

6

WHY HUMANS ARE NOT MACHINES

This chapter deals with the following topics: The historical origin of the mechanistic world outlook. How modern psychology still clings to this outlook. Why the content of thought cannot be explained in terms of mechanics. The difference between the content and the form of thought. The relationship between subjective and objective. Why the brain cannot form the basis of the mind. Why the computer model is inapplicable to humans. The connection between the mechanistic world outlook and mysticism. The weakness of the Piagetian approach. Finally, why the mechanistic outlook is so entrenched in modern psychology.

It would be true to say that contemporary psychology is characterised by a *mechanical* approach to its subject matter. Thus D.O. Hebb, a widely respected figure in the history of modern psychology, states categorically:

> There are two theories of mind . . . one in its clearest form is *animistic,* a theory of demonic possession: it assumes that the body is inhabited by an entity, a demon known as the mind or soul . . . The second theory is *physiological* or *mechanistic*: it assumes that mind is a bodily process, the activity of the brain or some part of that activity. This is *monistic* theory. Modern psychology works with monistic or mechanistic theory.[1]

A more recent textbook, commenting on the 'information processing' approach (often referred to as 'cognitive psychology') which, in terms of the number of scientific papers and books published, tends to dominate contemporary psychology, states:

> The methods and model building of cognitive psychologists subscribe to the 'man is a machine' view; but a machine with a difference. It is seen as much more

complex than that postulated by the Associationists and Behaviourists . . . the important thing is to understand the workings of the machine as accurately as possible.[2]

The well-known and influential Steven Rose sees human consciousness as arising from the mechanical interaction of individuals with their respective environments. Thus he states: 'Consciousness, in my opinion, is a continuous, unrolling, continuously developing activity of minds/brains in interaction with their environment, modified, either temporarily or permanently, by changing circumstances.'[3]

The purpose of this chapter is to show that the mechanical, 'man as a machine' view is both false and misleading.

It is necessary to discuss briefly the origin of the 'mechanical' viewpoint. An extremely important aspect of the Renaissance that accompanied the decline and break up of the Middle Ages was the development of natural science. A significant aspect of this development was the advance of *mechanics*, highlighted by the immense contributions of Newton (1642-1727). Undoubtedly the development of mechanics was closely linked to that of manufacturing industry, since the latter was characterised by the replacement of manual work by that performed by machines. The development of mechanics also led to the development of a *mechanistic world outlook*, exemplified by the views of philosophers such as Bacon (1561-1626), Hobbes (1588-1679) and Locke (1632-1704).

The mechanical world outlook was based on two related premises. First, that the objects studied were isolated entities rather than parts of much wider and integrated wholes which had their own laws of development and functioning, wholes to which the functioning and indeed the very existence of the various parts were subordinated. Second, that the functioning of objects was determined by their own internal structure. These two premises have to be considered in the context of the history of science. They were inevitable because of the extremely limited development of science prior to the Renaissance. Plants and animals had to be *classified* before any theory of evolution could be outlined. Similarly, stars and planets had to be observed and classified before any theories of their formation from nebulous gases could be developed. Newton's theory of the universe, which postulated the unchanging nature of the movement of the heavenly bodies, was essentially a *mechanical* model which considered the origin of stars and planets to be due to a divine act of creation rather than to any laws of the development of cosmic matter. At the same time, the observation and classification of objects could not but be accompanied by the notion that their functioning was due not to their relationships with other elements in a system but solely to their physical structure. It was believed that we could see with the eyes because of the structure of the eyes, breathe with the lungs because of the structure of the lungs and so on.

Natural science has of course made colossal advances since the Renaissance. Biologists now view organisms both as the products of evolutionary development and as elements in ecological systems. Similarly, astronomers now consider stars and planets not as fixed and unchanging entities but as aspects of the development of the universe as a whole. However, it has to be said that the discipline of psychology still remains dominated by the mechanistic world outlook — an outlook the overcoming of which is a necessary step if any real progress is to be made.

The implications of a mechanistic world outlook in psychology have to be made clear. As has been mentioned above, classical mechanics saw the functioning of physical bodies as being primarily dependent on their internal structure. The way in which a clock worked, for example, was determined — after it had been wound up — by the mechanical interaction of all its parts. The way in which its various parts interacted with one another was determined by their individual structures. This outlook has been expressed — in one way or another — throughout the history of psychology. In Freudian theory, the structure of the individual mind is such that, as a result of interaction with the 'social environment', the superego arises.[4] During the long period during which academic psychology was dominated by the outlook of behaviourism[5] the ways in which rats in cages 'adapted' to the environment by responding to 'reinforcement' represented the mechanical interaction between the structure of the rats' nervous system on the one hand and the structure of the 'reinforcing' environment on the other.

The profound impact on academic psychology made by the development of computer technology — exemplified clearly by the 'information processing' approach — might at first sight make it appear that the mechanistic world outlook has been discarded by modern psychologists. But this is not the case. Computers are in fact sophisticated machines, but machines none the less. They are machines whose programmes may be such that the structure of the programmes themselves change as a result of input fed into them in the course of their 'interactions' with their 'environment', that is, with the computer operator. In accordance with the logic of those psychologists with a mechanistic world outlook, human individuals are to be seen as computer-like bodies the structures of whose brains are such that the 'programmes' which control their behaviour are changed during and as a result of their interaction with their 'social environment'. Thus it is stated that:

> Computer models are not only relevant to . . . psychology, but are perhaps the most exciting new method of representing cognitive processes.[6] . . . information theory, feedback theory and computer algorithms, have suggested analogies for a model of human cognitive processes . . . the formalisation of cognitive processes as computer algorithms has forced the models to become more explicit simply because a computer needs every step to be spelt out unambiguously.[7] . . . a human being is a transmission device for receiving input signals, coding them, and processing them for output.[8]

The computer analogy is taken further. Some proponents of what is termed 'artificial intelligence' maintain that, at least in the future, computers may possess some form of 'consciousness' similar to human consciousness. An American author speculates thus:

> What, then, if a creature of similar behaviour (to that of a human being) and intelligence were to be fabricated from components of quite a different kind with a nervous system and brain based on electronic components instead of neurons, for example? Would it too possess consciousness and the subjective feelings that go along with it? For all we know today, surely this has to be considered to be a possibility. And how about existing electronic digital computers? Is it possible that, somewhere among their wires and transistors, there already stirs the dim glimmering of the same kind of sense of awareness that has become, for man, his most personal and precious possession? Fantastic? Perhaps . . .[9]

The view that computers can possess 'human' features has caught the imagination of the lay public. Weitzenbaum, in an amusing and instructive book[10] recounts how, just for fun, he devised a computer programme which mimicked a psychiatric interview. The 'psychiatrist' would 'talk' to the 'patient' via the screen while the latter would 'talk' to the 'psychiatrist' by means of the keyboard. Somewhat to Weitzenbaum's surprise, it was found that many people preferred to talk to the computer rather than to a real psychiatrist. Indeed, the programme was so successful that some hospital authorities actually proposed making psychiatrists redundant and replacing them with computer terminals. Proponents of 'artificial intelligence' are not only to be found in the West. They also exist in what was the USSR, where they exert considerable influence. It is stated that:

The construction of an artificial thinking system, built out of other elements, but in its total effect reproducing the highest programme — thought — is quite feasible . . . [A human being is] a system capable of perceiving external influences, extracting information from them, processing it through the formation of numerous models at different levels, and influencing the environment with multi-level programmes. In most general form man is a programme-controlled automation . . . Or to put it another way, man is a self-teaching and self-adjusting system . . . there can be no question of any 'free-will' as opposed to determinism.[11]

The view that 'intelligence' and 'consciousness' are properties of the physical structure of objects is of course a theme frequently found in science fiction. Some years ago the astronomer Fred Hoyle wrote a popular novel entitled *The Black Cloud* the central theme of which was that the world was encircled by a large cloud of particles from outer space. The particular arrangement of the particles, that is, the *structure* of the cloud, was such that the cloud itself possessed 'intelligence' and 'consciousness' and was able — as a conscious entity — to communicate with people on earth.

It would be incorrect to suggest that most contemporary psychologists take the writers of science fiction too seriously. It would also be incorrect to suggest that the great majority of them subscribe to the view that human individuals are no more than computers of a special type. Indeed, some psychologists have specifically warned against taking the computer analogy too far. However, despite many correct criticisms, contemporary psychology has been unable to pinpoint the fundamentally false assumption of those who seek to attribute 'intelligence' and 'consciousness' to the physical structures of inanimate objects like computers.

Before proceeding to a discussion on the computer analogy, it is necessary to outline why, in general, humans cannot be regarded as machines. It is also necessary to show why the human mind cannot, as Hebb and most other psychologists maintain, be regarded as 'a bodily process'.

The mechanistic outlook which dominates modern psychology views human beings as machines in the sense that their functioning is determined by their internal structure, which changes in the course of their interaction with their respective environments. However, the important point here is that the most significant actions of human individuals are governed by thought. People have mental values, knowledge, goals, plans to achieve these goals and so on. It is precisely their goals and plans to achieve them that guide and direct their most important actions. Moreover, these mental goals and plans to achieve them *do not obey the laws of mechanics.* One essential feature of *any* machine, however defined, is that its functioning is governed by fixed and rigid sets of rules. In contrast to this, however, the content of thought is not bound by any such rules. It is not bound by time and space. We can in a flash transfer our thought from the here and now to places far away, to the distant past or to the imagined future. To look at the question in another way, when we plan our future activity aimed at achieving a goal existing in the imagination, whether it be that of getting to work, finding a suitable marriage partner or composing a piece of music, *we ourselves make up our own rules* to govern our actions. A contemporary writer states that 'human behaviour is orientated towards future goals and is not determined by past facts as in the physical sciences' (e.g. in mechanics J.R.)[12] This is very well put!

Anyone subscribing to the 'man is a machine' approach would do well to consider the immense contribution to human knowledge made by the philosopher Descartes (1596-1650). For Descartes showed that the content of thought could not be equated with the structure of the body (brain). The body was a three-dimensional object, he maintained, whereas the content of thought was not three-dimensional. Of course, at the particular point in historical time during which Descartes lived, the only possible explanation for the relative concordance of thought and material reality was a religious one: it was God that ensured that we could use thought to comprehend the external world. But the fundamental idea of Descartes is still valid today, especially for the discipline of psychology. The brain is three-dimensional whereas thought is not. It is indeed a tragedy that so many psychologists consider that they have nothing to learn from the rich lessons afforded by the history of philosophy.

It should be noted that Hebb, in his statement about the nature of the mind, quoted on p. 75, (which clearly reflects the viewpoint of modern psychology), equates the two terms 'mechanistic' and 'physiological'. Whether or not the laws of neurophysiology can be interpreted in terms of Newtonian mechanics the present author is not competent to judge. But this is really not the issue here. What is important is the clear implication, on the part of modern psychology, that during the course of the body's interaction with its 'environment', input or 'information' enters the brain via the five senses where it is 'processed' by the structure of the brain in such a way that the mind comes into existence, develops and changes. If indeed this was an adequate explanation for the development of human minds, and if each human individual was no more than 'a transmission device for receiving input signals, coding them and processing them for output' then the conclusion would be inescapable: there is no real way of knowing the external world. Our knowledge would be restricted to the superficial appearance of things, as interpreted to us as separate individuals by the structure and physiology of our brains. In other words, our knowledge of the world would depend primarily on the workings of separate brains. However, this outlook is profoundly mistaken. For although knowledge is impossible without individual brains, at least its most significant aspects develop through history rather than through physiology.

Let it be recalled that humanity's very existence depends upon our continual mastery of nature, primarily through production. Our knowledge — particularly the knowledge embodied in the natural sciences — must therefore of necessity bear an objective relationship to the world upon which we act. Of course, human knowledge is always in a state of change and development. Thus quantum mechanics and relativity theory have been shown to reflect at least certain aspects of the world more accurately than Newtonian mechanics. The important point here is that the development of knowledge is an *historical* process closely interwoven with our *practical* mastery of various aspects of the world.

Each conquest of nature raises the possibility of further conquests and hence of the further development of knowledge. Yet at all stages of the development of knowledge it has constantly to be checked against the objective world through our actions upon that world. And such knowledge is essentially *social* and *collective*.

To return to the subject matter of the previous chapter, all human thought (including of course knowledge) is simultaneously social and historical on the one hand and unique and individual on the other. During the course of his or her own life-activity (nearly always co-ordinated with that of others) each individual 'gets caught up in' the historical development of knowledge. Even the unique knowledge of outstanding individual scientists (Darwin and Einstein are good examples) would not have been possible if they had not previously absorbed the relevant knowledge of others. A related question is that of the role played by concepts and categories of thought in the development of an individual's knowledge. What an individual scientist, for example, sees and hears is always interpreted in terms of such historically developed concepts and categories as 'causality', 'quantity', 'quality', 'relationship', 'correlation' and so on. It is precisely this question that is ignored by those who write of 'minds/brains' or who regard humans simply as mechanical 'transmission devices'.

Incidentally, if knowledge is indeed simply a question of 'information' being 'processed' by the structure of individual brains, not only would the external world be basically unknowable. It would also be extremely difficult for different people to share the same knowledge. For the following reason. It is now well known that there are enormous differences between the structure of individual brains. They differ in size, weight, number of nerve cells and so on. With the possible exception of identical twins, no two individuals possess identical brain structures. The very logic of those who subscribe to the 'man is a machine' view must therefore lead to an unavoidable assumption. This is that, since the structure of each machine (brain) differs, the same sort of 'information' contained in sensory input will be 'processed' (i.e., interpreted and evaluated) in different ways. Yet vital social activities such as those of production and the development of natural science could take place only if the concepts inherent in technical and scientific knowledge contained the same meaning for different individuals. Medical scientists, for instance, despite differences in the structure of their brains, all share an essentially similar basic knowledge of metabolism, anatomy, genetics and other aspects of medical science.

It would be opportune at this point to remark that those psychologists who subscribe to the 'man is a machine' view that the human individual is simply a 'transmission device' totally fail to explain to whom or to what the 'input signals', having been 'processed for output' are presented. They cannot offer an explanation, of course, because they cannot understand that our ability to see our own lives objectively — as if they were seen by someone else — arises not from the response of our brains to sensory input, but from the co-ordination of our own activity with that of others in ways which are determined by historically developed social relationships.

The view that thought and the mind can be explained simply by the individual brain's ability to 'process information' can rightly be termed a neo-Kantian outlook. The philosopher Kant (1724-1804) postulated that sensory input was structured by mental abilities which did not arise through social relationships. It was these abilities which structured sensory input in terms of categories like time, space and causality. All that natural science could hope to know, therefore, was the superficial appearance of the world. What underlies and gives rise to superficial appearance (termed by Kant the 'Thing-in-Itself') must forever remain unknowable. It was left to Hegel and, later, to Marx, to show that although only individuals could possess knowledge (there can be no knowledge without knowers), knowledge could never be *purely* individual. Rather, knowledge must represent an integral part of the objective movements of society and history, objective movements which constitute the very content of the life-activity of each and every individual. To return to Kant, there is a definite analogy between Kant's theory of knowledge and that of many modern psychologists. For Kant, scientific knowledge is limited to sensory input from superficial appearances plus unlearned, non-social categories of thought. For many modern psychologists, such knowledge is similarly limited to sensory input plus an individual non-social, non-historical 'transmission device for receiving input signals, coding them, and processing them for output'. Thus for modern psychologists, as for Kant, what it is that underlies and gives rise to superficial appearances (it is, after all, the task of science to find this out) is essentially unknowable. This is the very logic of the 'man is a machine' approach. We are no more than machines which interact with other machines (or with the 'social environment'), the form of interaction being determined by the internal structure of our 'mind/brains'. Here is a further example of the tragedy of modern psychologists failing to learn the important lessons afforded by the history of philosophy. To conclude this paragraph, it should be re-emphasised that although the ability of the brain to 'process information' is essential to thought, this ability cannot by itself serve as an explanatory principle. For at least the most significant aspects of the input which enters the five senses of every truly human individual (i.e., of every individual who has become the subject of his or her own life-activity) are interpreted and evaluated in terms of concepts, values and categories of thought which are essentially social and historical in origin. They are not ahistorical, as in the case of the Kantian categories. Neither do they arise from the structure of the brain as such, as is implied by those who regard humans simply as 'transmission devices'.

The totally unscientific nature of the 'man is a machine' approach of modern psychology is made clearer by an understanding of what the human mind actually is. From a Marxist standpoint, the first human minds arose through the practical activity involved in *social* labour. It is meaningless to write of 'minds/brains' as does Rose. Likewise it is incorrect to define mind — as does Hebb — as 'a bodily process'. Rather, the human mind represents *a form taken by the world external to the brain*. Not the world as such, of course, but the world as acted upon, experienced and inwardly recorded (via the sense organs) by the separate person. Our minds (thoughts, feelings, attitudes, values, knowledge and so on) are always *about* the world external to our brains (including various internal bodily states). We think about, have feelings about, have attitudes towards and possess knowledge of, various aspects of the world (real or imaginary) which are external to our brains. When we perceive an object, we perceive it, not as the subjective excitation of the optic nerve, but as something having objective existence outside our brains. Similarly, if we hit our thumb with a hammer, we perceive the pain as existing in the thumb rather than in those parts of the brain which are responsible for feelings of pain. Thus, although thinking can be defined as the activity of the brain — or of parts of it — the *content* of thought (the mind) can only represent aspects of the world external to the brain. Of course, there is considerable interpenetration between the physical state of the brain and the mind. But a consideration of this interpenetration will be deferred until the next chapter.

The nature of human minds can perhaps be made clearer still through a knowledge of the difference between the *content* and the *form* of thought. As has been stated above, thought is always about something in the world external to the brain. However, the process of thinking is the activity of the brain itself. The activity of the brain therefore constitutes the *form* taken by thought. Since the content of thought (mind) constitutes a form taken by the world — as acted upon and experienced by the separate person — the activity of the brain constitutes — so to speak — a form of the form of the external world. But the activity of the brain can never be equated with thought or the mind. Recall the insistence of Descartes that the body (brain) is three-dimensional whereas the content of thought is not. And it is precisely the content of thought which determines at least the most important aspects of what we do when confronted with the need for action.

The relation between the content and the form of thought is easier to understand through the realisation that the content of thought can take forms other than that of brain activity. The content of thought can become *materialised* and *objectified* through practical action. Thus if carpenters decide to make, say, a table, their practical action is guided by the content of their thought. They keep a mental image of the table which they have to make and it is this image to which they have to subordinate their practical activity until the task is completed. The content of their thought, therefore, becomes materialised and objectified in the completed table. The table thus becomes a *form* taken by the content of their thought. In other words it is not their brain cells that are transformed into the table, but their ideas which previously existed only in the form of brain activity. Similarly, when Charles Dickens wrote *The Pickwick Papers* his ideas (the content of his thought) about the adventures of Mr Pickwick and his companions became objectified in his manuscript. To take this example further, Dickens's ideas about the story first took the form of the activity of his brain cells. In transferring his ideas to the manuscript, the form taken by the content of his thought became that of his handwriting on the pages of the manuscript. Let it therefore be noted that the readers of Dickens's immortal tale are able to understand the content of his thought not by observing the activity of his brain cells but by perceiving the writing on the pages of the book.

The knowledge that thought (mind) can become objectified through practical activity raises a question which is fundamental to the development of a genuinely scientific psychology. This is that of the relationship of the subjective to the objective. For Marxists, the relationship can be expressed as follows: Individuals are forced by objective circumstances to undertake specific courses of action. They think (subjective) about what to do. This thought takes the form of the (objective) activity of the brain cells. A course of action leading to a mental goal is decided on (subjective). Practical activity (objective) guided by the mental goal and plans to attain it (subjective) is undertaken. The results of the successful attainment of the goal represent an objectification of the subjective. To illustrate this, consider the example of carpenters given in the preceding paragraph. Objective circumstances (request from a customer, need for money, etc.) causes the carpenters to decide to make a table. In their imagination they form an image of the completed table together with a plan to make it (subjective, taking the form of the objective activity of their brains). They subordinate their practical activity (objective) to the image (subjective) of the completed table. The completed table (objective) represents a form taken by their image of it together with their plans to make it (subjective).

It might be objected by some readers that, since it is impossible to think without a brain, the brain must be the basis of thought. But this is a false argument. It is false because it is one-sided. The brain and its ability to 'process information' is indeed necessary for thought. However, it would also be true to say that thought is equally necessary for the physical existence of the brain. For without thought human individuals could not survive as biological organisms. They could not act on the world in such a manner that their physical existence is ensured.[13] If people try to cross a busy motorway on foot without concentrating their minds on what they are doing the physical existence of their brains will be endangered. It needs to be realised that the physical existence of individuals and their thought do not even constitute different sides of the same coin, so to speak. This is because the difference between the two develops historically. Thus the thought of primitive hunter-gatherer tribes is rarely divorced from the practical activity of their daily lives. In contrast to this, in contemporary society there are to be found people like novelists and mathematicians whose physical existence is at times relatively divorced from the content of their thought. From what has been said above, it follows that, although the brain is essential for thought, it can never be the basis for the latter. Rather, the basis for both thought (mind) and physical existence (brain) can only be life-activity, a life-activity the content of which constitutes a definite part of ongoing history, that is, of social relationships and their means and media.

It is now possible to give a clear answer to the question of why humans are not computers. In addition to the above reasons concerning the false nature of the 'man is a machine' approach, the following two points need to be made. First, no computer, however sophisticated, can ever criticise its own programme. The ability to be self-critical implies the possibility of viewing one's own past, present and future life-activity objectively, from the side, as it were, as though it was that of another person. This is of course an essential aspect of human consciousness as previously defined. Computers can be programmed to criticise the programmes of other computers. They can also be programmed to change their own programme in response to pre-determined input. In such cases any changed programme must depend on a 'meta-programme' which, unlike human thought, must be governed by fixed and rigid rules. Here it should be repeated that humans, being the subjects of their own life-activity, make up their own mental rules which are not fixed and rigid. Computers, not being human, do not possess the ability to stand outside themselves, so to speak, in the imagination, and thus be able evaluate their programme objectively and critically, as though they were evaluating the performance of another computer. As has been stressed previously, this ability does not arise from the structure of the brain as such, or from its ability to 'process information', but rather from the co-ordination of the child's activity with that of others, that is, by the child's own actions being corrected by someone else. Just as the ability to be self-critical cannot arise from the structure of the brain as such, so such an ability cannot arise from the structure either of a computer or of its programme.

The second point to be made concerns the ability to set goals. Computers can of course be set specific goals of various kinds. They can be set the goal of solving mathematical problems or of providing a list of criminal suspects who have committed armed robberies and are very tall. As has already been mentioned above, they can also be programmed to change their own programme in response to specific outputs. What they cannot do, however, is to set themselves goals spontaneously, in a human way. All human beings possess the ability to set themselves goals without any direct prompting from others. Thus people can set themselves the goals of visiting relatives at the weekend, of placing a bet for a certain race, changing their job or composing a piece of music. Let it be recalled that the workings of any computer — however sophisticated — must ultimately be determined by fixed and rigid rules. In other words computers are of necessity the prisoners of their own programmes. In contrast to this, human thought — as Descartes showed — does not depend on such rules. The human mind is not — like a computer

— a three-dimensional object existing in time and space. The development of computer technology and of cybernetics has given rise to the widespread view that at least the most significant aspects of human behaviour are controlled by computer-like algorithmic processes leading to the achievement of goals existing in the imagination. This theme was first put forward by a seminal book *Plans and the Structure of Behaviour*,[14] which dealt a serious blow to the then dominant outlook of behaviourism. There is little in this approach with which Marxists would disagree.

The labour-process which is the basis of humanity's existence cannot take place without our ability to imagine a complete task and to work out plans, however rudimentary, for its completion. But the important question here is that of how goals and the plans to achieve them arise in the first place. Those who adopt a functionalist approach to psychology and who subscribe to the 'man is a machine' view can only have one answer, albeit implicit rather than explicit. This is that sensory input is transformed by the structure of the brain into mental goals (together with plans to achieve them) which are likely to lead to the survival of the organism. In contrast to this, Marxists would start from the premise that all thought is simultaneously both individual and social. For just as the ability to become the subject of one's own life-activity, that is, to look at one's past and future life-activity objectively, arises from being corrected and criticised by others, so the ability to formulate one's own plans or 'programmes' arises from activities involving definite social relationships. Past suggestions and criticisms made by others, together with information and viewpoints received from and expressed by others, are retained in the memory. These memories are brought back and used, in the individual's imagination, to work out definite plans of action. It is as if past discussions with others become 'internalised'. When working out plans for future actions, individuals often recapitulate, again in their imaginations, abbreviated forms of meetings at which common agreement is sought of various issues, such as a family discussion about the future of one of its members, trade union branch meetings, university seminars and so on. In fact without participating in external dialogue, listening to the suggestions of others and so forth, no individual would be able to carry out the *internal* dialogue so necessary for the formation of relatively complex plans of action. This question can perhaps be made clearer by reference to the content of many dreams, in which we often carry out conversations with or receive information from others. These others can be real or imaginary, living or dead. The important point here is that those with whom we interact in dreams represent — directly or indirectly — those with whom we interact in real life. In other words those we talk to, argue with or listen to in dreams could not exist in our imagination unless we had previously talked to, argued with or listened to real people in our waking lives. It should be recalled that many people actually obtain inspiration from dreams which resolve real life problems. During waking hours the process is relatively similar, although usually more oriented towards reality. For as a result of past relationships with others we acquire the ability to look for possible solutions to problems about what to do from various angles and standpoints which must, ultimately and usually indirectly, represent the standpoint of others. Thus a correct answer to the question of who or what programmes our behaviour depends on a rejection of the 'man is a machine' view in favour of that based on an understanding of the dialectical unity of individual and social thought.

It now becomes clear that the central question facing the discipline of psychology is not that of the relationship of the brain to thought, as is implied by those subscribing to the mechanical approach. The ways in which various physical states of the brain affect thinking and feeling of course constitutes a legitimate field of study. (This point will be taken up in the next chapter.) However, the *central* question facing a genuinely scientific psychology can only be that of the relationship of thought and mind to a life-activity the basis of which is social relationships and their means and media.

The mechanical approach to individuals in psychology is manifested in attempts to explain the ways in which concepts are formed. The most common current view is that we mentally abstract common features of separate objects. What these objects have in common then forms the basis for a concept. In other words, stimuli enter the brain via the five senses. The structure of the brain is such that it abstracts common features of objects, people and other aspects of the world in a purely mechanical fashion. It is stated that:

> The process of categorisation [i.e., of forming concepts] entails both generalisa-
> tion and discrimination. We categorise different animals as dogs by recognising
> features that are common to various dogs. In other words we generalise from one
> dog to another, abstracting features that are shared by different dogs . . . At
> the same time we discriminate or notice the difference between dogs and other
> animals . . . [we note] similarities among stimuli and [group] stimuli into
> categories . . .[15]

It is of course possible that psychology undergraduate students in artificial and contrived laboratory situations may learn certain concepts in the above manner. It is also possible that *some* concepts may also be learnt in the same way in everyday life. This having been said, it is necessary to state that the approach just described rests on an unstated but false assumption. This assumption is that what is seen is automatically understood. Thus in the above example, the words 'we generalise from one dog to another, abstracting features that are common to all dogs [and] we discriminate between dogs and other animals' clearly imply a previous understanding of what constitutes a dog. For without this previous knowledge we could not abstract from dogs alone rather than from dogs and other animals or indeed from inanimate objects. Just as we could not differentiate between dogs on the one hand and, say, hyenas or wolves on the other. It should be noted that there are far more 'common features' shared by the external appearances of Alsatians and wolves than are shared by the external appearances of Yorkshire terriers and Irish wolfhounds. Yet Alsatians, Yorkshire terriers and Irish wolfhounds are conceptualised (categorised) as dogs whereas wolves are not.

It also needs to be noted that the above-quoted author restricts his example to tangible objects such as dogs. How people acquire concepts such as 'God', 'justice', 'immortality' or 'the square root of minus one' by the abstraction of 'common features' is not explained.

From a Marxist standpoint, any understanding of at least the most significant concepts in our lives must start from a knowledge that concepts form important aspects of the means and media of the co-ordination of activities, that is, of social relationships. They are closely linked to language. Thus the concept 'give' is strengthened in the mind of the young child when he or she utters the word 'give' to the parents, thereby bringing about the coordination of activities (the parent gives, the child takes). The concept 'money' is strengthened in the young mind by actions involving both money and the activity of others. The child is, for example, sent to a shop to buy something from the shopkeeper and bring back the change. It is certainly doubtful if the concept 'money' is learned by the passive contemplation of various coins and banknotes and the mental abstraction of their common features. Quite apart from anything else, this sort of abstraction would necessarily involve a previous knowledge of the difference between a banknote and other printed pieces of paper of roughly the same size. The concept of 'dog' used in the above example is probably formed by the child participating in activities relating to dogs or at least observing these activities. Dogs have to be house trained, taken for walks, kept as watch dogs, avoided if fierce and so on. In other words, people engage in activities involving dogs which are different from, say, the activity of watching television programmes in which wolves and hyenas are to be observed. One further example: The concept of 'rain' would probably be explained by the current approach in terms of individuals contemplating various kinds of rain (drizzle, downpours and so on) and abstracting their common features. A much more likely explanation is that the concept is formed when we *do things* in relation to rain. We close windows to avoid it getting in, take shelter, put on raincoats and stout shoes and get the washing in off the line.

The view of concept formation put forward by the above-quoted author has as a major premise a particular model of the human individual. He or she is seen as an isolated and passive contemplator who sits in a armchair, as it were, observing various aspects of the world and abstracting their 'common features'. But it is necessary to re-state that we exist not by contemplating the world but by acting on it. Furthermore, few complex actions are possible without their co-ordination with those of others. In other words, concepts are for *doing things*, usually — directly or indirectly — in conjunction with others. It is precisely here that the learning of at least the most significant concepts is to be explained. A further feature of concepts about which a reminder needs to be made is their *historical nature*. To return to above examples, concepts such as 'God', 'justice' or 'the square root of minus one' are clearly products of history. Yet the current viewpoint at least gives one the impression that the formation of concepts is a *purely* individual matter, arising solely from the abstraction of 'common features' of what is observed. This viewpoint can in fact give rise to some amusement. For instance, one can try to imagine the above-quoted author trying to convince his readers that the concept 'ghost' is formed by the individual armchair contemplation of a varied assortment of spooks and spectres and the mental abstraction of what they have in common.

As mentioned briefly above, the current view of concept formation ignores the fact that concepts are essentially produced by *history*. The concept of 'God' could only arise at a definite stage in history as a partial attempt on the part of the human race to understand the world and its workings. Concepts such as 'justice' must be historical since much of what was considered just in, say, the days of the Roman empire would be considered unjust today. Those such as 'the square root of minus one' could only arise as a part of the historical development of mathematics. Even the concept of 'dog' must be historical in nature since different historical cultures have made use of dogs in different ways.

It is necessary to stress again that at least the most significant concepts in our lives represent part of the means and media of active relationships. Thus those such as 'God' and 'justice' are used by parents and teachers to encourage children to conform to certain rules. The concept 'ghost' (which must also have arisen, during a certain historical epoch, to explain aspects of the world) is used by older children to frighten or impress younger ones. That of 'the square root of minus one' is used by teachers involved in showing their pupils how to solve certain types of problems which arise in mathematics. It is necessary to recall that, used in a Marxist sense, the term 'consciousness' implies not only the ability to be the subject of one's own life-activity. It also implies the ability to perceive the world in terms of what it could become with human intervention. This in turn implies that many of the concepts which are of importance to the existence and development of the human race reflect the *social purpose of things*. This can be seen especially clearly when tools are considered. The concept of 'saw' (noun) is inseparable from the action of sawing, that of 'spade' from that of digging, that of 'hammer' from hammering and so on. Similarly the concept 'clothes' is inseparable from the need to wear them, that of 'house' from what people live in, that of 'bicycle' from the action of riding one and that of 'gun' from the action of killing people or game. Numerous similar examples could be given. From what has just been said it is clear that a knowledge of the nature of human consciousness is a necessary condition for an understanding of concepts. (And indeed of words denoting concepts.) For what has to be explained by psychologists is the ability of individuals to perceive the world, not only as it is, but also as it could become with conscious human intervention. It is also clear that those psychologists who start from the premise that human individuals are no more than isolated and passive contemplators whose brain structures make mechanical abstractions from superficial appearances cannot even begin to understand the true nature of concepts.

It may be concluded that any serious study of the formation of concepts in the minds of individuals must start from the assumption, outlined in the previous chapter, that human thought is simultaneously unique and individual on the one hand and social and historical on the other. The brain, together with its ability to 'process information', is of course essential to thought. But the way in which it functions (e.g. by its ability to abstract 'common features') is inadequate to explain the formation of concepts. Human individuals are not machines but the products and makers of history.

One important aspect of the mechanistic world outlook is its close connection with mysticism. This connection was highlighted by Descartes. By showing that the content of thought could not be explained in terms of mechanics, his work gave rise to the so-called mind-body problem.[16]

To illustrate the connection between mechanics and mysticism in modern psychology, it is necessary to return to the statement by Hebb quoted at the beginning of this chapter. After making clear that, in his opinion, there are two theories of mind, animistic and mechanistic, he goes on to say that the mechanistic theory 'is a working assumption only, which may turn out to be wrong, and the student as neophyte scientist need not — should not — believe it. In his private capacity he may believe in either of the two theories . . . there are men of the highest ability to be found on either side of the question (a great majority, probably, believing in the existence of the soul).'[17] Thus Hebb who, it should be recalled, is a very important figure in the history of psychology makes it absolutely clear that a mechanistic approach to human individuals leaves the door wide open for mysticism.

Despite the opinions of Hebb — and indeed of the many modern psychologists who share his views — it is clear that any genuinely scientific psychology worthy of the name must account for the fact that many human individuals possess religious beliefs.

Attempts have been made by earlier psychologists — for example Freud and Jung — to explain religion. That these attempts have been unsatisfactory is really beside the point. At least they tried. Modern psychology, however, totally avoids this very important psychological question.

From a Marxist standpoint, a scientific knowledge of religious beliefs implies, first and foremost, a clear understanding of their *historical development*, right from the belief of the earliest hunter-gatherer tribes in the existence of large numbers of spirits to present-day monotheism. It further implies the knowledge that the concept of supernatural God is no more than a historically developed personification — in the imagination — of those natural and social forces over which the human race has no conscious control.[18]

An important factor linking a mechanistic approach to that of mysticism is that of *choice*. As has already been stated, one of the significant features of historically developed human individuals is their ability to choose consciously one of alternative courses of action. In contrast to the Russian author quoted above, Marxists believe that individuals do possess free will, at least in the sense that we are free to make conscious choices. As compared to the free will that is inherent in human consciousness, machines — including computers — cannot make conscious choices. It needs to be re-emphasised that their performance is predetermined by their past. Any so-called 'choice' made by the most sophisticated computer is predetermined both by its programme and by its input.[19] It must therefore follow that anyone who adopts a mechanistic approach to human individuals can only really explain moral and other choices in terms of supernatural or mystical factors. It may be concluded that a mechanical approach to human individuals and a mystical approach to human individuals constitute dialectical opposites. One must necessarily imply the other.

No criticism of the 'mechanical' approach to human psychology would be complete without mention of the theoretical approach of Piaget, mentioned briefly in Chapter Four. Piaget has much in common with Marxism. For example he stresses the importance of *action* in the development of thinking of children. He also agrees with Marxists that individuals change themselves during and as a result of their practical activity. He correctly insists that human thought and knowledge cannot be understood simply in terms of what goes on in the heads of individuals. Rather, it has to be understood in terms of the individual's continual interchanges with the environment, the most important aspects of which are of course social. However, Piaget's approach, despite its sophistication, is essentially that of *mechanics*. He conceives of thought developing as a result of the interaction and interchange *between two natural systems*, the individual biological organism on the one hand and its environment on the other.[20]

It is necessary to consider this last point in some detail. Piaget maintains that during the development of logico-mathematical thinking (his principal field of study) certain 'intellectual structures' develop. 'Structures' in Piaget's theory are organised sets of 'operations'. The latter terms refers to mental actions which are reversible. An example is necessary. Mental operations such as multiplications and division are organised into a 'structure' because they can be reversed. Thus we know that because we can multiply 6 by 4 to obtain 24 the operation can be reversed by dividing 24 by 4 to obtain 6 and thus return to the original starting point (the number 6). What Piaget fails to appreciate, however, is that such 'intellectual structures' can only be meaningful to those possessing *consciousness*. Consciousness, of course, implies the ability of the individual to view his or her activity 'from the side' as it were, that is, to be the subject of his or her activity — including mental activity. To return to the above example, consciousness implies the ability of individuals to say to themselves: 'If I can multiply 6 by 4 to obtain 24, then I can also divide 24 by 4 to obtain 6.'

The weakness of Piaget's position now becomes clear. For consciousness is a product, not of the mechanical interaction between a biological organism and its environment. It arises in individuals as a result of their activity undertaken with others in historically developed social situations.

In a very limited sense, of course, Piaget is not incorrect. Individuals *are* biological organisms and they *do* interact with their environments. However, when studying the development of thought in individuals such an approach is inadequate and hence of necessity false. The only really adequate starting point is that of the *historical* individual whose life-activity constitutes a part of human history and who consequently develops the faculty of consciousness.[21] Any serious consideration of the mechanical outlook in psychology demands that a further question be raised. This is that of why the mechanistic world outlook still clings so tenaciously to the discipline of psychology. It should be noted that since it first flourished during the period of the Renaissance, this outlook has largely been discarded in many disciplines. For example in physics, chemistry, biology and mathematics. The development of cybernetics and of systems theory has undoubtedly hastened its decline. (Understandably, a mechanistic approach still prevails in engineering. Engineers are interested in how the internal structure of objects causes them to interact with other objects in space).

Why is it, therefore, that so many psychologists still regard people as mechanical objects while others, although possibly uneasy about the 'man is a machine' approach, are unable to take any effective stand against it? It is certainly not because all psychologists are stupid. Amongst their ranks are to be found some that are very intelligent. It is also not because of the existence of some widespread conspiracy to conceal the truth. Most psychologists are men and women of integrity. The answer to this question must be that the mechanical approach of modern psychology to human individuals is a reflection and a manifestation of the objective social relationships which exist in capitalist society. In other words, the same social relationships that give rise to the illusion that 'society' is something standing apart from individuals (see Chapter 5) also give rise to the illusion that human individuals are machines.

It is a characteristic feature of capitalist society that people are in effect seen by others as objects to be used and manipulated, much as machines are used and manipulated. In other words, they are perceived in terms of what can be got out of them.

This can be seen especially clearly in industry, in which workers become no more than objects subordinated to machines. Marx and Engels write:

> Owing to the extensive use of machinery, the work of the proletarians has lost all individual charm for the workman. He becomes an appendage to the machine.[22]

This reduction of individuals to no more than appendages to machines has been graphically illustrated by Charlie Chaplin in his classic film 'Modern Times'.

The cut-throat competition that characterises capitalism, summed up by the old saying: 'Every man for himself and the devil take the hindmost' implies that people are regarded as expendible objects. Generally speaking, they are of use only in so far as they possess money or can be used to make money for others. Marx and Engels write further:

> The bourgeoisie . . . has left remaining no other nexus between man and man than naked self-interest, than callous 'cash payment'. It has drowned the most heavenly ecstasies of religious fervour, of chivalrous enthusiasm . . . in the icy water of egotistical calculation. It has resolved personal worth into exchange value . . .[23]

During the periodic wars that represent inevitable concomitants of capitalism, millions of human beings are also regarded by generals and politicians as expendible objects. The appropriate term 'cannon fodder' has in fact entered the English language.

Since all these expendible objects are capable of movement and action, they are therefore seen simply as mechanical objects or machines, the functioning of which is determined by their internal structure.

It may be concluded that the reason that modern psychologists conceptualise human individuals as machines is to be sought in the objective social relations of capitalism. The latter cause individuals to be treated as expendible objects and they therefore become conceptualised as such.

Before concluding this chapter, attention has to be drawn to three choices that have to be made by those intent on developing a genuinely scientific psychology.

First. EITHER: The human individual is a machine that develops psychologically in interaction with similar machines, the form taken by the interactions being determined both by the structure of the brains of individuals and by the structure of the 'social environment'. OR: The human individual is a product of history and, by that fact, a maker of history.

Second. EITHER: Human consciousness is, as Rose maintains, a 'developing activity of minds/brains in interaction with their environment'. OR: Human consciousness is a product of the co-ordination of one's activity with that of others in historically developed social situations. It is not the product of the workings of a machine but of history, a history of which the life-activity of each individual constitutes a definite part.

Third. EITHER: The human individual, being a machine, possesses no free will. OR: The human individual, being the product of social relationships and of history, possesses free will as an essential aspect of human consciousness as previously defined.

Finally, it is necessary to return again to the statement of Hebb quoted at the beginning of this chapter. He maintains that there are two theories of mind, the animistic and the mechanistic. *Hebb is wrong.* There is a third theory of mind, namely the Marxist theory, which rests on the assumption that the human individual is neither a machine nor a body inhabited by a soul, but is a product and a maker of history possessing human consciousness. This book is written in the belief that the Marxist theory will provide the basis for the psychology of the future.

NOTES TO CHAPTER SIX

1. Hebb, D.O. *Textbook of Psychology*. Third Edition, Saunders, 1972, pp. 4-5.
2. Radford, J. and Govier, E. *A Textbook of Psychology*. Sheldon, 1980, p. 43.
3. Rose, S. *The Conscious Brain*. Penguin, 1976, p. 34.
4. See Chapter One, Note 6
5. See Chapter One, Note 7
6. Greene, J. and Holloway, C. *Cognitive Psychology*. Introduction. Part 1. The Open University, 1978, p. 72.
7. *Ibid*. p. 19.
8. *Ibid*. p. 15.
9. Wooldridge, D.E. *The Machinery of the Brain*. McGraw-Hill, 1963, pp. 238-9. Quoted in Mikhailov, F. *The Riddle of the Self*. Progress Publishers, 1980, p. 130.
10. Weitzenbaum, D. *Computer Power and Human Reason*. Penguin, 1984.
11. Amosov, N.M. *Modelling of Thought and the Mind*. Kiev, 1965. Quoted in Mikhailov *op. cit.* p. 250.
12. Delgado, J. *Physical Control of the Mind. Towards a Psychocivilised Society*. Harper and Row, 1969 pp. 224-5.
13. Of course, feral children and those possessing grossly deformed or severely damaged brains can exist as biological organisms — incidentally in the latter case always kept alive by others — but they can hardly be termed human in the sense that they are subjects of their own life-activity.
14. Miller, G., Gallanter, E. and Pribram, K. *Plans and the Structure of Behaviour*. Holt, Rinehart and Winston, 1960.
15. Wessells, M. *Cognitive Psychology*. Harper and Row, 1982, pp. 198-9. To their credit, a few modern psychologists have stressed the *social* nature of concepts. See, for example: S. Moscovici *Social Representations*. Cambridge University Press, 1963. Attention has also been drawn to the social nature of concepts by the work of Vygotsky. See, for example, Vygotsky, L. *Thought and Language*. M.I.T. Press, 1986.
16. For a discussion of the so-called 'mind-body problem' see Chapter 11.
17. Hebb op. cit. p. 4.
18. Of course, the question of why some individuals possess religious beliefs while others do not can only be answered by a separate examination of the life-activity of each of the individuals concerned. For a Marxist view of the origin and development of religious beliefs see, for example: Engels *Ludwig Feuerbach and the End of German Classical Philosophy*. Progress Publishers, 1946. Also: Engels *Anti-Duhring*. Lawrence and Wishart, 1954.
19. From the Marxist standpoint, the fact that humans can make choices does not of course imply that the activity of our brains is not governed by objective laws. When we make choices we cannot observe the particular brain activity which correlates with a definite choice. Quite apart from the

enormous complexity of brain processes, any attempt by people to observe their own brains while making a choice would change their own thinking and thus effect the making of the choice. They would thus be like cats chasing their own tails or people climbing up a ladder to look down on themselves. A further point that needs to be made is that, from a Marxist standpoint, individuals can only make choices within the framework of the concepts which they have acquired in the course of their own historical life-activity. Further, moral and other dilemmas can only arise within the framework of social situations which have objective existence independently of the individual's consciousness or will.

20. See, for example, Piaget, J. *Biology and Knowledge*. Edinburgh University Press, 1971.
21. A much fuller Marxist critique of this aspect of Piaget's outlook is to be found in Lektorsky, V. *Subject. Object. Cognition*. Progress Publishers, 1980.
22. Marx and Engels *Manifesto of the Communist Party*. Progress Publishers, 1977, p. 38.
23. *Ibid*. p. 42.

7

THE INTERPENETRATION OF
BIOLOGICAL AND SOCIAL FACTORS
IN THE INDIVIDUAL

In previous chapters the *historical* nature of the human individual has been stressed. It is necessary to recall, however, the somewhat obvious fact that individuals are biological organisms, obeying the laws of human biology. In Chapter Five it was argued that human thought is simultaneously unique and individual on the one hand and social and historical on the other. The purpose of the present chapter is to look at this argument in another way and to show that individuals must necessarily represent the point of interpenetration of the laws both of history and of human biology. A number of separate aspects of the question need to be considered. Amongst these are: Basic biological needs. How these are intertwined with social factors. How physical factors help to determine social roles. Social factors linked to puberty. How the form of thought influences its content and vice versa. Piaget's 'functional invariants' and their relevance to the 'functional autonomy' of motives.

A good starting point in considering the interpenetration of biological and social factors is a brief reminder of the existence of definite biological needs which cause individuals to engage in various forms of activity. The influence of social factors on these biological needs has to be pointed out.

The most obvious biological needs are those of air, food and water. Lack of these creates uncomfortable states of tension which individuals will seek to reduce. The biological need for sex is also obvious, although it needs to be remarked that without food and water individuals could not engage in sexual behaviour. Also obvious is the biological need for protection from extremes of temperature, as is the need for sleep.

One of the positive achievements of contemporary psychology is that it has highlighted a number of biological needs that are not so obvious as those just mentioned. Perhaps the most significant of these is the need for stimulation. In an interesting series of experiments researchers working under the auspices of D.O.Hebb subjected volunteers to conditions referred to as those of 'sensory deprivation'. These experimental subjects were deprived of visual, auditory and (as far as possible) tactile experience. After a period of time undergoing this experience the subjects became psychologically disoriented and disturbed, while in some cases hallucinations were reported.[1] Thus it is apparent that every individual requires, and will therefore seek, a certain level of sensory stimulation. What is more obvious is that individuals will avoid intense levels of stimulation. Thus we tend to avoid very loud noises and very bright lights. It can be concluded, therefore, that individuals will tend to seek sensory stimulation within definite limits — not too little and not too much.[2] Other studies have shown that innate tendencies exist to seek novel stimuli. Monkeys (our nearest evolutionary relatives) have been shown to work hard by, for example, pressing down a bar in order to be rewarded by the sight of a toy train or by the opportunity to manipulate mechanical puzzles.[3] Such a need obviously exists in humans and must play an important part in human exploration and discovery. Closely related to this is the need to avoid boredom and repetitive stimuli. Such needs as those of a definite level of stimulation and of novel stimuli, together with the avoidance of boredom, are sometimes collectively referred to as 'intrinsic motivation'.[4]

Biological needs are intertwined with social factors at every level. The elementary need to breathe is affected by bad posture and undue tensions in the intercostal muscles, both of which are produced either by socially-learned habits or by psychological tensions brought about by social situations. The natural processes of digestion are affected by social factors. Thus food eaten by someone on the verge of starvation will be digested in a different manner to that of food eaten by a glutton who is constantly overfed. Numerous similar examples could be given. Indeed, such intertwining of biological needs and social factors has given rise to the conception of 'socialised physiology', one of the major proponents of which was the psychiatrist Harry Stack Sullivan. The authors of a well-known textbook outline Sullivan's views on this topic thus: '. . . the interpersonal experiences of an individual may and do alter his purely physiological functioning, so that even the organism loses its status as a biological entity and becomes a social organism with its own socialised ways of breathing, digesting, eliminating, circulating the blood and so on.'[5]

The extent to which the 'intrinsic motivation' (e.g. the seeking of stimulation) referred to above is influenced by social factors is at present unknown.

It is obvious, however, that the way in which stimulation is sought, boredom relieved and so on can only be of a social character. People relieve boredom by watching television, engaging in sporting activity or conversation, reading a book or playing with their children. All activities like these represent parts of a life-activity the framework of which is historically developed social relationships together with their means and media.

Right from the very moment of conception, physical factors are influenced by social ones. Indeed, social factors help to determine the very genetic constitution of the human individual, half of whose genes come from the mother and half from the father. It is of course social factors which determines who mates with whom. One has only to look at South Africa, where mating between blacks and whites has been prohibited by law, to realise this. The physical development of the embryo and foetus in the mother's womb is also of course influenced by social factors. If the mother, while pregnant, receives inadequate nourishment or takes certain drugs, her child may well be born deformed or retarded.

The physical existence of individuals as biological organisms will influence the particular role they play in society. This role will tend to vary from culture to culture and from one sub-culture to another. It is clear that there are wide cultural variations in the roles expected of males and females. There are also wide cultural variations in attitudes towards both the young and the elderly. If children are unfortunate enough to be born ugly or deformed, they may well be teased or bullied by other children or even rejected by their parents. To the extent they are bullied or rejected they are likely to develop feelings of bitterness, resentment and insecurity in a manner that would not occur if they had been good-looking or not deformed. Although their feelings of bitterness and insecurity would not necessarily have developed if they had not been born ugly or deformed, these feelings cannot be directly attributed to ugliness or deformity as such. Of equal importance is the attitude of others towards ugliness and deformity. (It needs to be remarked that 'ugliness' is a social concept varying from culture to culture). The dialectical interpenetration of the biological and the social is here clearly revealed.

The dialectical 'unity of opposites' is further revealed by the thoughts, feelings and behaviour engendered by the onset of puberty. This is, of course, a biological phenomenon one aspect of which is feelings of sexual arousal. Individuals, however, cannot have sexual feelings without having definite attitudes towards them such as those of guilt, wonder, puzzlement and so on. In some cultures, guilt towards one's own sexual feelings at the time of puberty is widespread, especially in Catholic countries. But such attitudes are clearly social in origin. That this is so can be shown by cross-cultural studies. In advanced countries the period of adolescence which follows the onset of puberty is frequently accompanied by difficulties in establishing interpersonal relationships. These difficulties in turn lead to various forms of distress and confusion. In contrast to this, in many primitive tribes the stress and problems of adolescence so apparent in advanced countries are remarkable by their virtual absence, as anthropologists have testified.[6] Thus, the thought and behaviour of adolescents following the onset of the biological process of puberty cannot be explained simply in terms of biology. During this period of life social factors play an essential part. The biological and the social are fused together, as it were.

In the previous chapter, the distinction was made between the content of thought and its form. It will be recalled that the content of thought (what the individual thinks about) represents, not an awareness of the activity of the brain cells, but rather a form taken by the world (as acted upon and experienced by the individual) existing outside the brain. In contrast to this the activity of the brain itself represents the form taken by the content of thought. It is now necessary to draw attention to some of the ways in which the form of thought influences its content and vice versa.

One of the most obvious ways in which the form of thought affects its content is the decline of mental abilities that takes place with age. This reflects the inevitable physical deterioration of the body (including the brain) which is brought about by the various processes of aging. It is far easier to learn higher mathematics when one is nineteen than when one is 90. It is of course well known that the memories of elderly people are notoriously bad as compared to those of younger generations.

The physical deterioration of the brain that occurs with age is not, of course, the only way in which brain damage can be sustained. Thus severe blows to the head or bullet wounds can disrupt mental functioning. If the brain's frontal lobes are damaged, the individual's previous ability to subordinate short term to long term goals may be lost or impaired. Certain vitamin deficiences may lead to hallucinations. The lifting of inhibitions that results from the drinking of alcohol is of course well known, as is the disruption of normal behaviour patterns by the taking of drugs such as L.S.D.[7]

A number of examples can be given of the way in which social factors can influence the activity of the brain. As has already been mentioned, social factors which cause women to be undernourished or take certain drugs while pregnant can result in the child's brain failing to develop as it should. This may cause the child's mental development to fail to proceed as it otherwise would.

Similarly, of course, inadequate nutrition when young can cause children to grow up mentally retarded, as often happens in the so-called 'Third World'. It is of course social factors which cause people to drink alcohol. Excessive alcohol intake not only releases the mind from inhibitions. It can also cause physical damage to the brain. Similarly the social factors which cause people to take certain drugs are responsible for the ways in which normal brain functioning is disrupted by these drugs. Social factors causing people to become neurotic can lead them to consult a psychiatrist. The latter can then cause them to submit to electro-convulsive therapy, which in turn can physically damage their brains. This damage can lead to further social problems.[8]

The above examples indicate that there is considerable interpenetration between the content and the form of thought. However, it is important for the development of a genuinely scientific psychology that a clear distinction be made between the two.

The importance of understanding biological factors when considering the form taken by thought has been highlighted by Piaget, mentioned previously in Chapters Four and Six. Although he failed to see the limitations of the 'adaptation model', his views in some respects came close to Marxism.[9] Piaget started his career as a biologist. This led him to suggest that aspects of psychological functioning could be understood in terms of what he referred to as 'functional invariants'. As the term itself implies, these are unvarying properties of all biological matter. The two most important of these are 'adaptation' and 'organisation'. In the sense used by Piaget, 'adaptation' implies the ability of the organism to change itself during and as a result of its own activity in a manner likely to ensure its survival. In contrast, the term 'organisation' implies the integration of all parts of the organism into a coherently functioning system. The two 'opposites' are dialectically united. The organism can adapt because it is organised and by adapting it becomes better organised. At the same time, however, the two opposites often pull in opposite directions, as it were. Thus the tendency to change comes into conflict with the tendency of the organism to conserve intact its own internal structure. To put it another way, the tendency to change comes into conflict with the tendency to conserve what already exists and vice versa. This is very important from the standpoint of the discipline of psychology. For these two tendencies are manifested in the activity of the brain (representing the form taken by thought) which must reveal itself in the content of thought and in behaviour generally. Generally speaking, it is desirable that there should be a balance between the two tendencies. On the one hand it is necessary to change in the course of one's own activity[10] and thus to profit from experience. On the other hand such change should not be so great that the changes brought about by previous activity are completely lost or reversed. To put it another way, the ability to learn from immediate experience should not be such that the lessons afforded by past experiences are lost.

It is of course well known that young children acquire new behaviour patterns very easily. Yet even at an early age certain what may be termed 'personality characteristics' can become stabilised and relatively enduring. Thus Adler maintained that what he termed the 'life-style', that is, the way in which individuals evaluate and compensate for their own inferiorities, became relatively stabilised by the age of about five.[11] Many other writers have also drawn attention to the stabilisation of certain behaviour patterns at about this age.[12]

The stabilisation of behaviour patterns brought about by the biological tendency to conserve what already exists can help to explain many ways of behaving which otherwise would remain almost inexplicable. Thus many petty criminals will keep on committing offences which cause them to be frequently imprisoned. They cannot learn from past mistakes. Similarly gamblers who regularly lose money are often unable to learn more satisfactory behaviour patterns. About the time of the end of the second world war many Nazi SS troops, instead of surrendering, risked loss of life and limb by carrying on fighting even when they knew for certain that they had lost the war.

Piaget's identification of the tendency of the biological organism to conserve intact its own patterns of functioning has given a theoretical underpinning to one of the principal conceptions of the personality theorist Allport. This is that of what Allport termed the 'functional autonomy' of many human motives.[13] The term 'functional autonomy' refers to motives which acquire an existence independent of the particular activities during the course of which they first appeared.[14] This implies that means to ends become ends in themselves. An example is necessary to make this clearer. Many individuals set out to make large sums of money in order to buy, not only the necessities of life, but also luxuries. Yet amongst such people there are many examples of those who, in the course of making money in order to buy things, acquire the functionally autonomous motive of making money simply for the sake of making money. The means (making money) to the end (buying necessities and luxuries) becomes an end in itself. The particular mode of functioning (making money) becomes stabilised and hence acquires a relative independence from the previous motive of making money simply in order to be able to buy things.

A theoretical conception of the stabilisation of behaviour patterns to form 'functionally autonomous' motives permits a deeper understanding of the totally inadequate nature of the 'functionalist' approach discussed in Chapter Three. For it is clear that there must be many such motives that are not adaptive in the normal biological sense, that is, they they do not necessarily lead to the survival of the individual. On the other hand such a theoretical conception also strengthens the Marxist view that in each stage in history individuals are able to come forward to play an active role in the development of humanity's ability to create the conditions of its own life. For without the 'functionally autonomous' motive of making money for its own sake it is unlikely that the early industrialists would have had the initiative and drive to create modern industry. Similarly without the 'functionally autonomous' motives that lead to self-sacrifice and martyrdom those historically necessary revolutions which enabled humanity's abilities and capacities to develop unhindered could not have occurred. For example, capitalism could not have developed unhindered in Britain if it were not for the martyrs of the Cromwellian revolution.

It is thus clear that Piaget's identification of the two important biological tendencies, that of changing and that of conserving intact, constitutes a significant contribution towards an understanding of human behaviour and thinking.

To sum up this chapter, the development of a genuinely scientific psychology is inconceivable without the premise that there is a continual dialectical interpenetration of biological and social (historical) factors in human individuals. It needs to be reiterated that the ongoing history of the human race is not something to which individuals 'adjust' or 'adapt'. It is not something which forms a backdrop, as it were, against which human beings enact their individual lives. Rather, ongoing history constitutes the very content of individual life-activity, a life-activity of organisms obeying the laws of human biology. The human individual is thus the point of interpenetration between the laws of history and those of human biology.

Before concluding this chapter, it is necessary to recall that — from a Marxist standpoint — human history constitutes an extension of natural history. The ways in which biological and social factors interpenetrate in individuals must therefore represent a necessary aspect of the development of humanity's ability to create and re-create — from the Stone Age to the Atomic Age — the conditions of its own existence. It is only from this standpoint — rather than a functionalist one — that such interpenetration can be understood.

Finally, since there is so much confusion and misunderstanding amongst psychologists on this point, it is necessary to reiterate once again: Although the brain is essential to thought, the latter is not and can never be produced by the brain *as such*. As has already been remarked in the previous chapter, thought and the physical existence of the body (brain) are mutually interdependent. Without the brain there can be no thought and without the thought that guides and directs our behaviour there can be no physical existence of the brain. Both thought and physical existence share the same basis — that of life-activity. To look at the matter in another way, all thought must represent a reflection — however distorted a reflection it may be — of the world external to the brain. It can only represent a form taken by the external world — a world acted upon and experienced by the separate person, who thinks with the aid of historically developed concepts and categories of thought. If changes take place in the physical structure of the brain such as those brought about by old age, drugs, injury or disease, these changes may well bring about corresponding changes in the content of thought. Nevertheless — and this is what is really important here — the content of thought must always remain a form of, and a reflection (however distorted) of the external world. It can never be attributed *directly* to the brain.

It is clear that the interpenetration of biological and social (historical) factors in the human individual constitutes an essential question for those intent on developing a genuinely scientific psychology. A clear understanding of such interpenetration opens the way for further clarification. Conversely, lack of clarity can and does lend to further confusion.

NOTES TO CHAPTER SEVEN

1. See: Hebb, D.O. *Textbook of Psychology*. Saunders, Third Ed., 1972, p. 210.
2. There appear to be wide variations in the level of stimulation which different individuals will tend to seek. Eysenck has in fact postulated the existence of what he terms a 'personality dimension' involving these variations. See, for example: Eysenck, H.J. *The Biological Basis of Personality*. Thomas, 1967.
3. See, for example: Butler, R. *Curiosity in Monkeys*. Scientific American, February 1954.
4. The question of the precise relationships between the levels of stimulation sought, the need for novel stimuli and the avoidance of boredom is a question which is outside the scope of this book. A good account of 'intrinsic motivation' is given in: Milner, A. *Physiological Psychology*. Holt, Rinehart and Winston, 1970, Chapters 17,18.
5. Hall, C. and Lindsey, G. *Theories of Personality*. Wiley, 3rd. Edit., 1978, p. 181.
6. See, for example: Malinowski, B. *Sex and Repression in Savage Society*. Meridian Books, 1955.
7. At this point it is perhaps necessary to re-emphasise that the brain *as such* does not produce thought. The content of thought always represents, in however distorted a manner, a form taken by the material world. The proverbial drunkard who 'sees' pink elephants could not 'see' them unless he had previously seen, heard of or read about elephants.
8. Although electro-convulsive therapy (ECT) is not now used as much as it has been in the past, its application throughout the world is still relatively widespread. This is despite warnings of its dangers in reputable scientific journals. For example, an article in the official journal of the Royal College of Psychiatrists concludes with the words: 'ECT patients' inferior . . . performance does

suggest that ECT causes permanent brain damage.' (Templar, D., Ruff, C. and Gath, D. 'Cognitive Functioning and Degree of Psychosis in Schizophrenia given many Electroconvulsive Treatments'. *The British Journal of Psychiatry*, October 1973.)

9. Further comment on Piaget's work will be made in Chapter Eleven.

10. It will be recalled from Chapter Four that the ability to change oneself during one's own activity consitutes one of the essential prerequisites for the development of human culture based on production.

11. See Brown, J.A.C. *Freud and the Post-Freudians*. Cassell, 1963, p. 39.

12. See, for example: Bloom, B. *Stability and Change in Human Characteristics*. Wiley, 1964.

13. See Allport, G. *Pattern and Growth in Personality*. Holt, Rinehart and Winston, 1961.

14. The term 'motive' is used here in the sense of the definition of Miller, Gallanter and Pribram. These theorists define a motive as a goal together with a plan to achieve it. See Chapter Six, Note 14.

8

DOING AND THINKING

The aim of this chapter is to discuss the vital psychological question of the relationship between doing and thinking. More specifically, it is to discuss the relationship between practical purposive behaviour and abstract thought. In the context of the subject matter of this chapter — and indeed of the whole book — the term 'practical activity' refers to the active changing of the concrete material world. The adjective 'purposive' denotes that during their practical activity individuals are guided by a mental image of the results of their actions, together with a mental plan of how to proceed. The term 'abstract thought' refers to thought which is not directly associated with immediate sense-perceptions.

Aspects of the relationship to be discussed are: Practical activity and abstract thought as dialectical opposites. Practical activity and personality characteristics. Why practical activity is of more importance than thought itself in the development of personality and the mind. How a Marxist approach contradicts a further premise of modern psychology. Finally, why modern psychologists fail to see the true relationship between doing and thinking.

It is a regrettable feature of contemporary psychology that, apart from a few notable exceptions, inadequate attention has been given to this question. However, it is difficult to understand the thinking and behaviour of individuals unless the relationship between their practical activity and their thought is better understood.

The relationship between practical activity and abstract thought is a dialectical one, involving a unity of and a conflict between the two. Practical activity is not abstract thought and abstract thought is not practical activity. At the same time their unity and conflict is expressed in the relationship between them. Any change in practical purposive activity — at least beyond a certain limit — must of necessity rely on a change in abstract thought.

Conversely any change in abstract thought — again at least beyond a certain point — must of necessity rely on a change in practical activity.

That changes in practical activity require changes in abstract thought is obvious. All practical purposive activity involves foreknowledge (an important aspect of abstract thought) and without change in foreknowledge no significant change in practical activity is possible.

That changes in abstract thought require changes in practical activity is perhaps less obvious. It might of course be argued that individuals can add empirical facts to their memories *ad infinitum* without any corresponding change in their practical activity. But the important point here is this: any really significant changes in the concepts and categories of thought of individuals and any significant development of new forms of their thinking can take place only when they are confronted by objective circumstances in which their existing forms of thinking, concepts, categories, values and so on prove inadequate for the task at hand. This means that the practical purposive activity needed to cope with any new objective circumstances requires new forms of abstract thought (such as foreknowledge and values) to guide it. It is worth repeating two quotations already given in Chapter Four: 'The origin of thought is always the presence of a task.' (Luria)[1] and 'I only know an object to the extent to which I act upon it' (Piaget).[2] Here it would perhaps be useful to remind ourselves that individuals do not maintain their own material existence in the world simply by thinking about it. They have to do things in objective situations which confront them independently of their own will in an ever-changing world. And doing new things demands new forms of abstract thought.

The dialectical relationship between practical purposive activity and abstract thought can be represented diagramatically thus:

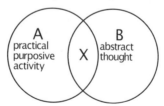

In regions A and B changes in either practical purposive activity or abstract thought do not depend on changes in their opposite. In region X any change in one depends on a change in the other. The relative sizes of the three regions have no significance.

Examples are necessary in order to make clearer what has just been said. Novice surgeons will of necessity have to carry out many and varied operations (practical activity) before they become proficient. At the same time their ability to perform operations — especially the more complicated ones — will depend on their reading of textbooks of surgery (abstract thought). Conversely their ability to understand these textbooks (abstract thought) will be limited by the amount of direct experience of performing operations (practical activity). To put it another way, the reading of textbooks of surgery will increase the ability of surgeons to perform operations in a way that would not otherwise be possible. Conversely, the performance of operations will increase their ability to understand textbooks which otherwise would be too difficult. In an analogous manner students learning say, electrical engineering will have to learn to undertake the practical activity of constructing electrical circuits. They will also have to learn the theoretical aspects of their subject (abstract thought). It is of course possible to construct a very elementary circuit without much theoretical knowledge of electricity. Likewise it is possible to understand Ohm's Law without constructing electrical circuits. But the construction of complex electrical apparatus and circuits cannot be carried out without a knowledge of theoretical principles, just as an understanding of the more advanced principles of electrical engineering cannot be achieved without experience of the practical construction of apparatus and circuits.

The term 'practical activity' has been defined above as 'the active changing of the concrete material world'. However, it is now time to add a qualification. For the ability of human beings to carry out practical activity as defined can lead to the ability to carry out practical activity at a purely mental level. This finds its dialectical opposite in abstract theoretical concepts. As an example, consider the practical activity of mathematicians. The latter learn to understand the theoretical propositions of higher mathematics by the practical mental activity of solving mathematical problems. At the same time, however, the ability to solve practical problems relies upon an understanding of these propositions.

An understanding of the relationship between doing and thinking, between purposive practical activity and abstract thought, can lead to an understanding of another virtually identical relationship. This is that between practical purposive activity and what may be termed 'personality characteristics'. The latter term includes, for example, the knowledge, skills, values, goals, attitudes, likes and dislikes of individuals.[3]

The relationship between practical activity and personality characteristics is therefore such that although changes can occur in one without the other being changed, beyond a certain point any change in one depends upon a change in another. The relationship between the two can therefore be represented in a diagram very similar to that showing the relationship between practical purposive activity and abstract thought:

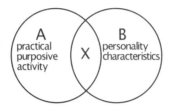

In regions A and B changes in practical purposive activity or in personality characteristics do not depend on changes in their opposite. In region X any change in one depends on a change in the other. As in the previous diagram the relative sizes of the three regions have no significance.

The term 'personality characteristics' includes of course the mental goals which the individual strives to achieve. Since goal-directed activity constitutes the most significant aspect of adult human behaviour and since the undertaking of practical activity is the essential prerequisite for the attainment of goals, the dependence of practical activity on an individual's goals, together with the individual's values, attitudes and so on, is obvious. Less obvious, however, is the dependence of goals on practical activity. To illustrate this last point, consider the example of many young people who, with the best of motives, aspire to become leading politicians. They believe that once they are in a position of authority they can contribute to the well-being of the population as a whole. However, they find that on the way they have to overcome many unforeseen and unexpected obstacles. They also find that in order to overcome these obstacles they have to engage in all sorts of devious practices and skulduggery, which they can initially rationalise on the grounds that 'the end justifies the means' and that once they have a lot of power they can do a lot of good. This in turn leads to a situation in which the nefarious forms of practical activity which they have to undertake causes their values and hence their goals to change. From young people intent on making a better life for others they become cynical politicians intent on feathering their own nests. The dialectical relationship between means and ends, discussed in the previous chapter, is of course of great relevance here.

An understanding of the dialectical relationship between personality characteristics and practical activity must lead to the raising of the question of which of the two opposites is ultimately decisive in the life-activity of individuals. It is widely believed that the principal aspects of the behaviour of individuals are determined by their ideas, values and other aspects of their personality characteristics. It is of course true that what an individual does in a given situation is determined by his or her personality characteristics as defined above. Thus someone who appreciates Beethoven will be more likely to attend a local concert at which Beethoven's Fifth symphony is being played than someone with no interest in classical music. However, superficial appearances can be deceptive. To return to a vitally important point that has already been reiterated in this chapter, it is objective circumstances existing outside the will and consciousness of individuals that cause them to develop new forms of practical activity (and hence new personality characteristics) in order that they may cope with the tasks at hand. To return to a previous example, if children have to engage in practical activity involved in coping with parents who reject them they will develop personality characteristics different from those who engage in the practical activity involved in coping with parents who give them adequate love and guidance.

The relationship between thinking and doing, or between abstract thought and personality characteristics on the one hand and practical activity on the other, is made clearer by an understanding of the relatively obvious fact that the human race survives not primarily because human individuals think, but primarily because they do things. Before people can engage in say, mathematics, religion or the appreciation of poetry they have to eat, live in houses and obtain clothes to wear. Furthermore, these material necessities of life are produced by physical action. Although it may require thought to guide it, it is this physical action which is decisive. For thought by itself cannot produce food, houses and clothing. The conclusion can therefore be drawn that, for the survival of the species *Homo sapiens*, thinking is for doing rather than vice versa. That this is so can be verified by empirical observation. The very perception of the world by individuals is ultimately determined by what they are trying to do. Thus if a certain crowd is being observed by four different people, one a medical student, another a fashion designer, the third an evangelist and the fourth a pickpocket, the first will see the crowd in terms of what ailments people have, the second in terms of what they are wearing, the third in terms of potential souls to be saved while the fourth sees it in terms of possible victims. As with perception so with many attitudes and values. Thus if kindly and considerate individuals are conscripted to fight in a war they will, if forced to engage in direct combat for a long period, discard many of their past attitudes and values and instead develop a cynical and callous attitude towards human suffering. It is clear that their new personality characteristics enable them better to carry out the practical activity of killing and maiming others. Similarly, if a relatively trusting and friendly man is unfortunate enough to get sent to prison, important aspects of his personality may be transformed. If he finds he has to engage in practical activity involved in coping with demoralised and vicious fellow prisoners he will, for example, find himself becoming deeply distrustful of others and will come to regard the world as a hostile and threatening place. On his release from prison he will, at least for a period of time, find it far more difficult than formerly to form close friendships and to trust others.

It would be useful to look at the above question in another way. Whenever purposeful activity of a directly physical nature is carried out, the human body develops certain characteristics. Carpenters will develop strong forearms while postmen will develop strong legs. It is clear that this strengthening of various parts of the body assists in the performance of practical activity. By analogy, many 'personality characteristics' arise in the course of practical activity in a manner which assists in the carrying out of that activity. The above examples of soldiers and a prisoner have already illustrated this, but further examples would not be amiss. Nurses engaged in the care of obnoxious patients tend to regard them as being less obnoxious than would those who do not have to care for them. Similarly domestic servants will tend to regard their employers with genuine feelings of respect and even of affection, even if the latter are hated by most people who know them.[4]

What has just been said makes it clear that the development of abstract thought and 'personality characteristics' such as those given in the above examples cannot be explained by the 'functionalist' approach of modern psychology. In other words the abstract thought, attitudes, values and so on of individuals cannot be explained in terms of their contributions to individual biological survival.[5] Rather they are to be explained in terms of the positive assistance they provide in the attainment of the mental goals which individuals strive to attain in objective situations. From a Marxist standpoint, which seeks to explain the existence of the human race in terms of labour (production), the ability of individuals to subordinate their attitudes, values and so on to mental goals is an essential aspect of the labour process. Recall the words of Marx, already quoted in Chapter Four:

> At the end of every labour process, we get a result that already exists in the imagination of the labourer at its commencement. He not only effects a change

of form in the material on which he works, but he also realises a purpose of his own that gives the law to his *modus operandi* and to which he must subordinate his will.[6]

The words might also be added '. . . and to which he must subordinate the development of his personality characteristics.'

A knowledge of the relationship between abstract thought and practical activity renders possible a clearer understanding of a further basic premise of at least most modern psychologists. This is that the more complex aspects of human behaviour are to be explained by mental goals, together with plans to achieve them. This premise was in fact the central theme of Miller, Gallanter and Pribram's seminal work *Plans and the Structure of Behaviour*[7], which dealt a severe blow to the then influential outlook of behaviourism.

It is necessary to point out that the above premise is one-sided because at least the more complex of an individual's goals depend on an *understanding* of the various ideas, concepts and categories which constitute essential aspects of his or her goals and plans. And such an understanding can only arise, directly or indirectly, from practical activity. Thus the more complex behaviours of human individuals cannot be explained simply in terms of their goals and plans as such. They can be explained only by their life-activity, of which their goals, plans, ideas, concepts and categories are manifestations.

One remaining point needs to be made. This concerns the question of why it is that most modern psychologists fail to understand — or attempt to understand — the decisive part played by practical activity in the development of abstract thought and personality. From a Marxist standpoint, this question is analogous to that of why society is seen as something standing apart from individuals and that of why individuals are conceptualised as machines.

The implied belief that there is no necessary connection between thought and practical activity is closely linked to what is termed the philosophical outlook of idealism. This implies that the concrete, material world represents a projection of thought. The converse of idealism is the outlook of materialism, which expresses the belief that all thought is a reflection — however distorted — of an external world which has an objective existence independently of thought and knowledge. In its modern form, the idealist outlook finds expression in the belief that thought originates in the brain as such.

For Marxists, the idealist philosophical outlook — right from Plato onwards — represents a manifestation and a reflection of the division of labour which is inherent in all class society. More specifically, it represents the division of society into those engaged in mental work and those engaged in manual work.

Thus in slave society slaves did the manual work while those of the slave-owning class engaged in the supervision of slaves, artistic pursuits, affairs of state and so on. In feudal society the serfs produced the necessities of life while their lords administered the country. Under capitalism there are to be found dustmen, bricklayers, and carpenters on the one hand and managers, lawyers and politicians on the other. Thus superficial appearances can well create the impression that, from the standpoint of the survival of the species, those engaged in mental work are more important than those engaged in manual work. Herein lies the secret of the origin and survival of the idealist philosophical outlook.[8] And it is precisely this outlook which prevents modern psychologists from understanding the dependence of thought upon practical activity.

It is clear that the dialectical relationship between purposive practical activity on the one hand and abstract thought and personality characteristics on the other, between doing and thinking, is and will remain a vital question for any genuinely scientific psychology.

NOTES TO CHAPTER EIGHT

1. See Chapter 4, Note 3.
2. See Chapter 4, Note 1.
3. Instead of the term 'personality' that of 'mind' might be used here. However, the present author has decided to use the former term. For the following reason. The term 'personality' is usually used to denote physical as well as psychological characteristics. Thus Eysenck defines it as the 'organisation of a person's character, temperament, intellect and physique'. (See Chapter Three, Note 6). Since many physical characteristics often change during and as a result of purposive practical activity it is felt that the use of the term 'personality' rather than that of 'mind' would be appropriate.
4 The notion of feelings, attitudes, etc. being of such a nature that they assist in the carrying out of practical activity is implicit, if not explicit, in the works of Festinger. See Festinger, L. *A Theory of Cognitive Dissonance*. Stanford University Press, 1957.
5. To return to a point made in Chapter Three: numerous instances can be shown of human behaviour not conforming to the views of those who subscribe to the 'functionalist' hypothesis. These include behaviour which is aimed at the achievement of a mental goal. Thus soldiers whose goal it is to win a battle will often consciously sacrifice their own lives. Similarly, high-powered businessmen, constantly prone to stress, will consciously risk ulcers, strokes and heart attacks in order to make much more money than they need for their physical survival.
6. See Chapter Four, Note 29.
7. See Chapter Six, Note 14.
8. Marxists believe that, in the future world socialist society, the division between mental and manual labour will tend to disappear. This is because a vastly increased productivity of labour will lead to a drastically reduced working week. This in turn will lead to conditions in which dustmen and bricklayers will have sufficient leisure time to write novels or compose music. Conversely, there will be no reason why architects, having designed a house, could not acquire valuable experience by actively helping to build it.

9

METHOD

The aim of this chapter is to contrast the empiricist methodology of contemporary psychology with that of Marxism and to demonstrate the superiority of the latter.

The following topics will be covered: Knowledge as an historical process. The relative separation of thought from action. The role of theory in the development of science. Empiricism as a theory of knowledge. Weaknesses in the theory of empiricism. Logical positivism. The view of Karl Popper. The practice of cognition. Why the human individual, seen as a particular expression of the universal, cannot be understood empirically. Why it is necessary to understand, not only regularities in behaviour, but also irregularities. How empirical methods cannot predict the emergence of new psychological characteristics. Modern psychology as 'a collection of specialisms'. Finally, the relation between 'concrete' and 'abstract' knowledge, also that between 'essence' and 'appearance'.

It is necessary to start with a brief exposition of the Marxist theory of knowledge, dialectical materialism.[1]

For Marxists, the nature of human knowledge cannot be separated from that of the human race. As has been outlined in Chapter Two, humanity exists as a part of nature using tools to master nature and thus to wrest from it our human needs. The making and use of tools is essentially a social and historical process. It is during this historical process that knowledge develops. The development of knowledge therefore constitutes a definite part of the historical development of the human race. It follows that to understand the nature of knowledge one must understand the nature of the human race and its history.

The historical struggle of the human race to master nature is a continuous process. During its course new knowledge arises and much previous knowledge is either rejected as wrong or regarded as inadequate or in need of modification.

Knowledge is therefore a process. Just as humanity's struggle to master nature is never-ending (every new conquest opens up new fields to be conquered), it must follow that our knowledge can never be completed. It depends upon and reflects human activity as a whole, which is unending. It can therefore only be of a relative nature, that is there can be no absolute and final truth. This does not, however, imply that there is no objectively true knowledge. It is objectively true that six divided by two equals three, that water is composed of hydrogen and oxygen, that dinosaurs once lived on the earth and that the heart pumps blood round the body. Likewise it is objectively true that the basis of human society is production and the relations of production and that capitalism arose out of the contradictions inherent in feudalism.

It will be recalled from Chapter Four that the possession of consciousness, implying the ability to view one's own activity objectively, was an essential prerequisite for the development of culture based on production. This ability in turn implies a relative separation of thinking about an action before actually carrying the action out. Of course, since human activity is essentially social in nature, the thought necessary for a future action can be undertaken by people other than those actually performing it. Thus an architect can design a building and then superintend its actual construction by bricklayers, carpenters and others. This human ability to separate thought about an action from the action itself finds its expression in the dialectical relationship between theory and practice. From the Marxist standpoint, it is this dialectical relationship which constitutes an essential aspect of the development of human knowledge and which forms the real basis for scientific advance.[2] What is implied here is this: When confronted with the need to investigate aspects of nature, scientists use abstract, theoretical thought to predict what will happen when they carry out practical activity (as often takes place in experimental laboratories). They then observe the results of their practical activity or practice and compare these with their previous theories, rejecting or modifying the latter if necessary. Those who make theoretical contributions to science are not, of course, necessarily the same as those who engage in experimental work or who make empirical observations. Einstein, for example, showed theoretically that the mass of objects increased as they approached the speed of light. It was not until some decades later that other scientists, possessing the technology to accelerate sub-atomic particles to high velocities, empirically confirmed this particular aspect of Einstein's theoretical contribution. The Marxist view of the progress of scientific knowledge can be depicted diagramatically:

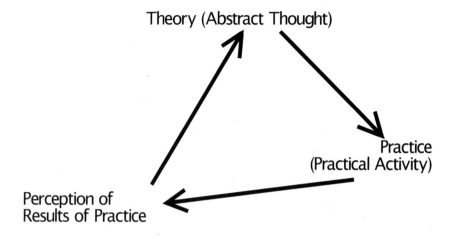

Theory guides and gives rise to practice. The results of practice are perceived. These perceptions are then posited upon theory, which is modified if necessary.

Lenin, interpreting the idealist philosopher Hegel in a materialistic way, outlines the Marxist view of scientific knowledge thus:

> From living perception (of the results of practice) to abstract thought, and from this to practice — such is the dialectical path of the cognition of truth, of the cognition of objective reality.[3]

For Marxists, the role of theory in the development of science is fundamental. For while we can observe the world and note the appearance of things, it is theory which enables us to understand what underlies and gives rise to whatever appears before us. After all, if our knowledge of the world coincided with the immediate appearance of its various aspects, there would be no need for science at all. If chemists see compounds reacting they do far more than note any change in colour or temperature. They attempt to explain the reaction in terms of abstract molecular theory. Likewise when physicians encounter patients with acute abdominal pains they do more than note that the patients are experiencing pain. They attempt to understand the pain in terms of a theoretical understanding of what can go wrong with the human body. The aim of science, therefore, must be such that theory enables us to understand that which is not immediately observable. Theory must, of course, be tested out through our practice and our observation of this practice. Nevertheless, Marxists insist, theory has a relative independence from practice and observation. To return to the example of Einstein given above, at the time when he demonstrated theoretically that objects travelling at high speed increased their mass there was no conceivable way in which this aspect of his work could be tested through practice. It is precisely on this question of the relative independence of theory from practice and observation that fundamental differences arise between the Marxist method on the one hand and the empiricist methods which dominate contemporary psychology on the other. The methodology of empiricism is discussed below.

Empiricism is a theory of knowledge the main premise of which is that 'sense experience is the only source of knowledge' and that 'all knowledge is founded on experience and is obtained through experience.'[4]

There is little doubt that the theory of empiricism does tend to dominate modern psychology. A popular textbook, published in 1970 and still reflecting the view of the majority of psychologists, shows this with great clarity:

> Two points of view dominate science: the empiricist and the hypothetical-deductive. No perfect differentiation can be made between the two, but, briefly, the empiricist approach is to look first for regularities among observable phenomena and then infer conclusions from them . . . A hypothesis, on the other hand, derives from an explanatory theory which may be true or false, but which is made up by the investigator and which he will then test by some kind of experimental procedure . . . it must be remembered that the hypothesis is usually based . . . on some empirical observation.[5]

The above paragraph correctly draws attention to the fact that the hypothetical-deductive method cannot automatically be equated with that of empiricism. However, it should be noted that the hypotheses of modern psychologists are 'usually based . . . on some empirical observation.' It is therefore permissible to state that, generally speaking, modern psychologists tend to subscribe to the empiricist theory of knowledge as defined above.

Marxists consider that empiricism as a theory of knowledge originally played a most significant role in human history. As an important part of the ideology of the rising English bourgeoisie, it challenged the medieval scholasticism that dominated intellectual thought in the Middle Ages. The early empiricists like Bacon and Hobbes rejected the view of scholasticism that knowledge developed through the interpretation of holy writ and insisted on the importance of the actual observation of the real world. This having been said, however, the fact remains that empiricism as a theory of knowledge is inadequate and hence false.

One of the most telling refutations of empiricism as a theory of knowledge is the history of mathematics. Generally speaking, mathematical knowledge does not arise from sensory experience. The theorem of Pythagoras, which shows that in any right-angled triangle the square of the hypotenuse is equal to the sum of the squares of the other two sides, is impossible to prove empirically. Of course, empirical investigation may well show that all existing right-angled triangles share this property, but it cannot demonstrate why it could not be otherwise. Similarly, the differential calculus can give us information about the rate of growth of many variables not directly accessible to observation. Yet the basic assumption of the calculus, that a curve can be divided into an infinite number of straight lines, is an assumption that cannot be based on empirical evidence.

It would indeed be true to say that sensory experience, which empiricists claim is the only reliable source of knowledge, often gives us information about the world which is false. As an example, consider Newton's first law of motion. This law states specifically that if a body is moving at a constant velocity it will keep moving in a straight line at the same velocity unless it is acted upon by an impressed force. This is of course belied by sensory experience. If we push, say, a wheelbarrow over a flat surface and then stop pushing it, it will stop. Similarly, if we throw a ball into the air it will drop to the ground and eventually come to rest. There is nothing in our sense-experience to tell us of the correctness of Newton's law. Rather, the opposite is the case.

What has just been said emphasises the relative independence of abstract, theoretical thought from sensory experience. This is of course what empiricists specifically deny. Thus the authors of the above-quoted textbook state categorically: 'We acquire a theory which works well until further (empirical) facts are discovered.'[6] This statement implies that there is no need to evaluate a theory critically on purely theoretical grounds. It only needs to be criticised if and when it is contradicted by empirical 'facts'. In other words, for empiricists, scientific theories can arise only through the generalisation of empirical facts. This empiricist view of theory is in fact echoed by the modern school of logical positivism, which in effect represents a more sophisticated version of empiricism as compared to the traditional empiricist outlook of Locke and Hobbes and which influences at least some psychologists. The principal premise of this school is that scientific knowledge has to be based on statements which can be verified by empirical evidence. A modern Marxist writer sums up the method of this school:

The rapid development of fundamental research in the twentieth century has clearly shown the untenability of logical positivism based on radical empiricism . . . The entire history of modern science, starting with the development of the quantum theory and the theory of relativity and ending with cybernetics, is a repudiation of the tenet of empiricism. It is not accidental that most contemporary philosophers of science reject the reduction of theoretical knowledge to empirical knowledge . . . Yet this general premise is still a long way from regular criticism of empiricism as the core of positivist philosophy, as well as from a comprehensive theory of scientific knowledge and its consistent substantiation.[7]

The school of logical positivism is of interest not least because amongst its ranks was once to be found Karl Popper, a well-known figure whose later views on scientific methodology are today accepted by many psychologists. Despite the fact that Popper broke with logical positivism, he continued to share its belief in the fundamental importance of empiricist methodology. In contemporary psychology, he is best known for his insistence that a theory can be genuinely scientific only if it is capable of being disproved by empirical observation. The importance of Popper's empiricist methodology is attested to by the authors of the textbook quoted above:

One of the hallmarks of a scientific theory is that it is testable. As Popper . . . has said: 'A theory which is not refutable by any conceivable event is non-scientific. Irrefutability is not the virtue of a theory (as people often think) but a vice . . . Every genuine test of a theory is an attempt to falsify it, or to refute it.'[8]

For Marxists, Popper's criterion of a scientific theory is just as untenable as is the empiricist belief that theory can only advance if it is based on empirical observations. For there is nothing in the history of science to support his view. Darwin's theory of evolution certainly cannot be disproved empirically. It can, however, be tested in practice by both animal and plant breeders. To return once more to a previous example, at the time when Einstein first theorised that the mass of an object increased as its velocity approached that of light, there was no conceivable way of disproving his theory by empirical means. Yet Einstein could hardly have been accused of not being a genuine scientist. The Marxist assumptions that the making and use of tools was a crucial factor in the emergence of the human race and that the basis of any given form of socio-economic system is the relations of production cannot be empirically disproved. Yet — Marxists insist — there is no other way of even beginning to understand what ultimately underlies and gives rise to the multifaceted and seemingly chaotic superficial appearance of human society and its history.

What is implied by Popper's criterion of scientific knowledge is that there can be no objectively true knowledge. By the term 'objectively true knowledge' is meant knowledge reflecting objects, processes, relationships and so on which have objective, material reality existing independently of human thought or will. From the standpoint of a genuinely scientific biology, the Darwinian theory that birds and mammals evolved from reptiles represents knowledge that is objectively true. Yet from Popper's standpoint such knowledge is not scientific. By the same token, the principal theory put forward by the present author, namely that the basis of the mind is material life-activity and that, in turn, the basis of human life-activity is the ways in which and the means by which people co-ordinate their activities, cannot, from a Popperian standpoint, be considered to be scientific. Yet without this objectively true knowledge there can be no penetration beneath superficial appearance and hence no satisfactory understanding of human minds.

From a Marxist standpoint there is a further reason for rejecting Popper's approach. The logic of his standpoint must lead to the conclusion that all hypotheses must be either true or false. This ignores the contradictory development of human knowledge. For hypotheses can be simultaneously partly true and partly false. When this occurs, the task of a scientist is not to reject the hypothesis but to transcend it (in the Hegelian sense). In other words they have to incorporate what is true in the old hypothesis into a fresh one and thus make the old a part of the new.

Despite the vigorous defence of empiricism as a theory of knowledge by psychologists, logical positivists and others like Popper, the whole history of science shows that enormous theoretical advances can and have been made without corresponding sensory experience. Einstein revolutionised physics, not by performing experiments or by making empirical observations, but solely by sustained and immense intellectual effort.[9] Darwin, while making numerous scientific observations, obtained much of his inspiration from the work of the clergyman Malthus, who postulated that wars were necessary to stop the human population from outgrowing the existing food supply. It was this view which gave Darwin the idea of the struggle for the survival of the fittest. Another source of inspiration was from geology, which had shown that geographical aspects of the world such as mountain ranges had not always existed. It was this which led him to suspect that at least some biological species had not always existed.[10] A further example of the relatively independent role of theory is afforded by modern physics. For the decisive steps forward in physics are today made not by empirical observations but by purely theoretical advances in mathematics which are needed by physicists in order to be better able to conceptualise their subject matter.[11]

It is now necessary to draw attention to one of the consequences of accepting the empiricist view that the only theories that have scientific validity are those derived from empirical evidence. This is the inability to use the philosophical categories of the Universal, the Individual and the Particular discussed in Chapter Five in order to achieve a better understanding of human individuals. It will be recalled that every individual is a particular expression of the universal. To return to examples used previously, the historically developed institution of marriage finds its expression in the particular behaviour patterns of individuals who engage in or at least think about marriage. Similarly the universal of religion finds its expression in the religious beliefs (or non-beliefs) of particular individuals. It is clear that an understanding of particular individuals demands an understanding of the various universals these express through their thought and behaviour. Yet universals such as those in the above examples cannot be understood empirically but only theoretically. The universal of marriage can be comprehended only through its historical development, that is that it arises as a part of the superstructural aspects of definite socio-economic societies based on relations of production. Similarly the universal of religion can only be understood through a theoretical understanding of the historically developed concept of a supernatural God. (As has already been stated in Chapter Six, Marxists believe this to be the personification, in the imagination, of those natural and social forces which individuals can neither understand nor control.)

What has been said in the preceding paragraph implies that in the process of understanding a particular (empirically perceptible) individual, the perception of the individual has to be linked in thought to the abstract, theoretical knowledge of the relevant universal or universals. An understanding of this linking of the empirically perceptible to the theoretical in thought leads to the more general methodological question of how what is empirically perceived can be understood. To answer this question, Marxists, deriving inspiration from Hegel's *Science of Logic*[12] have developed a method referred to as 'the practice of cognition'. What this implies is the following: When an object, person, situation or other phenomenon is perceived, the perceiver has to refrain from making an immediate interpretation or judgement. Rather, he or she needs to take sufficient time to remember and consider all knowledge that he or she possesses that may be relevant to whatever is perceived. What is empirically perceived is then linked in thought with past, abstract knowledge. In other words, snap judgements (which may be mistaken) need, if possible, to be avoided, since the initial impression of things can be extremely misleading. (Since the content of thought is essentially social, the practice of cognition can frequently involve more people than the immediate perceivers. What is perceived by one individual may be understood by others who can explain what has been perceived in terms of theoretical knowledge.)

What has just been said may appear commonplace, yet the making of snap judgements based on immediate impressions is very common, not least in the natural sciences and in contemporary psychology.[13] An example from natural science is necessary to show how misleading snap judgements can be. When considering the action of walking, all that is empirically perceived is the physical movements of the legs and feet. Someone not trained in the practice of cognition might well infer that the action of walking can be attributed solely to these movements. However, if time is taken to link in thought what is empirically perceived to theoretical knowledge, then a totally different conclusion will be reached. For the theoretical knowledge of Newton's third law of motion, namely that action and reaction are equal and opposite, will lead to the conclusion that the action of walking results not only from bodily movements but also from the reaction of the ground to the action upon it.[14] Numerous other examples could be given, not least from psychology. Thus if we encounter individuals who frequently and violently denounce cruelty, we might at first conclude that they are very kind people. However, if we take the time to link our initial impressions of them to a theoretical knowledge of the nature of reaction formations[15] then we might well conclude that at least some of them are as cruel as those whom they denounce.

It is the hope of Marxists that the future will see the practice of cognition taught in schools just as say, reading and arithmetic are taught now. In the meantime, its importance both in the discipline of psychology and in science generally needs to be emphasised.

At this point it would be useful briefly to contrast the two theories of knowledge, that of empiricism and that of Marxism (dialectical materialism). Empiricists maintain that sense-experience is the only basis for and a sufficient cause of knowledge. Scientific theories can arise only through a generalisation of empirical facts. Furthermore, such theories are not changed unless 'further facts are discovered'. In contrast to empiricists, Marxists conceive of knowledge as arising from a dialectical conflict between theory and practice. Human beings are not passive contemplators who mentally generalise perceived 'facts' into theories. Rather they are active participants in the changing of the material world. In this activity they are guided by theories which are changed or modified if necessary in the light of the results of their practical activity. Theory is the dialectical opposite of practice in that its development is not directly dependent on the perception of the results of practice but, on the contrary, is relatively independent of it.[16]

The emphasis placed, in preceding paragraphs, on the relative independence of theory from practice and observation has been very necessary. The principal reason for this is that contemporary psychologists consciously deny the need to consider questions such as the nature of humanity, its origin and history and the history of its thought. These questions cannot of course be discussed without an abstract, non-empirical, theoretical approach. It is stated that:

> The term 'experimental psychology' has been used for several decades to refer to scientific psychology . . . as opposed to kinds of psychology based mainly on philosophic . . . considerations.[17]

It should be recalled that the principal concern of philosophy — at least from the time of the early Greek philosophers until Hegel — has been precisely that of the nature of the human race and its thought. From the Marxist standpoint, these 'philosophical considerations' are absolutely essential for the development of a genuinely scientific psychology. A further point that needs to be stressed is that it is impossible for anyone, whether scientist or layperson, not to have philosophical assumptions or 'considerations'. This second point needs to be discussed further.

One of the basic assumptions of contemporary psychologists is that psychology should be and is a discipline using the methods of the natural sciences. Thus:

> The decisive development in the history of psychology was the application of the general methods of the natural sciences to the study of mind.[18]

This outlook is underlined by the related view that 'psychology has its roots in biology'.[19] It is necessary to stress that the assumption that 'the mind' can be studied by methods of natural science is a manifestation of a definite philosophical outlook. This is that of *mechanics*. As has already been outlined in Chapter Six, the mechanical world outlook takes as its starting point the premise that the world consists of bodies which interact with other bodies, the form of interaction being determined by the internal structure of the bodies. For a psychology which 'has its roots in biology' the inevitable logic of the mechanical approach is that the human body (with its brain) produces thought in mechanical interaction with other human bodies or with the 'social environment'.

It is not of course suggested here that psychologists should not concern themselves with the functioning of the human brain and body. A knowledge of what parts of the brain are associated with various behaviours is genuine scientific knowledge. So is a knowledge of the role of the endocrine glands in emotion. Indeed, such research as that carried out by psychologists leading to the development of psychological tests for brain damage constitutes an extremely valuable contribution to science. However, what is important here is this: The *content* of human thought (a vitally important field of study in any genuinely scientific psychology) cannot be understood simply in terms of the brain or of its mechanical interaction with the environment. As has also been outlined in Chapter Six, the content of thought results from objective life-activity, the very content of which in turn *is human history*. And history, let it be recalled, cannot be explained in terms of the mechanical interaction of bodies or in terms of what is empirically observable, but only in terms of theoretical thought, which must include philosophical 'considerations' about the nature of humanity.

What has just been said emphasises the fact that it is impossible for any scientist not to be influenced by fundamental philosophical assumptions and 'considerations'. Therefore, when psychologists deny — as most do — that they take philosophical 'considerations' into account, what they unconsciously imply is that they start both from a mechanical world outlook and from the related theory of knowledge of empiricism.[20]

Any discussion of scientific method in psychology must lead to the question of how the human individual is theoretically presented. Here the two methods, the empirical and the mechanical on the one hand and the Marxist on the other, stand in sharp contrast. For the former method, the individual is seen as a biological organism interacting mechanically with the environment. This interaction is essentially a purely spatial one. The dimension of time is ignored, or at least restricted to a description of how mechanical interactions change in the course of time. In contrast to this, the Marxist method starts from the development of human life-activity in time as well as in space. Furthermore, instead of starting from the individual biological organism interacting with (or adjusting to) the environment, Marxists start from the development of society and history, of which the individual biological human organism is an integral and subordinate part. (Human society, let it be recalled, is a whole which constitutes much more than the sum of its constituent parts.) Ongoing history is objectified in the historically developed forms of social relationships (parent/child etc.) together with their means and media, which guide and direct individual life-activity in such a way that the individual becomes what he or she is. The human individual is not, therefore, simply a biological organism adapting to his or her 'social environment'.[21] Rather, he or she is a one-sided expression of ongoing and multi-faceted history. As such, he or she develops the faculties of consciousness and creativity and, by that fact, becomes a maker of history as well as its product. It follows, therefore, that to present the human individual theoretically it is necessary to consider him or her as someone who enters human society at a definite point in its historical development and who, one-sidedly and in a unique way, expresses this historical development. (Let it be recalled once more that ongoing history constitutes the content of the lives of each and every individual. Or, to put this differently, the life-activity of each particular individual must constitute a unique expression of the universal of ongoing history.)

Thus the empirical method in psychology takes as its starting point the empirical observation of human individuals, with the hope that certain explanatory principles and theories can be arrived at on the basis of these observations. In contrast to this the Marxist method starts from a theoretical comprehension of the individual as a product and hence a maker of history. What has just been said does not of course imply that psychologists should neglect the observation of human individuals. Indeed, for Marxists, experimentation and observation forms a significant part of the development of science, including psychology. But what is important here is that what is observed is understood. Are complex human behaviours to be understood as adaptations to a social environment or are they to be seen as a part of ongoing history? It is obvious that a clear theoretical starting point is just as essential as is the making of empirical observations. Furthermore, the theoretical assumptions, be they explicit or implicit, of psychologists will ultimately determine what sort of observations they think they should make and, indeed, what they believe the discipline of psychology should include within the framework of its studies.

The empiricist view that the starting point for the discipline of psychology should be the observation of individuals and that its task should be 'to look first for regularities among observable phenomena and then to infer conclusions from them' leads to difficulties other than those already mentioned. For example, while it is quite correct to look for regularities in behaviour and thinking, it is also the irregularities that have to be explained. For a genuinely scientific approach, exceptions to rules should be just as important as the rules themselves. Deviations from the average have to be accounted for as well as the average itself. This can be done only by using an historical approach, that is by the realisation that the widely differing life-activities of individuals all have one common root in historical time. This common root is of course the continuous resolution of the basic contradiction of the human race: that between the need to pass on the skills of production from generation to generation and the inability to fix these genetically. As stated previously, this resolution takes the form of the passing on, from generation to generation, of those objective social relationships which cause individuals to undertake a life-activity which makes them what they are. An analogy from biology will help to make this clearer. Differences and similarities between the various classes of an animal or plant species have to be understood not merely by empirical observations of these differences and similarities. They also have to be understood theoretically as variations in evolutionary time of the one original species. What has to be explained, therefore, in both biology and human psychology, is an essential *unity in diversity*. In biology, this implies the differences between the various classes which represent forms of the same species. In psychology, it implies differences in the life-activity of individuals — and hence of their 'personality characteristics' — which represent but different forms of the resolution of the initial historical contradiction.

A related problem of those empirical psychologists who 'look . . . for regularities among observable phenomena' is that their thinking is confined solely to the present. Their method cannot be used to predict the emergence of new psychological characteristics. To return to the previous analogy, any biologists who restricted themselves to purely empirical methods could not predict the emergence of new classes of a species or, for that matter, of new species. It should be recalled that one of the principal tasks of genuine science is to use abstract, theoretical thought to predict what will happen in the future, and thus to prepare either scientists themselves or others for possible active intervention. From the Marxist standpoint, it is to be hoped that future changes in social relationships leading to the abolition of humanity's alienation (see Chapter Ten), also to the abolition of the nuclear family in favour of a more humane method of child rearing, will lead to the development of new psychological needs, abilities and other 'personality characteristics' which cannot be inferred from any empirical observation of the here and now.

The methodology of empiricism in psychology finds its reflection in a more or less explicit disavowal of the need to comprehend the human race (and hence human individuals) theoretically. Thus, despite the pleas of those like Neisser for an understanding of 'fundamental questions of human nature' (See Chapter One), the authors of the previously-quoted textbook tell their readers:

The reader will notice a comparative absence of theoretical discussion. This is deliberate. The creation of large-scale general theories has gone out of fashion in psychology now in favour of limited and precise theories dealing with specific problems.[22]

The 'large-scale general theories' referred to are of course those dealing with humanity and its 'nature'. It thus becomes clear that contemporary psychologists avoid 'fundamental questions of human nature' by splitting psychology into what have in fact become a number of relatively independent disciplines. The same textbook continues:

> We could with some justification characterise present-day psychology as a collection of specialisms, united only by the logic of their (empirical) methods, within which individuals worry over limited sets of problems. . . . The practice of carving up university courses into chunks labelled Learning, Perception, Physiological Psychology. . . . Social Psychology and so on . . . reflects . . . a discipline broken down into specialisms. . . . In short . . . psychology is a group of specialisms.[23]

From the Marxist standpoint, a genuinely scientific approach is the opposite of that which has just been described. Rather than taking as a starting point the separation of studies of various aspects of behaviour and thinking, what is needed as a starting point is a theoretical comprehension of the relationships between learning, perception, behaviour in various social groups and so on. For all these aspects have a common root. That root is in fact humanity's origin and development through labour, from which arises all our various psychological abilities such as those just mentioned. Thus humanity's struggle to master nature primarily through labour represents, as it were, the root and trunk of human psychology, while the various separate aspects of psychology like learning, perception and so on represent but different branches existing as parts of the same tree. And for the different branches to be properly understood the tree as a whole has to be understood.

The difference between the Marxist method and that of empiricism is made clearer by a consideration of the philosophical categories of the abstract and the concrete. The latter term is often used (wrongly) by empiricists to denote that which is immediately observable. This is of course the view of what is often referred to as 'common sense'. What is observed of an object is regarded as 'concrete' knowledge of that object. For Marxists, however, the aspects of an object which are observed constitute an abstraction. They are an abstraction because there must inevitably be other aspects of the object as a whole which either have not been observed or which are not directly observable. Any real knowledge of the whole object (which constitutes what Marxists refer to as concrete knowledge) must therefore imply a combination of abstractions, including those of a purely theoretical nature.

The real relation between the abstract and the concrete can in turn be made clearer by the use of two further philosophical categories, namely those of essence and appearance. While the latter term is self-explanatory, the term 'essence' requires explanation. 'Essence' refers to all those aspects of an object, (situation, person, process, etc.) which cause its existence to depend on other aspects of the world. To put it perhaps more simply, the term 'essence' refers to those aspects of an object (situation, person, process, etc.) which are essential to its existence. 'Essence' may be contrasted to 'appearance' which, although a form taken by essence, may be accidental, fortuitous and unessential to the existence of the object. Here it becomes obvious that only a knowledge of the essence of an object can constitute concrete knowledge. Since all objects (situations, persons, processes etc.) have complex and many-sided relations with various aspects of the world, all genuinely concrete knowledge must represent the coming together of many abstractions. To put it another way, since the world (including society) constitutes a unified and integrated whole, with every part interdependent with other parts, each individual part must constitute an element of a system or of systems. And to understand any aspect of the world it is necessary to understand the system (or systems) of which it constitutes a part. This can only be done through abstract, theoretical thought. The appearance of an object cannot therefore be the basis for a concrete knowledge of it. (Marx referred to the 'imaginary concrete', since seeing an object is not the same as understanding it). It can only represent a one-sided abstraction. (It should be recalled that if a knowledge of objects coincided with their appearance, then there would be no need for science). To return to a previous example, the essence of the action of walking (a 'system') constitutes the muscular action of the legs and feet together with the reaction of the ground to the action of the feet. Yet the appearance of the action is solely the movement of the legs and feet. The appearance is thus an abstraction from the essence, which needs to be linked in thought to another abstraction, namely the theoretical knowledge of Newton's law that action and reaction are equal and opposite. It is thus only a combination of abstractions that gives us a concrete knowledge of the essence of the process of walking.[24] Similarly, of course, the observation of human individuals can only represent abstractions from their total life-activity. A concrete knowledge of them (i.e., knowledge of their essence) requires that the abstractions made in observing them be joined in thought with abstract theoretical knowledge of their respective life-activities (i.e., knowledge of which particular one-sided aspects of ongoing history they are a manifestation of). The practice of cognition to which reference has been made is of course relevant here.

A knowledge of the categories of 'abstract' and 'concrete' assists in the understanding of the basic psychological question of what constitutes human nature and how it is manifested in individuals. Empiricists, confusing the abstract with the concrete, would, if pressed to face up to the question, start from a series of empirical observations (abstractions). These would lead to the assumption that human nature was something existing in the biological structure of individuals, something inherent in the genes which enabled people to adapt to their respective environments. In contrast to this Marxists start by recognising that a concrete knowledge of human nature is arrived at by a combination of abstractions. These abstractions must include a knowledge of humanity's origin through labour and the knowledge that we exist as a species not by adapting to the environment but by mastering it. Also necessary is a knowledge that the relations of production alone form the basis of every socio-economic formation. Furthermore, knowledge is necessary of the fundamental difference between a human being possessing consciousness and a member of the species *Homo sapiens*. (See Chapter Four. For empiricists a newborn baby is human. For Marxists a child becomes human only to the extent that he or she acquires consciousness). From a combination of abstractions such as these it can be deduced that human nature is not something inherent in the genes of each individual. Rather, the essence of human nature is labour. It is manifested in the life-activity of individuals (including their consciousness) the basis of which is objective social relationships ultimately arising from the relations of production.[25]

To conclude this chapter, it would be useful to summarise some of the most important points. The theory of knowledge of empiricism is based on the assumption that sense-experience is a sufficient and only cause of knowledge. Scientific theories can arise only as a generalisation of empirical observations. There can be no independent, or relatively independent, theoretical advances apart from this generalisation. Thus existing theories remain unchallenged until and unless 'further facts are discovered'. Empiricist psychologists join with Popper and with modern 'philosophers of science' in rejecting as being outside the realms of science any attempt to understand theoretically the origin and historical development of the human race.

The Marxist theory of knowledge, dialectical materialism, starts from the premise that an understanding of the nature of knowledge is inseparable from an understanding of the origin and development of humanity through labour. The human race does not exist by adapting to nature but by a continuous struggle to master it, primarily through production. In this struggle for mastery theory guides practice (in science this practice often involves experimentation) while perception of the results of practice are posited on existing theory, changing or modifying the latter if necessary. In sharp contrast to empiricists, Marxists insist on the relative independence of theory from practice and observation. The history of science verifies this relative independence.

The practice of cognition, involving the linking in thought of what is empirically observed with whatever is theoretically known about it, constitutes an important aspect of scientific methodology.

What is immediately perceived of an object (situation, person, etc.) can only be an abstraction. To obtain a concrete knowledge of the object (situation, person, etc.) it is necessary to link this abstraction in thought to other abstractions, including those of a purely theoretical nature. Concrete knowledge of an object implies knowledge of its essence (its essential rather than its incidental qualities; its essential relations with all other aspects of the world). Essence should never be confused with appearance, which can only appear in knowledge as an abstraction from the concrete.

The logic of the open disavowal of 'philosophical considerations' by empiricist psychologists leads to the reduction of the discipline of psychology to a 'collection of specialisms'. From the Marxist standpoint, however, a genuinely scientific psychology should start from a definite theoretical basis, namely that of the understanding of humanity's self-origin through labour. Psychological aspects of human functioning such as perception, memory, thinking and falling in love all have to be understood as manifestations of the resolution of the original contradiction, namely that between the need to transmit production and other skills from generation to generation on the one hand and the inability to fix these genetically on the other.

Although most empiricist psychologists would dismiss the question of human nature as being only a 'philosophical consideration', the logic of the empirical method in psychology, that is the emphasis on direct observation (the 'imaginary concrete') together with the limitation of theory to the generalisation of empirical 'facts', must lead to the assumption that human nature is something in the physical structure of individuals. Together with the assumption, explicit or implicit, that humanity exists by adapting to the environment, their only explanation of human nature could be that it constitutes the ability, inherent in the genes, to adapt to the environment.

From the Marxist standpoint, human nature is social labour. It is manifested in individuals not in any genetic, inherent biological tendency, but in objective social relationships (ultimately dependent on relations of production) which form the basis of individual life-activity and hence of the individual's psychological qualities.

NOTES TO CHAPTER NINE

1. Dialectical materialism is the Marxist theory of the human race and of its knowledge. The term 'materialism' refers to the philosophical outlook the principal premise of which is the objective existence of the material world independent of our consciousness or will. From the materialist standpoint all thought is a reflection, however distorted, of this material world. Materialism can be understood as the opposite of idealism, the philosophical outlook which starts from the premise that the material world is a projection of thought. In its crudest form, idealism finds its expression in the belief that the material world is a projection of the thought of God. The term 'dialectical' implies the self-movement of nature. The new develops out of the self-movement of the old. Thus the solar system arose from the self-movement of a cloud of nebulous gases. Living matter arises from non-living matter. New animal — and plant — species arise from the self-movement of more primitive species, amphibians arising from fishes, mammals from amphibians and so on. Humanity arose from the self-movement of a species of ape. Capitalism arose from the self-movement of feudalism and — Marxists believe — world socialism will arise from the self-movement of capitalism. An understanding of dialectical materialism is made easier by contrasting it to mechanical materialism. The latter outlook views the world and its various parts as machines. Any machine — from a simple lever to a computer — is an object devoid of self-movement. In order to move, a lever needs mechanical pressure applied from without while a computer needs electricity. Newton's conception of the solar system, with planets moving in unchanging orbits — the first initial movement being made by God — was essentially a mechanical conception. But for Marxists the world as a whole, including human history, must always be in a state of self-movement, however imperceptible aspects of this self-movement might be. An essential feature of the outlook of dialectical materialism is the insistence, not only that the world is in a constant state of self-movement, but also that it constitutes an integrated and coherent whole, with the existence of each of its constituent parts being dependent upon other parts. To repeat a phrase that has been used before, the whole is more than the sum of its parts. For an introduction to dialectical materialism as the Marxist theory of the human race and of knowledge see Engels, F. *Anti-Duhring*. FLPH, Moscow, 1954. Engels *Ludwig Fuerbach and the End of German Classical Philosophy*. Progress Publishers, 1978. Also Oizerman, T. *Dialectical Materialism and the History of Philosophy*. Progress Publishers, 1982.
2. The 'dialectical relationship' referred to here implies that theory and practice are opposites — they are mutually exclusive. Nonetheless any change in one must — after a certain level has been reached — bring about a change in the other. It will be recalled from the previous chapter that an analogous dialectical relationship exists between the abstract thought and the practical activity of individuals.
3. Lenin, V.I. 'Conspectus of Hegel's book "The Science of Logic" '. *Collected Works*. Vol. 38. Lawrence and Wishart, 1961, p. 171.
4. *Dictionary of Philosophy*. Progress Publishers, 1984, p. 123.
5. Wright et al. *Introducing Psychology. An Experimental Approach*. Penguin, 1970, pp. 18-19.
6. *Ibid*. p. 19. My emphasis.
7. Naletov, I. *Alternatives to Positivism*. Progress Publishers, 1984, p. 10.

8. Wright et al. *op cit.* p. 19.

9. See, for example, Holton,G. *Thematic Origins of Scientific Thought: Kepler to Einstein.* Harvard University Press, 1973.

10. See Darwin, C. *Autobiography and Selected Correspondence.* Dover Press, 1958.

11. See, for example, Horz, H. et al. *Philosophical Problems in Physical Science.* Marxist Educational Press, Minneapolis, 1980.

12. Hegel, G.W.F. *Science of Logic.* Muirhead Library of Philosophy, 1969.

13. An absence of a clear understanding of the practice of cognition is evident in modern psychiatry. Psychiatrists frequently make hurried diagnoses, often on the basis of one interview. Their patients are variously labelled 'schizophrenic', 'paranoid', 'manic-depressive' and so on. Once the diagnosis is made, the patients are stuck with the label, which will affect the way in which they are treated. In other words, there is little or no attempt to join the impressions of the initial psychiatric interview either with additional knowledge of the patient's history and current social situation or with theoretical knowledge of what types of social situations lead individuals to come under the care of psychiatrists.

14. This is, of course, a further example of how empirical knowledge, by itself, can be misleading.

15. Reaction formation: A psychological mechanism the function of which is to deny to oneself one's own unpleasant or undesirable characteristics.

16. The application of the Marxist method to problems of psychology is well exemplified by the training of relatively large numbers of blind deaf-mutes referred to in Chapter Four. Here the psychologists involved started, not with any theory based on a generalisation of empirical facts, but with the Marxist theoretical premise that the life-activity of individuals takes place within the framework of objective social relationships together with their means and media. Doubtless Popper and his many supporters in university psychology departments would object that since the Marxist premise cannot be falsified it is therefore unscientific. Nevertheless, in this outstanding psychological 'experiment' the theory has been tested out in practice. The proof of the pudding is in the eating!

17. Wright et al. *op. cit.* p. 9.

18. *Ibid.* p. 16.

19. *Ibid.* p. 26.

20. The untenable nature of empiricism as a theory of knowledge finds its reflection in the works of a number of contemporary writers often referred to as 'philosophers of science' (Kuhn, Feyerabend, Lakatos, Quine, Bunge and others). Brief mention has to be made of these as no doubt some psychologists (although probably only a small minority) are influenced by their views. Perhaps the majority of these writers, well aware of the basic weaknesses of classical empiricism, in one way or another come close to certain Marxist positions. Their principal difference with Marxism is their belief that the nature of scientific knowledge is revealed through a study of science *per se.* In contrast to this Marxists, as has been stated above, start from the premise that the nature of human knowledge (including scientific knowledge) is revealed through a study of the human race, its origin and historical development together with the origin and development of its thought. In other words, Marxists believe that philosophy is a branch of human knowledge which has an existence relatively independent of natural science. Humanity and its history has to be understood before the nature of its scientific knowledge can be understood. For a comprehensive exposition of the relationship between Marxism and the modern 'philosophy of science' see Naletov *op. cit.*

21. The concept of individuals adjusting to their environments may of course be used under certain circumstances. Children can be said to adjust to a new school situation. People can be said to adjust to a new situation following the loss of a loved one. Once again, however, the important point here is this: Being products of history individuals possess the ability to master their respective environments rather than adjust to them.

22. Wright et al. *op. cit.* p. 11.

23. *Ibid.* p. 25.

24. For a concise but thorough exposition of the categories of 'abstract' and 'concrete' see Ilyenkov,

E.V. *The Dialectics of the Abstract and the Concrete in Marx's 'Capital'*. Progress Publishers, 1982.
25. For empiricists, human nature can never be labour since they can observe thousands of individuals who do not participate in the processes of production. Here is a good example of the fact that genuine scientific knowledge requires abstract thought to penetrate beneath superficial appearance (the imaginary concrete, which in reality can be no more than an abstraction) and to provide an understanding of the essence of things, that is of what underlies and gives rise to superficial appearance.

10

A MARXIST APPROACH TO
PERSONALITY THEORY

The break up of contemporary psychology into a 'collection of specialisms' should not be allowed to conceal the fact that since the time that Freud first started to develop his theoretical views, there have been a relatively large number of what have become known as 'theories of personality'.

The aim of this chapter is to do no more than outline at least certain aspects of some of the principal theories and to comment on them briefly. The need for these brief outlines and comments is twofold: first, to show how such theories should be approached from a Marxist standpoint; second, to emphasise that a study of what is generally meant by the term 'personality' involves definite assumptions, be they explicit or implicit, about human nature and how it is manifested in individuals.

It will be recalled that, for contemporary psychology, 'large scale theories have gone out of fashion'. This refers, of course, to personality theories like those of Freud. It would perhaps be useful briefly to indicate the periods during which the theories discussed in this chapter were developed. Freud started to develop his theory towards the end of the last century and at the beginning of the present one. Adler and Jung followed soon after. Those who became known as neo-Freudians — Horney and Fromm — were once Freudian analysts in Germany who emigrated to the U.S.A. when Hitler came to power. Here, working with the American Harry Stack Sullivan, they developed theorectical views which differed in important respects from those of Freud. About this time another American, Allport, also developed a theory which became influential. Modern theorists include Kelly, Mowrer and Eysenck. Another modern psychologist of whom mention will be made is Skinner who, although not strictly speaking a personality theorist, has developed views which, implicitly if not explicitly, constitute basic assumptions about human nature. A brief outline will now be made of each theory in turn, together with relevant comment.

FREUD

Probably the best-known aspect of Sigmund Freud's theory of personality is his insistence on the unconscious nature of many aspects of psychological functioning. In his model of the human mind, a definite portion of it, known as the id, was unconscious. It was unconscious in the sense that the individual was unaware of its contents. It represented the only part of the mind that was innate and hence unlearned. The most significant aspect of the contents of the id, from the standpoint of personality development, was what Freud termed the Oedipus complex. This was a sexual attraction for the parent of the opposite sex, which led to corresponding feelings of jealousy for the parent of the same sex. Also significant in the id was an unconscious urge for self-destruction, which became transformed or 'displaced' into feelings of aggression directed against others. The id also contained other biological urges such as those for food and water. It was 'powered', as it were, by 'psychic energy' which was derived from bodily processes and which also 'powered' the mind as a whole. The id operated according to the 'pleasure principle'. This implied that the discharge of the tensions built up by the psychic energy underlying the need for food (hunger was a manifestation of this psychic energy), for sex and for aggression were all pleasurable.

The pleasure principle was manifested by the thrusting into consciousness of images (such as occurred in dreams) that would release the tensions built up by psychic energy. However, the images could not of course release tension by themselves. An image of food will not relieve the tension of hunger. This implied that psychological processes were necessary to discharge the tensions of the id in the real, material world. A hungry person has to find and eat food, and hence to cope with reality. It was this need that gave rise to the emergence of the next portion of the mind, known as the ego, which, in contrast to the id, contained conscious mental processes. It was the task of the ego not only to discharge the tensions of the id in a satisfactory manner but to distinguish between the images of the id on the one hand and the real world on the other. In further contrast to the id, which operated the pleasure principle, the ego operated what Freud termed the 'reality principle', since its task was to cope with the world of reality.

To put matters another way, the task of the ego was to restrain the impulses arising from the id until situations had been found in which the id could operate the pleasure principle and discharge its tensions in a satisfactory manner.

Freud saw that the real world in which the ego operated was in fact a social world. Therefore to operate effectively the child, with his or her developing personality, had to internalise the moral prohibitions and ideals of society, as interpreted primarily by his or her parents. This internalisation formed the basis for the third and last portion of the mind, which Freud termed the superego. The superego basically consisted of two parts. The first of these was the conscience, which made the individual feel ashamed whenever he or she transgressed society's moral rules and standards. The second was the ego-ideal, a sort of ideal standard to be lived up to, which made individuals pleased with themselves whenever they conformed to social morals and values.

According to Freud's theory, the three portions of the mind or personality worked in harmony. However, parallel to this harmony there were innumerable conflicts. The ego was in conflict with the id, since the latter constantly strove to discharge its psychic energy while the former tried to hold it back until an appropriate time and place had been found. The ego was also in conflict with the superego, since while the latter strove to do what was morally right, the former strove to do what was expedient. The most significant conflict of all, however, was that between the id and the superego. As has been stated, the id contained both aggressive drives and the Oedipus complex both of which, being socially reprehensible, were offensive to the superego. This was especially true of the Oedipus complex. One of the principal tasks of the ego, therefore, was to ensure that the contents of the id were discharged in a manner acceptable to the superego. The ego's principal mechanism which it used in attempting to carry out this task was that of repression. In other words it tried to repress from consciousness the unwanted contents of the id. However, the ego's attempts at repression could never be fully successful and the Oedipus complex kept slipping into consciousness, as it were, albeit in disguised forms such as occurred in dreams.

All art, Freud maintained, was nothing more than a disguised or 'sublimated' form of the partially repressed Oedipus complex. This aspect of his theory Freud considered so important that he maintained that the adult personality represented — in large measure — the attempted resolutions of the fundamental conflict between the id and the superego. These attempted resolutions, according to Freud, took place during childhood and remained relatively fixed thereafter.

The above thumb-nail sketch of Freud's theory of personality can do no more than form the basis for a number of points — although important ones — to be made. But it should be noted that, despite the fact that Freudian theory has few followers today, Freud made a number of positive contributions. He was the first to really focus attention on the widespread nature of unconscious motivation, that is on the fact that people often did things for reasons of which they were unaware. By showing that many physical disorders were of psychological origin he did more than anyone else to develop the field of psychosomatic medicine. He was also one of the first to demonstrate the importance of the early years of a child's life for the formation of personality characteristics. Furthermore, the whole richness of Freud's clinical experiences is such that they undoubtedly deserve further study.[1]

From a Marxist standpoint, many criticisms of Freud could undoubtedly be made. However, only three of these are of a really fundamental nature. The first of these is Freud's total ignorance of humanity's self-origin through labour. As has been pointed out in Chapter Four, for the human race to develop from the animal kingdom through the making and use of tools and for the relatively continuous development of production and of the productive forces, on which our existence as a species depends, it has been and is necessary for human individuals to possess certain characteristics. One of these is an absence of any innate tendencies which would preclude the possibility of the learning of the enormously varied social roles which individuals have had to play throughout history. Such innate tendencies as those of self-destruction and the Oedipus complex, which form such an essential component of Freudian theory, would undoubtedly have precluded the possibility both of humanity's self-origin through labour and the subsequent development of production. Freud was unable to see human history other than as an expression and reflection of innate unconscious tendencies in all individuals. In other words, he could not see human history as an extension of natural history beginning with and following our origin through labour. It follows from this that Freud thought of personality as being significantly influenced by innate factors (that is the inborn urge to self-destruction and the Oedipus complex) rather than as the product of objective situations which make individuals carry out definite activities which cause them to become what they are.

The second fundamental criticism to be made of Freud is his fixed dichotomy between the biological and the social in the individual. The social, in Freud's theory, is of course incorporated into the individual personality in the form of the superego. The biological, on the other hand, remains fixed as the innate and unlearned drives of the id. Although the id and the superego are in constant conflict, the two remain unchanged by this conflict. It is as if both id and superego are separate machines which interact with each other, the form of interaction being determined by their respective internal structures which remain unchanged by the interaction. This view of Freud is of course basically the same as that of the majority of contemporary psychologists, who conceptualise the individual as a biological organism which has to adapt to society. In other words society is seen both by Freud and by the contemporary supporters of the outlook of functionalism (see Chapter Three) as an entity which imposes itself on the biological individual. For Freud, the development of both the ego and the superego represent adaptations to an external world which is seen to be predominantly social.[2]

As has been argued forcefully in Chapters Six and Seven, it is impossible to separate the biological and the social in the individual. The biological and the social are opposites which interpenetrate dialectically. Biological needs such as those for food, shelter from the elements and sex are simultaneously needs for specific social relationships.

Human society constitutes the sum total of social relationships. These social relationships are of course relationships between biological individuals, whose basic organic needs cannot be met other than through social relations. For these organic needs to be met individuals have to enter into social relations that earn them money (such as the employer and the employee relationship) to buy the necessities of life. Alternatively they have to maintain relationships with others on whom they are objectively dependent (such as relations between husband and wife or between parents and offspring).

Any conceptions of society being imposed on the biological individual and of the biological individual adapting to some nebulous 'social environment' must necessarily be both false and misleading.

The third criticism to be made here can be implied from the second. For Freud, the decisive aspect of the organic needs of individuals, from the standpoint of personality development, is sex. For Marxists, however, the decisive aspect cannot be sex. Rather it must be the need for food and shelter. For unless these needs are met the individual will perish. In contrast to this, individuals can be denied sex but they can still survive as biological organisms. It follows, therefore, that the social relations into which people enter to satisfy their needs for food and shelter must be the decisive relations which ultimately determine the development of personality. Furthermore, the social relations entered into by individuals in the satisfaction of their needs for food and shelter must at least influence the form taken by both sexual and other relationships. Individual life-activity constitutes an integrated and coherent whole. Therefore all other social relationships cannot but be dependent — directly or indirectly — on those through which food and shelter are provided.

In conclusion, any serious study of Freud will reveal that his theory of personality manifests at least some of the main weaknesses of contemporary psychology as a whole. Despite this, however, Freud remains an outstanding figure in the history of psychology who raised a number of important questions.

JUNG

Although Carl Gustav Jung is not as well-known as is Freud, the impact of his work on twentieth century Western culture has been considerable. His theory of personality is best known for what he termed the 'collective unconscious'. Like Freud, Jung believed that the most significant aspects of personality were hidden from consciousness. However, in Jung's theory these unconscious aspects were very different from those postulated by Freud.

The most significant feature of Jung's 'collective unconscious' was the existence of what he termed archetypes. These were innate. They represented the racial memories of humanity which had become physically embedded in the brain. In other words, the experiences of individuals that had occurred throughout countless generations found their expression in an inherited and unconscious tendency to repeat these experiences. For example children, who had had more or less the same experiences with their mothers from the beginning of human history, inherited a predisposition to behave in specific ways towards the mother. It was this predisposition that constituted the mother archetype. Throughout history, generations of individuals have watched the sun rise and set. This gave rise to the sun archetype, which found expression in the sun-worshipping that has taken place in primitive cultures and in certain more modern images and conceptions of a supreme deity. Our evolutionary origin from non-human species found its expression in the 'shadow' archetype, which represented the allegedly animal or anti-social side of our nature.

Much of Jung's extensive and prolonged research was concerned with discovering the existence and nature of archetypes. For several decades he studied ancient myths and rituals, history, literature, alchemy, astrology and other aspects of human culture. Apart from those mentioned, he claimed to have identified the archetypes of birth, re-birth, death, power, magic, the demon, the old wise man and the earth mother.[3] What convinced Jung of the correctness of his beliefs was the fact that throughout history similar themes kept on re-occurring in the myths, literature, religious beliefs, rituals and so on of otherwise widely differing cultures.

Just as Freud considered the identification of the Oedipus complex as his greatest achievement, so Jung considered his to be that of the alleged discovery of the archetype of the 'self'. It was this archetype that gave unity and integrity to the personality as a whole. According to Jung, the self archetype caused each individual to strive unconsciously to give expression to all the archetypes. He maintained that neuroses arose through some archetypes being given more expression than others which were thereby inadequately expressed. It was the function of the self archetype to ensure that each archetype received adequate expression. Furthermore, it was also the function of the 'self' to ensure that all archetypes, once they were adequately expressed, acted as parts of a well-balanced, coherent and integrated personality. Indeed, it was Jung's belief that the basic human motivation was the striving for an integrated personality.

Although Jung postulated the existence of other aspects of personality, these were not considered as important as the archetypes of the collective unconscious. There is therefore no need to mention them in this brief outline, which is adequate for the purposes of this chapter.

It should be noted that Jung's theory of personality has given rise to, or has at least influenced, more recent theories of 'self-actualisation' such as that of Maslow (see below).

The first criticism to be made of Jung from a Marxist standpoint is precisely the same as that made of Freud. This is that any fixed and rigid innate behaviour patterns, such as those implied by the alleged existence of archetypes or by the Oedipus complex, would have made impossible both the self-origin of humanity through labour and the subsequent historical development of culture based on production. The human race can only survive, let it be repeated, through the ability of children and adults to learn an infinite variety of production and other necessary skills. The existence of Jungian archetypes would certainly have precluded this ability.

The second criticism to be made is that Jung conceptualised personality as something existing purely inside the individual, being physically embedded in the brain. The fact that individuals change and develop during the course of their activity and that this activity results from objective social situations, imposed on the individual independently of his or her will, is virtually ignored. From the Marxist standpoint, this is probably the most important criticism that could be made of Jung.

Despite the above criticisms, what is interesting about Jung's theory of personality is his recognition of the essentially historical nature of human thought. Of course, Jung saw this as arising from the physical structure of a brain which has developed throughout the centuries. In other words, he saw the historical and social nature of thought in a highly distorted and inverted way. But he saw it none the less. An interesting and instructive analogy can be drawn here between Jung and Hegel. The latter postulated the existence of what he termed the 'Absolute Idea' (really another name for God). The development of history represented the ever-increasing manifestation of the same 'Absolute Idea' in the minds of individuals. It was left to Marx and Engels to turn Hegel's ideas the correct side up, as it were, and to show that the thought of each individual reflected, in however distorted and one-sided a fashion, the objective movements of history.[4] It is now the responsibility of present and future psychologists to realise the significance of this aspect of Jung's contribution and to appreciate fully the social and historical nature of human individuals and their thought.

A further interesting aspect of Jung's theory is that of the striving for an integrated personality. While there are good grounds (see above) for rejecting the conception of archetypes — including that of the self — Jung's idea of integration into a coherent and well-balanced whole may well be regarded as a distorted and inverted view of the essential unity and integration of individual life-activity. Every aspect of an individual's total life-activity must — however indirectly — be related to all other aspects. The dialectical relationship between practical activity and personality characteristics discussed in Chapter Eight is of course relevant here.

To sum up, while Marxists would undoubtedly reject the basic assumptions of Jung's theory, there still remains something from which we can learn.

ADLER

Alfred Adler became well-known when he led the first serious breakaway from Freud's psychoanalytic movement to form his own school known as Individual Psychology. He decisively rejected Freud's conceptions of innate and unconscious strivings such as that of the Oedipus complex. Instead, he postulated that the main source of human motivation lay in a striving to compensate for inferiority.

Adler's conception of compensation for inferiority first arose when he was a physician in general practice. He noted that bodily weaknesses were compensated for by beneficial changes. Thus if a lung or a kidney became damaged, the other lung or kidney became correspondingly strengthened. If a bone was broken and subsequently healed, the point of fracture became stronger than it had originally been. Adler also noticed that psychologically, weaknesses led to gains. Thus blind people would develop acute senses of touch, hearing and smell. Many famous orators were people who had once suffered speech defects but who had become able to overcome them in such a way that they were able to speak much better than the average person.

Whence came this tendency to compensate for inferiority? Adler maintained that it was part of life itself; in other words a fundamental tendency inherent in all biological matter. Since all individuals were to a greater or lesser extent, and in one way or another, inferior to others, the personality reflected attempts to compensate for these inferiorities.

All individuals were considered to be capable of altruistic and socially responsible behaviour. It was the task of therapists and teachers to help individuals with neurotic problems or anti-social behaviours to compensate for their inferiorities in other, more satisfactory ways.

Adler was, unlike Freud, an optimist about human nature. He opposed the latter's view that the individual was at the mercy of unconscious and largely unknowable instinctual urges over which he or she had no permanent control. He refused to believe that the individual was at the mercy of his or her past. Rather, he insisted that what really mattered was not the past itself but the way in which the individual evaluated the past. Thus past misfortunes could and should be regarded not as misfortunes as such, but as experiences from which it may be possible to learn important lessons. Similarly individuals who make serious mistakes in their lives may, if they learn the appropriate lessons, be far better able to cope with life than those who have never made such mistakes.

In contrast to Freud and Jung, Adler placed great emphasis on the role of an individual's consciousness. As may be inferred from preceding paragraphs, what really mattered to Adler was not inferiorities as such, but the way in which the individual consciously evaluated and compensated for them.

Further aspects of Adler's theory have already been mentioned in Chapters Five and Seven.

There is much in Adler's theory with which Marxists would agree: First, his insistence on the absence of complex, innate and predetermined behaviour patterns. Second, his insistence that what matters about the past is the way in which it is evaluated in the present. Marxists have long postulated a dialectical relationship between the past and the present. The past, which cannot be changed, leads up to the present situations which we have to confront. However, our conscious learning of the lessons afforded by the past can influence the way in which we are able actively and consciously to change the present. Third, Adler's insistence on conscious rather than unconscious mental processes. This implies the individual's ability to evaluate objectively his or her own inferiorities and past experiences. In other words this implies the ability to see oneself and one's activity from the side, as it were. Fourthly, Adler's belief, implied from what has been said before, that individuals can, consciously and actively, change the world. They are not, therefore, either the victims of internal, unconscious urges nor are they the passive recipients of environmental pressures to which they must 'adjust' or 'adapt'

From the Marxist standpoint, therefore, much of what Adler has said is correct. However, his theory can be criticised for what it fails to say. The central criticism is that it fails to face up to the relation between the social and the individual. Indeed, the very title of Adler's school, 'Individual Psychology', reflects a belief that the content of thought is a purely individual matter. In other words Adler failed to grasp that the content of thought constitutes a dialectical unity between the unique and individual on the one hand and the social and historical on the other. This is of course reflected in his view of consciousness. For while he conceptualised individuals as possessing the ability to view their life-activity objectively, 'from the side', he neglected to mention that consciousness also implies the ability to perceive the world with historically developed knowledge of what it could become with human intervention.

To sum up. While Adler undoubtedly made a significant contribution towards an understanding of human individuals, his theory of personality leaves a wide gap to be filled.

HORNEY

Karen Horney was one of a number of psychologists and psychiatrists who became known as neo-Freudians. This term was first used to denote those who were originally Freudian analysts but who, while still subscribing to many of Freud's views, rejected some of his basic principles. Later the term was also used to include those like Harry Stack Sullivan (see below), who worked with the original neo-Freudians but who had never been Freudians themselves.

Horney was critical of Freud for a number of reasons. Probably the most important of these was Freud's ignorance of the findings of anthropologists. The latter had shown the enormous variation in cultural and moral norms of peoples in different parts of the world. Many of these cultural and moral norms were very different from those of the upper middle class Viennese who became Freud's patients. It was knowledge of anthropological findings that no doubt played an important role in the development of Horney's own thinking. She eventually rejected Freud's conception of innate unconscious aggressive drives, together with the Oedipus complex. Nonetheless, Horney shared with Freud the latter's belief in the importance of unconscious motivation, of which mention is made below.

One of Horney's major contributions was her conception of what she termed 'basic anxiety'. This is a feeling experienced by young children who have lost, or who have never experienced 'the blissful certainty of being wanted'. In other words the child feels helpless and isolated in a hostile world, in which the security of the child's relationship to the parents is disturbed or non-existent. Horney maintained that a relatively large proportion of children suffered, in one degree or another, from basic anxiety and that attempts to overcome this feeling would lead to important and relatively permanent personality characteristics.

Psychological strategies to overcome basic anxiety were termed by Horney 'neurotic needs'. Their identification by Horney constituted an important aspect of her theory. They included the neurotic need for power, that for prestige and that for perfection and unassailability. There was a total of ten such needs. They were termed 'neurotic' since they were self-defeating. In other words, in striving for such needs the individual created situations which led to his or her basic anxiety being increased. Thus childhood strategies aimed at relieving basic anxiety were carried on into adulthood.

The ten neurotic needs were regarded by Horney as being unconscious. It is because of this that she shared Freud's belief in unconscious motivation. However, Horney saw that if children are raised in a home in which there is love, tolerance, respect, trust and hence feelings of emotional security, there need be no basic anxiety and hence no neurotic needs. She therefore saw unconscious motivation as arising from objective social relationships rather than from instinctual urges. In this of course she differed fundamentally from Freud — and indeed from Jung.

There is little in Horney's theory with which Marxists would disagree. It is obvious that young children who are denied adequate love and guidance will feel anxious, insecure and threatened. Likewise it is clear that such children will adopt psychological strategies such as those described by Horney aimed at reducing these feelings. Furthermore, they will in all probability not be aware of the full implications of these strategies. Having said this, however, it needs to be pointed out that Horney's theory is extremely limited. She restricts herself to an account of how children who lack adequate love may develop certain personality characteristics. Thus there is no account of the development of the personalities of children who do not suffer from basic anxiety. Above all, there is no attempt to raise the crucial question of the relation of the individual to the social. For what is implied in Horney's writings is a model of a human individual who 'adapts' to the 'social environment' — in her particular case an individual who 'adapts' by developing 'neurotic needs'.

To return to the influence of the work of anthropologists on Horney. Although she was not alone in stressing the importance of their findings, she did help to draw attention to the discipline of psychology of the importance of cultural variables. It would therefore be appropriate at this point to quote a relevant passage from J.A.C.Brown's well-known work *Freud and the Post-Freudians*:

> The Freudian assumption of the fixity of human nature began to fare badly in the 1930s when Ruth Benedict and Margaret Mead produced a series of studies which demonstrated how very flexible human nature is when observed against different cultural backgrounds. Margaret Mead, an American anthropologist, found for instance that the storm and stress which is taken for granted as typical of adolescence in Western civilisation does not occur amongst girls in Samoa, where custom permits early sexual experience. Similarly, sexual differences between male and female cannot be said to be due to innate biological factors, as Freud supposed, if, as Mead found in New Guinea, neighbouring tribes with differing cultures show variations in masculine and feminine traits which in some cases amount almost to a reversal of the roles as we know them. 'The Arapesh ideal is the mild, responsive man married to the mild, responsive woman; the Mundugumor ideal is the violent aggressive man married to the violent aggressive woman. In the third tribe, the Tchambuli, we found a genuine reversal of the sex-attitudes of our own culture, with the woman the dominant, impersonal, managing partner, the man the less responsible and the emotionally dependent partner.' These cultural differences extend into all fields of personality; the Arapesh are cooperative, unaggressive, and gentle towards their children, the Mundugumor uncooperative, aggressive, and harsh. Aggression is so distasteful to the Arapesh that it appears to hold an equivalent position to that of sex in Victorian society, and enterprise, self-assertion, competitiveness, or anger are strongly disapproved of, so that the mere sight of anyone in a temper shocks them profoundly. Children are never punished and during its early life it is incessantly suggested to the child that everything is 'good — good sago, good house, good uncle, and so on. Amongst the Mundugumor, on the contrary, 'social organisation is based on a theory of a natural hostility that exists between all members of the same sex, and the assumption that the only possible ties between members of the same sex are through members of the opposite sex'. The late Ruth Benedict, another American anthropologist, found that the Zuni Indians of New Mexico resemble the Arapesh of New Guinea in their lack of assertiveness and initiative

— the Zuni try to lose a race, and insist on not occupying positions of importance, so that leaders have to be forcibly put in positions of authority and are poorly regarded once they are there. While we in Europe and America strive to collect money, the Kwakiutl of Puget Sound prefer to burn it and tear it in pieces at their 'potlatch' ceremonies, and the Dobu live in such a state of persecutory suspicion that a European psychiatrist would unhesitatingly diagnose any Dobuan outside his own society as a paranoiac requiring psychiatric treatment. War is unknown amongst the Eskimos, and suicide amongst many other tribal communities. Bali, says Roheim, is '. . . the unthinkable; a schizophrenic culture'.[5]

Although it would perhaps be unwise to take all these reported anthropological findings at their face value, all that has been said in the above quotation is sufficient to indicate the wide variations in personality between those living in different cultures. It needs to be recalled that before Horney's time cultural variables were frequently ignored by psychologists.

Horney should be remembered both for her criticisms of Freud — including Freud's neglect of cultural variables — and for her concept of 'basic anxiety'.

SULLIVAN

Harry Stack Sullivan, often referred to as a neo-Freudian, was an American born and bred psychiatrist. Thus, although he was both a contemporary and a collaborator of Karen Horney and Erich Fromm (see below), he differed from the latter in two significant respects. Firstly, he had never been a Freudian analyst. Secondly, he had not been forced, as had Horney and Fromm, to emigrate to the U.S.A. on Hitler's rise to power. Nevertheless, as will be pointed out below, the influence of Freud can be seen in his theory of personality.

In one important respect Sullivan's theory of personality comes close to Marxism. This is his insistence that it is vacuous to speak of personality as something that exists apart from social relationships. He defines personality as: 'The relatively enduring pattern of interpersonal situations which characterise a human life.'[6] The unit of study is therefore the interpersonal situation rather than the person. Even in nocturnal dreams, the individual exists together with others in interpersonal situations. Interpersonal situations may take place with imaginary figures such as the Virgin Mary or the hero of a novel. Sullivan defines psychiatry thus: 'Psychiatry is the study of phenomena that occur in interpersonal situations, in configurations made up of two or more people all but one of whom may be more or less completely illusory.'[7]

As has already been stated in Chapter Seven, Sullivan maintained that interpersonal relationships gave rise to what may be termed 'socialised physiology'. The individual becomes a social organism with socialised ways of digesting, eliminating breathing and so on. Similarly: 'Perceiving, remembering, thinking, imagining and all the other psychological processes are interpersonal in character'.[8]

Sullivan, like Horney, attaches great importance to anxiety, which he conceptualises as a feeling of interpersonal insecurity. Severe anxiety, he maintains, is so disruptive of normal behaviour that he likens it to a blow on the head.

One important aspect of Sullivan's theory is his conception of the 'self-system'. As the term implies, this consists of the ideas which the young child acquires about himself or herself. It arises, according to Sullivan, as a result of anxiety. In order to avoid interpersonal insecurity the child acquires conceptions of a 'good-me self' and a 'bad-me self' which eventually fuse together to form a unified 'system'. By playing the role of the former rather than the latter the child thereby conforms to the parents' wishes and thereby avoids interpersonal insecurity. What is important here is this: Where there is inadequate love and guidance the self-system becomes overvalued. In other words, family situations in early life which result in a lack of interpersonal security give rise to a strong self-system which will tend to minimise insecurity and anxiety. The child therefore grows up feeling that the self-system needs to be valued, since in the past it has minimised anxiety. This, however, means that he or she will lack — at least to a certain extent — the ability to be self-critical and thus to fully profit from experience. Sullivan thus maintains that in contemporary capitalist society an over-valued self-system becomes 'the principal stumbling block to favourable changes in personality.'[9] In view of the interpersonal insecurity experienced, in one degree or another, by young children today this particular aspect of Sullivan's theory deserves serious consideration.

The influence of Freud on Sullivan is shown by the latter's conception of the individual operating on a tension-reduction principle. (Freud believed that the individual was driven by attempts to reduce the tensions built up by the contents of the 'id'.) Sullivan believed that there were two sources of tension which the individual sought to reduce: first, organic tensions such as the need for food; second, the tension of anxiety produced by interpersonal insecurity.

There are a number of aspects of Sullivan's theory other than those mentioned here. However, enough has been said to at least indicate how a Marxist evaluation should proceed.

From a Marxist standpoint, Sullivan's insistence on the decisive importance of interpersonal situations (social relationships) constituted a big step forward in the history of psychology. However, the important question here is that of what actually occurs to individuals within the framework of interpersonal situations. As has been outlined in previous chapters, for Marxists what is important is that it is interpersonal situations which cause individuals to undertake a life-activity such that, through this activity, they become what they are psychologically. Here it might be suggested that this can be inferred from Sullivan's theory. But this question is of such crucial importance that it needs to be spelled out. It needs to be spelled out because it is through their life-activity that individuals acquire both consciousness and creativity and thus become able to change the world purposefully.

What has just been said is relevant to any consideration of Sullivan's conception of the individual operating on a tension-reduction principle. In view of the all-pervading outlook of functionalism in psychology, it could well be implied from Sullivan's theory that the individual adapts to interpersonal situations by undertaking such behaviour as would lead to a decrease in interpersonal insecurity and hence of anxiety. This of course leads back to the decisive question of whether the human individual is just a biological organism adapting to the 'social environment' or someone who consciously and purposefully changes the world of which he or she is an integral part. A closely related question, which Sullivan ignores, is of course that of the objective relationship between the individual on the one hand and society and its history on the other. It cannot therefore be deduced from Sullivan's theory that all individuals are products and hence makers of history.

Despite the above criticisms, Sullivan's theory constitutes an important contribution. There is much of interest in his writings.

FROMM

Erich Fromm, one of the so-called neo-Freudians, worked closely with both Horney and Sullivan. However, while Horney and Sullivan had been heavily influenced by both Freud and Adler, Fromm was influenced by both Freud and Karl Marx. Indeed, Fromm tried to bring about a synthesis of the theories of both Freud and Marx, making plain that he considered the latter to be a clearer thinker than the former.

Fromm was especially influenced by Marx's conception of the alienation of individuals under capitalism. The term 'alienation' is often used in a very wide and loose sense. Strictly speaking, in the Marxist sense it refers to the alienation of the worker from whatever he or she produces, also of the worker from his or her own labour-power, which during the process of production belongs not to the worker but to the employer. In a loose sense it is also used to denote the feelings of aloneness and helplessness of the individual in the face of historical and economic forces over which he or she has no control[10] In what is probably his best known work *Fear of Freedom*[11] Fromm contrasts the serf in feudal society to the individual in contemporary capitalist society. While the former felt secure in the knowledge that he knew precisely where he stood in relation to others in society, the latter felt alone and isolated. As individuals gained more social freedom, so they felt more alone.

Fromm devoted much of his writings to the personality types which reflected humanity's alienation under capitalism. He identified four such types: The receptive (those who were dependent on others). The exploiting (those who use and abuse others for their own ends). The marketing (those prepared to 'bargain' their personalities in exchange for what they want). Finally, the productive (normal individuals who are capable of genuine love and affection for others). Here is of course an example of how the universal (alienation under capitalism) is expressed in particular individual character or personality types.

Fromm correctly stresses the historical nature of personality, pointing out the differences in personality of individuals living in different historical periods. As has been already stated in Chapter Five, he has drawn attention to the role of child-rearing practices in moulding the type of personalities needed for the smooth running of whatever form of society exists at the time.

However, despite all such important and correct contributions, Fromm's theory contains an unresolvable contradiction. This is because he also puts forward views about the relationship between the individual and society which have far more in common with Freud than with Marx.

It was of course an essential aspect of the outlook of Marx that the human race constituted a definite part of nature. Fromm, on the other hand, emphasises a divorce of ourselves from nature:

> Humans in becoming human have been torn from the animals' primary union with nature . . . humans with their power to reason have lost this intimate interdependence with nature.[12]

Fromm indeed essentially reflects Freud's view, criticised above, that society is something imposed on a biological individual. 'By making demands that are contrary to their nature, society warps and frustrates humans.'[13] Humans, according to Fromm, have an animal nature which gives rise to organic needs.

They also possess specifically human needs among which Fromm identifies that for relatedness (implying the need for satisfactory human relationships), that for transcendence (implying the overcoming of one's animal nature and being creative), that for rootedness (implying the felt need to belong), and that for a frame of orientation (implying a need for a stable and consistent way of understanding the world) together with the need for identity (consisting of a clear system of ideas about oneself). It has to be understood that Fromm considered these needs as an essential form of human nature. It also has to be understood that when Fromm refers to the historical character of personality, what he really implies is that in various forms of society, these five human needs find expression only through the specific needs and demands of the relevant form of society. It is thus clear that both Freud and Fromm share a common belief that something inherent in human beings — with Freud the id, with Fromm the five needs — comes into conflict with society.

Before proceeding to a more fundamental criticism, it needs to be pointed out that the five needs which Fromm considers to constitute an ahistorical 'human nature' are in fact the product of the development of the human race through definite socio-economic systems. Here Fromm is guilty of an astonishing ignorance of anthropology, which shows quite clearly that, for example, in very primitive hunter-gatherer tribes the need for identity is conspicuous by its absence.[14]

The most fundamental criticism that can be made of Fromm from a Marxist standpoint is that for Fromm, human nature consists of the five needs enumerated above. In other words, Fromm conceptualises human nature as something inherent in each individual, just as did Freud. In contrast to this Marxists insist that human nature is labour. Further, since labour is essentially a social and historical process the skills of which are transmitted from generation to generation, human nature (or the human essence as it is sometimes termed) resides not in human individuals as such but in the historically developed social relationships which force individuals to undertake those forms of activity that cause them to become what they are. As Marx points out:

> The human essence is no abstraction inherent in each individual. In its reality
> it is the ensemble of the social relations.[15]

Thus both Freud and Fromm stand diametrically opposed to Marx. For the former two human nature is a purely individual matter. For the latter it is historical and social, although of course it finds expression in the life-activity of individuals.

A further and related fundamental difference between Marx and Fromm lies in their respective attitudes to the relationship between the individual and society. For Fromm, society reflects attempts by individuals to give expression to their human nature and its five needs. Thus the transition from capitalism to socialism, which for Marx arises from the objective contradictions of capitalism, is seen by Fromm as being the result of enough individuals deciding to express their individual human nature in new ways.[16]

Here it needs to be reiterated that, from the Marxist standpoint, human history is a part of natural history. The laws of historical development which underlie the transition from one socio-economic system to another are laws which are just as objective as those which underlie the development of new biological species. It is 'social being' which 'determines consciousness' rather than the other way round as implied in the theory of Fromm.

Despite the claims of Fromm to be a follower of Marx, it is clear that his basic assumptions about humanity are very far from Marxism. Nonetheless, his writings do throw important light on the way in which the alienation of individuals under capitalism is manifested in the human personality.

ALLPORT

Gordon Allport was an American psychologist who became an influential personality theorist. He was a contemporary of the neo-Freudians discussed above.

His theory is best known for three important features. Firstly, his concept of the 'functional autonomy' of motives, secondly his insistence on the uniqueness of each individual. Thirdly, his belief that the concept of 'trait' is useful for an understanding of the human personality.

Allport's conception of the 'functional autonomy' of motives has already been discussed in Chapter Seven. As has been outlined, the term implies that motives do not have to be explained in terms of childhood origins. If people play football, chess or a musical instrument they do so simply because they like doing so. It is not necessary to explain behaviours like these in terms of other, unconscious motives.

The importance of Allport's views on this aspect of human motivation can best be understood when seen in the context of the widespread influence of Freud which still existed when Allport made his contribution. Freud, of course, maintained that the most significant aspects of human motivation were to be explained in terms of the unconscious repression of the Oedipus complex during childhood.

Allport's insistence on the uniqueness of each individual can only be welcomed from a Marxist standpoint. This aspect of Allport's contribution is important as a reaction against two trends in contemporary psychology. First, that of behaviourism, which implies that individuals can be moulded by environmental pressures to an almost infinite extent. This implication in turn suggests that many individuals could, in principle, be made to become almost carbon copies of each other. Second, the trend which maintains that the personality of individuals can be quantified with almost mathematical precision by means of what are termed 'personality questionnaires'. The rationale underlying the questionnaires is that 'scores' can be made of 'personality variables' such as introversion, extraversion, neuroticism and so on and that the resulting scores describe the personality as a whole. If this were true, of course, literally millions of individuals who would answer the questionnaire in the same way would be judged to possess the same personality. Allport's insistence on the uniqueness of each individual therefore serves a useful purpose. Every individual must be unique for two reasons. First because his or her life-activity can only represent an extremely one-sided aspect of ongoing history. Second, as has been outlined in Chapter Seven, every individual, as a biological organism, interpenetrates in the course of his or her life-activity with historically developed social relations and their means and media. This interpenetration must of course be partially determined by the biological features of the individual. These must necessarily include his or her genetic constitution. And the latter is, with the exception of identical twins, absolutely unique to each individual.[17]

With regard to the third best-known feature of Allport's theory, any discussion of the value of the concept of 'traits' to describe the personality of individuals is really outside the scope of this book.

Any brief evaluation of Allport's theory would be inadequate without a consideration of his definition of personality. This has already been quoted in Chapter Three as an example of the 'functionalist' approach to psychology, but it would not be amiss to quote it again: 'Personality is the dynamic organisation within the individual of those psychophysical systems that determine his unique adjustments to the environment.' Three points need to be made about this definition. First, Allport's term 'dynamic organisation' reflects the fact that within the individual there are two opposing tendencies, that to change and that to conserve intact whatever already exists. This has, of course, already been discussed in Chapter Seven. Second, the use of the term 'psycho-physical systems' reveals a great theoretical weakness, since it implies that thought is the product of the individual brain. Here Allport shows his inability to understand the dialectical nature of human thought. From the Marxist standpoint, thought is of course simultaneously social and historical on the one hand and unique and individual on the other. The contribution of the activity of the brain to thought is solely that of taking a form of its content. Third, the 'functionalist' assumptions of Allport are fully revealed by his view that the individual 'adjusts' to the environment. It is thus clear that just as Allport fails to understand the dialectical nature of thought, so he cannot understand that the human individual is both a product and a maker of history rather than a biological organism which adapts to its environment.

Allport was a prolific writer, commenting on various aspects of psychology. There is much in his writings which is both interesting and instructive. However, despite his positive contributions, including those mentioned above, it is clear that he has little in common with a Marxist approach to psychology.

MASLOW

Abraham Maslow was an American theorist whose writings became popular in the period after the second world war. Some of his most important conceptions were derived from those of another theorist, Kurt Goldstein. The latter put forward views sometimes referred to as 'organismic theory'. The term 'organismic' implies the essentially integrated and organised nature both of the body and of the human personality, which operates on the principle that the whole constitutes more that the sum of its parts. Related to this was the conception of 'self-actualisation'. This implied an inherent tendency to actualise potential. In other words, people enjoyed doing what they were capable of doing.[18] These aspects of the outlook of Goldstein and Maslow undoubtedly reflect the influence of Jung.

One aspect of Maslow's theory which has aroused much interest is his conception of a hierarchy of needs. At the bottom of the hierarchy are basic physiological needs such as those for food and sleep. Above this comes the need for safety and security. This implies, for the young child, adequate love and guidance. Next comes the need for love and belongingness, implying the need for friends, membership of some social group and affectionate relationships. The fourth order of needs is composed of what Maslow terms 'esteem needs', the satisfaction of which entails prestige and recognition from others, together with feelings of self-confidence and adequacy. Lastly there is the need for self-actualisation. As stated above, this implies a need to actualise one's potential. Maslow himself writes:

A musician must make music, an artist must paint, a poet must write if he is to ultimately be at peace with himself. What a man can be he must be. This need we may call self-actualisation.[19]

Maslow conceptualises a hierarchy of needs because it is difficult to satisfy needs high in the hierarchy unless and until those lower in the hierarchy have been met. Unless basic physiological needs are met it is difficult to meet 'esteem needs'. Similarly, it is difficult to actualise one's full potential if one lacks safety and security.

Maslow regards 'self-actualisation', together with the other needs outlined above, as a definite part of an inborn 'human nature'. He writes that he maintains 'a strong belief that man has an essential nature of his own, some . . . psychological structure that may be treated analogously with his physical structure, that he has needs . . . that are genetically based [and which are] good or neutral rather than evil.'[20]

There is much in Maslow's theory with which Marxists would agree. The 'organismic' approach which he shared with Goldstein clearly reflects the integrated nature of human personalities and of individual life-activity. His conception of a hierarchy of motivational needs undoubtedly approximates the truth. It is of course self-evident that unless basic physiological needs are met few other needs can be satisfied.

Both Maslow and Goldstein deserve credit for their conception of 'self-actualisation'. As has been pointed out in Chapter Seven, the human brain is in a constant state of activity. This must result in the individual continually doing things, even if only at a mental level. Indeed, without the tendency to actualise potential, the essential human characteristics of consciousness and creativity, the importance of which constitute a major theme of this book, would be impossible. However, perhaps a slight reservation needs to be made. While it may undoubtedly be true that 'a musician must make music, an artist must paint, a poet must write . . .' it is not always the case that people enjoy what they are good at doing. A good burglar, fearful of going to prison, may not enjoy what circumstances have made him do. Likewise soldiers who become good at surviving in battle by killing and maiming others may well not enjoy the carrying out of what is necessary.

The last point leads to a consideration of a basic weakness in Maslow's position. This is his failure to focus attention on the significance of the relative dependence on basic physiological needs of those higher in the hierarchy. What is meant here is not simply that needs higher in the hierarchy cannot be met unless and until physiological needs are satisfied. Rather, it is that the activity involved in satisfying basic physiological needs will heavily influence the form taken by say, the need for self-actualisation. In order to satisfy one's basic physiological needs, one has to enter into definite social relationships with parents, with employers (who pay one a wage) or with a marriage partner who can provide financial security. Since life-activity constitutes a unified and integrated whole it is these sorts of activity which will at least heavily influence the ability and the desire of the individual to become (to return to Maslow's example) a musician, an artist or a poet.

A further weakness in Maslow's position is that he fails to understand that such motives as 'esteem needs' are historically developed rather than innate. Like the need for identity postulated by Fromm, they are not found in very primitive hunter-gatherer tribes.[21] Likewise Maslow's belief that humans are born 'good' or 'neutral' rather than 'evil' ignores the fact that 'good' and 'evil' are both historically developed concepts. What is considered good or evil differs from one socio-economic system to another. Thus in ancient Rome it was considered 'good' to enjoy watching Christians being fed to the lions. Nowadays, of course, it would be considered 'evil'.

The very concept of an innate, genetically-based human nature put forward by Maslow of course contradicts the insistence by Marxists that human nature is not something residing in individuals. Rather, it consists of those historically developed social relationships, together with their means and media, which force individuals to undertake activity that causes them to become what they are psychologically.

To sum up. While Maslow's contributions certainly cannot be ignored, Marxists would be highly critical of some of his formulations. On top of this he avoids basic questions such as that of the relation of the individual to the social.

SKINNER

B.F. Skinner was of course a very well known figure in contemporary psychology. He himself denied any claim to the title of 'personality theorist'. Rather, he regards himself as a technologist of behaviour. However, he is included in this brief overview of personality theorists since his outlook essentially constitutes a theory of human nature.

Skinner's main interest centred on what is termed 'operant conditioning'. Although this has been mentioned previously a brief recapitulation would not be out of order. The principles of operant conditioning are usually explained by the use of an example. The most widely used is that of a hungry rat inside what is known as a 'Skinner box'. This box contains a bar. When the rat presses the bar it is rewarded or 'reinforced' by food. It is found that this 'reinforcement' (food) increases the probability of the rat pressing the bar again. The term 'operant' is used since the rat operates on its environment by pressing the bar. So-called 'negative reinforcement' occurs when the rat, instead of being given the food when it presses the bar, is given, say, an electrical shock. This negative reinforcer (the shock) has the effect of reducing the probability of the rat pressing the bar again.

For many years Skinner and others have worked on sophisticated variations of what has just been outlined. Much of their work has centred on the effect of what are termed 'schedules of reinforcement'. There is, for example, a 'fixed ratio' schedule of reinforcement in which reinforcement takes place, say, every fifth time the rat presses the bar. There are also 'fixed interval' schedules in which the rat is reinforced say, every two minutes. There are also variable ratio and interval reinforcements. What Skinner and others have discovered is that there are definite and precise lawful relations between the various schedules of reinforcement and the pressing of the bar.

Skinner maintained that the 'rat in a Skinner box' model is widely applicable to humans and that very many aspects of human behaviour can be explained in terms of operant conditioning. Praying, for example, is explained by Skinner thus: If people pray for something to happen which then does happen, the activity of praying is thereby reinforced. Conversely, of course, if what other people pray for does not happen, then these other people will tend either not to pray so much or else stop praying altogether.

There is little doubt that the principles of Skinnerian operant conditioning do apply to humans to a certain extent and in some degree. It is of course well known that young children will tend to do as they are told if they are rewarded for so doing and if they are punished for doing the opposite. If they want attention and cry, and if their crying is answered with immediate attention, crying is thereby reinforced. In future, they will tend to cry whenever they want attention, much as a previously reinforced rat will press the bar when hungry.

It can perhaps be said that Skinner deserves credit for drawing attention to the fact that we tend to repeat actions that have proved rewarding in the past. In other words, present and future actions are often determined by feedback from previous actions. However, a little caution is necessary here. For while Skinnerian operant conditioning can definitely be said to be a form of feedback, not all feedback is operant conditioning. For example, for operant conditioning to be successful, the reinforcer (food given to the rat) has to be given within a definite time of the rat pressing the bar. In humans, however, there are many types of feedback which can be effective long after the original action. If students give essays to lecturers for comment, the time lapse between the writing of the essay and the receipt of comments which may lead to better future performance is relatively unimportant.[22]

The last point leads back to the question of the mechanical approach to human individuals discussed in Chapter Six.

A machine, let it be recalled, possesses the quality of interacting with other machines, the form of their interaction being determined by the internal structure of the machines. In other words, the working of machines is determined by fixed and rigid sets of rules.

A rat in a Skinner box can of course be regarded as a machine. Its entirely lawful response to various schedules of reinforcement results solely from the structure of its nervous system which, machine-like, obeys fixed rules. In contrast to this, as has already been stressed in Chapter Six, the most significant aspects of human behaviour are carried out with historically developed consciousness. This implies the ability to see one's own activity objectively, from the side, as it were. It follows, therefore, that humans possess the ability to understand what is going on in an 'operant conditioning' situation and to decide consciously whether or not to respond to the potential reinforcement.[23]

It is clear that Skinner completely fails to understand the essential difference between humans and other animal species. He unquestioningly accepts the functionalist, Darwinian assumption that the human race exists, like other species, primarily through the adaptation of individuals to their respective environments rather than through the historical mastery of nature through production. He is unable to comprehend the essentially historical nature of humanity, that is that human history represents a part of natural history.[24] Thus he fails to see human individuals as both the products and the makers of history.

A closely related and fundamental error of Skinner is that the very logic of his outlook is to divide human society into two: those who are reinforced and those who do the reinforcing. This is an error about which Marx wrote:

The materialist doctrine that men are the products of circumstances and upbringing and that, therefore, changed men are products of other circumstances and changed upbringing, forgets that it is men who change circumstances and that the educator must himself be educated. Hence, this doctrine is bound to divide society into two parts, one of which is superior to society (in Robert Owen, for example). The coincidence of the changing of circumstances and of human activity can be conceived and rationally understood only as revolutionising practice.[25]

To paraphrase a part of what has just been quoted from Marx, it might be said that 'those who do the reinforcing must themselves be reinforced'. Thus Skinner cannot explain himself in terms of his own theory.

In contrast to Skinner, however, Marxists consider that it is historically developed life-activity that endows individuals with the consciousness and creativity to 'change circumstances' and in the course of so doing, to 'change themselves'.

Skinner's contribution to the discipline of psychology cannot be ignored. His work has at least given rise to the development of teaching machines and programmed texts. However, Marxists have to reject the theory of human nature which is implicit in his writings. For it cannot be accepted that society is composed simply of individuals who adapt to their respective environments largely by means of operant reinforcement.

EYSENCK

H.J. Eysenck is Britain's best known psychologist. For this reason it is necessary to mention his theory.

The main aspect of Eysenck's approach to personality is his belief that it can be reduced to three what he terms 'dimensions of personality'. These are first, a bi-polar dimension of Introversion-Extroversion, second that of Neuroticism and third that of Psychoticism. Most of his attention has been focused on the first two.

Eysenck's third dimension, that of psychoticism, has to be viewed in the light of his belief that there is no relationship between neurotic and psychotic behaviour. Let it be pointed out now that many psychologists and psychiatrists fail to see a clear-cut distinction between the two. They often find it difficult to distinguish a point at which neurotic behaviour ends and psychotic behaviour begins.[26]

Eysenck's is essentially a biological theory of personality. Differences in introversion-extroversion and in neuroticism, he believes, are due to genetically determined differences in the nervous system. Thus the dimension of neuroticism implies a genetically determined susceptibility to stress. The dimension of introversion-extroversion implies genetically determined differences alleged to underlie certain behavioural variables. The most important of these variables, from Eysenck's standpoint, is a susceptibility to classical conditioning.[27] Whereas introverts are easily conditioned extroverts are hard to condition. Two important conclusions follow from this, Eysenck maintains. First, introverts who are high scorers on one of Eysenck's tests for neuroticism (he has developed questionnaires the answers to which are alleged to give accurate measurements of the 'dimensions' of personality) are prone to develop such neurotic disorders as phobias (unnatural fears). This is because, according to Eysenck, phobias can be explained in terms of classical conditioning. As an example, an introverted pedestrian who sees a cat just before being knocked down by a motor car will develop a phobia for cats, the sight of a cat being analogous to the sound of the bell in Pavlov's experiment. Second, extroverts rather than introverts are prone, when young, to develop into psychopaths. The latter are defined by Eysenck as those who lack a strong conscience. One's conscience, according to Eysenck, results from classical conditioning. The moral prohibitions of parents and teachers become, through classical conditioning, associated with feelings of anxiety, the former being regarded by Eysenck as also analogous to the sound of Pavlov's bell.

Perhaps the first comment to be made about Eysenck's theory is that of how little information it even purports to give us about the enormously complex and varied nature of human life. Thus although he maintains that introversion-extroversion is a major personality 'dimension' the fact remains that the great majority of the population are neither particularly introverted nor extroverted. Again, a large section of the population is either not neurotic at all or at least not significantly so. Similarly, only a small proportion of the entire population can be classified as psychotic.

If an individual answering Eysenck's questionnaires gives answers indicating that he or she is slightly introverted but not at all neurotic or psychotic, what do we thereby know about him or her? Very little. We do not know whether he or she is lazy or hardworking, well educated or semi-literate, kind or cruel, sad or happy and so on. Furthermore, it should be noted that throughout the world literally millions of people would be likely to attain the same score as in the above example. Yet in many respects all these people would be as unlike each other as chalk from cheese.

Generally speaking, the same criticisms that have been made of Skinner apply to Eysenck. Just as certain behaviours, especially of young children, tend to resemble those of Skinner's rats, so certain human behaviours resemble those of Pavlov's dogs. Thus when hungry we tend to salivate at the sight and sound of food being prepared. However, here again it is necessary to recall that humans possess consciousness and hence the ability to view objectively their own behaviour. Consciousness enables us — at least within certain relatively wide limits — to decide what aspects of the environment we respond to with feelings such as fear. Human beings are of course regarded by Eysenck — as by Skinner — as no more that biological machines which respond in a mechanical fashion to environmental changes. Marxists, however, regard humans as makers of history possessing the conscious power of decision.

The logic of Eysenck's position must lead to a similar outlook to that of Skinner regarding the relationship of the individual to society. For if the decisive aspects of human behaviour are determined by classical conditioning, then society must represent an entity standing above the individual which administers the conditioning to him or her. Classical conditioning therefore must represent a way in which the individual 'adjusts' or 'adapts' to the environment in a typical 'functionalist' manner. This is clearly shown, for example, in the actual definition which Eysenck makes of personality:

> Personality is the more or less stable and enduring organisation of a person's character, temperament, intellect and physique which determines his unique adjustments to the environment.[28]

Here Eysenck totally fails to conceptualise the individual as a maker of history. Rather he sees the individual simply as one who 'adjusts' to history and society. However, it needs to be re-emphasised that the human individual can never 'adjust' or 'adapt' to a society which he or she continuously creates and re-creates.

In addition to the above quoted definition of personality, Eysenck also defines the human individual. 'To the scientist,' he writes 'the unique individual is simply the point of intersection of a number of quantitative variables.'[29]

In other words, the unique individual simply represents a number of scores on various tests for psychological variables such as neuroticism, introversion-extroversion, intelligence and so on. This definition, which really tells us more about Eysenck than about human individuals, deserves brief comment.

Eysenck is of course an empiricist. He believes that all we can really know is derived from superficial appearances of the world. Scientific knowledge of individuals is restricted to the observation of individuals. Including of course such aspects of human behaviour as the completion of 'personality question-naires', which is no doubt what he has in mind when he writes of 'quantitative variables'.

But as has been pointed out in the previous chapter, the task of science is not to restrict itself to superficial appearances. Rather, it is to use abstract, theoretical thought to comprehend what underlies and gives rise to superficial appearance. In psychology, this entails, for example, a theoretical understand-ing of what universals find expression in particular individuals, of the simultaneously individual and social nature of human thought, of the relation between natural history and human history and so on. At this point it might be argued that Eysenck does indeed use theoretical thought to explain say, differences in the ease with which one responds to classical conditioning in terms of physiological variables.[30] However, the important point here is that any personality theory worthy of the name must account for the actual content of individual life-activity — what the individual actually does throughout his or her life. And this is precisely what Eysenck does not do. He cannot, because he is unable to comprehend the basic psychological fact that the content of the lives of individuals constitute an integral part of ongoing human history.

To sum up from the Marxist standpoint, Eysenck's theory has little merit. Perhaps it can be regarded as being of use in that it expresses, in a succinct manner, all the theoretical weaknesses of contemporary psychology. With great clarity, Eysenck shows that the human individual is regarded as no more than a biological machine which 'adjusts' to its environment just as did Pavlov's dogs.

KELLY

George A. Kelly was a relatively modern American personality theorist. His work has given rise to what is termed 'personal construct theory'.

Kelly rejects both psychoanalytic and behaviourist (e.g. Skinner, Eysenck) models. Freudian psychoanalytic theory he sees as essentially a model of a battlefield, 'a dark cellar in which a maiden aunt and a sex-crazed monkey are locked in mortal combat, the affair being refereed by a rather nervous bank clerk.'[31] Alternatively, behaviourist theory is seen as possessing a model resembling 'a ping-pong ball with a memory'.[32]

Kelly's own 'model man' is conceptualised as 'man the scientist'. By this Kelly implies that people in general (including scientists) have theories about the world. They then conduct 'experiments' and make observations of the results of these. It is these observations which will either verify or disprove their 'theories', which can then be amended or discarded if necessary.

During the course of their 'experiments' people use what Kelly refers to as 'constructs'. These may be described as bi-polar concepts. Examples are love-hate, man-woman and day-night. Constructs are more than concepts, however, for two principal reasons. The first is that constructs are essentially predictive instruments. Thus if we construe someone as honest rather than dishonest we are essentially predicting that he or she is at least likely to make an attempt to repay a loan. The second reason is that constructs are organised into systems or sub-systems. Thus if we construe someone as nice rather than nasty we tend also to construe him or her as kind rather than cruel and as polite rather than rude. In other words the three constructs nice-nasty, kind-cruel and polite-rude are to be regarded as together forming an organised sub-system. Here Kelly shows that he is among those who subscribe to the idea of an integrated, coherent and organised personality.

Kelly makes plain his belief that the construct system of each individual is unique. Hence the term 'personal construct theory'.

According to Kelly, when an individual predicts (construes) events — including those brought about by his or her own actions — there are three possible outcomes. The construct can be validated, it can be invalidated or it can be found to be inappropriate to the situation. The example is given of a hopeful young man who takes a young lady back to his flat and construes her as 'willing rather than unwilling'. If an affair commences, then the construct is validated. If, on the other hand, she slaps his face and rings for the police then the construct is invalidated. A third possibility is that the 'young lady' turns out to be a transvestite. Here the young man's construct 'willing rather than unwilling' ceases to be appropriate to the situation.[33]

There is much in Kelly's theory with which Marxists would not disagree. Various aspects of the world are indeed understood in terms of their opposites. Boys are understood as not being girls, death is understood as the opposite of life and so on. Kelly is also to be commended for pointing out the tendency for an individual's thought to act as an organised and integrated whole. His stress on the uniqueness of each individual is correct.

However, Kelly's weakness is that of an empiricist. He conceptualises 'man the scientist' as someone akin to a contemporary psychologist. The latter, it will be recalled from the previous chapter, has a view of the development of scientific knowledge which is totally false. For empiricists, the only valid theory is one which represents a generalisation from sense-perceptions. Theories are changed only if contradicted by further sense-perceptions. In other words, theory remains unchanged 'until further (empirical) facts are discovered'. The relatively independent development of abstract, theoretical thought which characterises natural science and mathematical science is ignored.

Kelly's 'model man' is someone whose constructs change only when sense-perception changes. There is no room in his theory for creative thought. His theory could not possibly explain, for example, the abstract, creative thought of Einstein and Darwin mentioned in the previous chapter. It is clear that, strictly speaking, Kelly's model should not be termed 'man the scientist' but rather 'man the empiricist'.

Kelly himself reveals his empiricism when he writes: 'Our emphasis upon the testing of constructs implies our reliance upon the principles of empiricism . . . in this respect we are in the tradition of American psychology.[34]

The present author does not feel competent to undertake a full assessment of Kelly's use of the term 'construct'. It has already been mentioned that since many things are often understood in terms of their opposites, the use of the term to denote concepts of a bi-polar nature may prove to be a useful conceptual tool. However, it has to be pointed out that Kelly avoids the crucial question of the essentially historical nature of concepts (and hence of constructs). While he does not explicitly deny their historical nature, any student of Kelly's theory might well be forgiven for thinking that constructs arose simply in people's heads as a result of their individual experience. Yet the obvious fact remains that it would have been impossible for people living say, a hundred years ago to possess constructs such as 'computer-not computer', 'biotechnology-not biotechnology' or 'Charlie Chaplin-not Charlie Chaplin'.

Perhaps the most serious criticism that can be made of Kelly's theory is that he fails to recognise the decisive importance of objective situations which impel individuals to undertake definite forms of practical activity and hence to develop themselves psychologically. His model of 'man the scientist' seems to assume that the 'scientist' is free to do what he or she likes. Scientists are of course free, within certain limits, to decide consciously what aspects of their field they want to investigate, what experiments to carry out and so on. Yet they are always constrained by objective situations (availability of funds, time, the current state of knowledge etc.). More importantly, it is the objective situations which they have had to confront during the course of their life-activity which has caused them to develop themselves as scientists.

To sum up Kelly's theory. It can be said that although he has raised important questions, his work falls far short of what is required for even an elementary understanding of the human personality.

It needs to be re-emphasised that the outlines of each personality theory given above should in no way be taken to be adequate expositions. Neither should the brief comments which follow each outline be taken as fully-fledged Marxist evaluations. They can only be, at best, general guidelines as to where to begin. A thorough and comprehensive Marxist evaluation of the many aspects of Freudian theory alone would require a whole volume, or perhaps several volumes.

Enough has been said to indicate that, from the Marxist standpoint, each personality theory (including those that have not been mentioned in this chapter) represents, in one way or another, a positive contribution to human knowledge. Some more than others, of course. For what it is worth, the present author considers that he has learned the most from Freud and Adler, together with the neo-Freudians Horney, Fromm and Sullivan. He has learned least of all from Eysenck.

The majority of personality theorists discussed in this chapter adhere, implicitly or explicitly, to the basic but false functionalist hypothesis that human society consists solely of individuals whose mode of existence is that of 'adapting' or 'adjusting' to their respective environments. Possible exceptions to this general rule are Jung, Adler and Maslow. It needs to be pointed out, however, that none of these three theorists has ever explicitly condemned the functionalist hypothesis.

With the exception of Jung, no personality theorist has been able to understand the fundamental psychological truth that human thought is simultaneously unique and individual on the one hand and social and historical on the other. However, as has been pointed out earlier, Jung saw things upside down, as it were. He saw social and historical thought as arising from the physical structure of the brain rather than from the transmission of ideas from generation to generation through the medium of historically developed social relationships.

Finally, it needs to be noted that all personality theorists, without exception, avoid recognising the basic premise necessary for a correct understanding of human personalities. This is, of course, that the basis of human personalities lies, neither in innate thought nor in the ability to adapt or adjust to the environment. Its basis can only lie in those objective social situations which force individuals to undertake such practical activity that causes them to become what they are psychologically.

It is clear that a correct evaluation of personality theories must form an important aspect in the future development of a genuinely scientific psychology.

NOTES TO CHAPTER TEN

1. It should perhaps be noted that Russian psychologists and philosophers, many of whom claim to be Marxists, have so far totally failed to provide a satisfactory evaluation of Freud and his work.
2. Here it might be remarked that Freud conceptualised the individual personality as being rather like the anarchist who constantly strives to throw off the constraints of society in order to 'do my own thing.'
3. See Hall, C. and Lindsey, G. *Theories of Personality*. Wiley, 1978, 3rd Edition.

4. 'The mystification which dialectic [the self-movement of nature, history and thought] suffers in Hegel's hands, by no means prevents him from being the first to present its general form of working in a comprehensive and conscious manner. With him it is standing on its head. It must be turned right side up again, if you would discover the rational kernel within the mystical shell.' Marx *Capital* Vol. 1. Foreign Languages Publishing Company, 1969, p. 20.

5. Brown, J.A.C. *Freud and the Post-Freudians*. Cassell, 1963, pp. 121-123.

6. Sullivan, H.S. *The Interpersonal Theory of Psychiatry*. Norton, 1953, p. 111.

7. Sullivan, H.S. *The Fusion of Psychiatry and Social Science*. Norton, 1964, p. 33.

8. Hall and Lindsey *op. cit.* p. 183.

9. Sullivan, H.S. *The Interpersonal Theory of Psychiatry*. Norton, 1953, p. 169.

10. For a good exposition of Marx's concept of alienation see Meszaros, I. *Marx's Theory of Alienation*. Merlin, 1970.

11. Fromm, E. *Fear of Freedom*. Rinehart, 1941.

12. Hall and Lindsey, *op. cit.* p. 171.

13. *Ibid.* p. 173.

14. See, for example, Mikhailov, F. *The Riddle of the Self*. Progress Publishers, 1980, Chapter Three: 'When Consciousness is Conscious of Itself.'

15. Marx 'Sixth Thesis on Feuerbach' In: Engels, F. *Ludwig Feuerbach and the End of German Classical Philosophy*. Progress, p. 67.

16. See Hall and Lindsey *op. cit.* pp. 173-174.

17. It is well to recall that even identical twins are not born biologically equal. Their respective position in the womb will affect their pre-natal development.

18. See, for example, Goldstein, K. *The Organism*. American Book Company, 1939.

19. Maslow, A. *Motivation and Personality*. Harper, 1954, p. 91.

20. *Ibid.* pp. 340-341.

21. See Mikhailov *op. cit.* Chapter Three.

22. See, for example, Annett, J. *Feedback and Human Behaviour*. Penguin, 1968.

23. Relevant to this discussion is the old psychological joke about one rat boasting to another that he now had his psychologist so well conditioned that every time he pressed the bar the psychologist gave him food!

24. Skinner's functionalist approach is of course manifested in the fact that rats, learning to press a bar in order to obtain food, display behaviour likely to lead to their individual survival.

25. Marx 'Third Thesis on Feuerbach' In: Engels, F. *Ludwig Feuerbach and the End of German Classical Philosophy*. Progress, 1978, p. 66.

26. See, for example, Ullman, L. and Krastner, L. *A Psychological Approach to Abnormal Behaviour*. Prentice Hall, 1969. Also: Laing R.D. and Esterson A. *Sanity, Madness and the Family*. Penguin, 1970.

27. See Chapter One, Note 7.

28. Eysenck, H.J. *The Structure of Personality*. Methuen 1953 p. 2.

29. Eysenck, H.J. *The Scientific Study of Personality*. Routledge and Kegan Paul, 1953 p. 18.

30. See, for example, Eysenck, H.J. *The Biological Basis of Personality*. Thomas, 1969.

31. Bannister, D. 'A New Theory of Personality'. in: B. Foss (Ed.) *New Horizons in Psychology* Vol. 1. Penguin, 1972, p. 363.

32. *Ibid* p. 363.

33. *Ibid* p. 366.

34. Kelly, G.A. *The Psychology of Personal Constructs*. Vol.1. 'A Theory of Personality.' Norton, 1965, p. 17.

11

SOME APPLICATIONS

In previous chapters a number of important aspects of human psychology have been discussed. A number of conclusions have also been drawn. Such conclusions would be of limited value, however, if they could not lead to definite applications.

It is the purpose of this chapter to indicate how a Marxist approach can be used both to understand various aspects of human behaviour and thinking and, if possible, to use this knowledge in a practical way. A few of the points have already been made in preceding chapters. However, since most of the ideas outlined in this book will be relatively new to most readers, a little repetition will not be amiss.

Aspects of psychology to be mentioned here are: aggression; the tendency to conform to the nuclear family; the role of exchange in interpersonal relationships; religious behaviour; how individual behaviour under capitalism reflects the conflict between humanity's productive forces and the relations of production; the alienation of thought; art, music and literature; the unity and integrity of life-activity; how and to what extent the thinking and behaviour of individuals can be changed; the 'nature-nurture' controversy and, finally, the 'mind-body' problem.

A useful starting point would be a reminder that, from the Marxist standpoint, certain forms of behaviour and thinking cannot be understood unless and until human society is understood. To put it another way, in terms of the philosophical categories of the particular, the individual and the universal, the life-activities of particular individuals cannot be understood unless they are seen as aspects of the universal of history. This is especially true of those aspects of behaviour regarded by probably the majority of lay persons — and indeed by many psychologists — as the product of some innate and unchanging 'human nature' residing in all individuals. Two such aspects of human behaviour especially come to mind. These are first, aggression and second, the desire to enter into the monogamic relationships which lead to a nuclear family. It is necessary to discuss these in turn.

Aggression directed towards others is of course a widespread human characteristic. It has been manifested throughout history. Those who have been unable to break from the strait-jacket of empirical methodology may well be forgiven for believing that aggression (i.e., behaviour implying a conscious desire to harm others) is innate. For even in the classless society of primitive communism, hunter-gatherer tribes were often forced to fight rival tribes for hunting and other rights. Using the empiricist principle of formulating theories on the basis of abstracting common features of superficial appearances, many people have been led to accept that 'each one of us harbours within himself those same savage impulses that lead to murder, to torture and to war.'[1] This acceptance is so widespread that the findings of psychologists studying child development that: 'The newborn . . . has no innate tendencies to love, fear, approach or avoid people'[2] are almost totally ignored.

Any serious consideration of human aggression must of necessity take as one of its starting points the relation of the universal to the individual particular case. The universal, of course, can only be understood theoretically rather than empirically. As has been outlined in Chapter Nine, abstract theoretical thought is essential to understand what underlies and gives rise to superficial appearance which can, taken by itself, be very misleading. It is hard to envisage any other aspect of human psychology other than aggression which illustrates this general principle so clearly.

The universal to be considered here can only be that of human society in its whole historical development. Its history is expressed through the behaviour and thinking of particular individuals, many of whom have been, at one or other stage in their lives, aggressive towards others. Here it is necessary to return to a point made in Chapter Two concerning human society. From the Marxist standpoint, the basis of human existence is production. In the process of production individuals have to enter into definite relations with one another, termed relations of production. It is these relations which form the basis for any socio-economic system such as slave society, feudalism or capitalism. Upon the relations of production rest the ideological and social superstructure consisting of beliefs, values, the form of the family, education, art, literature, morality and so on. In other words every ideological and social superstructure represents, however indirectly, the socio-economic base that constitutes the ongoing relations of production. It is this Marxist conception of human society that enables human aggression to be understood. For all hitherto existing economic systems, from primitive tribal communism to contemporary capitalism, have required aggression to be a definite part of their ideological and social superstructure.

As has also been noted in Chapter Two, primitive tribal societies are noted for their internal co-operation. This co-operation is a necessary condition for existence, since the means of production are so primitive that only by co-operative effort within the tribe can the necessities of life be obtained. By and large, aggression within the tribe is negligible. However, it has to be recalled that the first form of human society, primitive communism, existed as a collection, often spread over wide areas, of relatively independent and self-sufficient tribes. The integrated world economy that exists today was of course not even dreamed about. It must have been inevitable, therefore, that clashes between tribes occurred over territory, since the original mode of existence of the human race was one of hunting and gathering. It is not difficult to imagine that some tribal territories periodically became depleted of whatever was hunted or gathered. Similarly it can be understood that therefore those tribes which inhabited these territories, in order to survive, had to move elsewhere. If the only new territory available was that already occupied by another tribe, then that tribe had to be driven out or wiped out by means of war. This form of aggression, therefore, was due, not to any innate urge to commit aggression against others. Its occurrence was due to the need of the tribe to survive.

The first form of class society, slave society, could of course exist only on the basis of aggression against the slaves. Indeed, the extensive wars that eventually exhausted and brought down the Roman empire were primarily waged to obtain fresh supplies of slaves. As has also been mentioned previously, slave society, however brutal, was a necessary historical stage in the development of humanity's productive forces. It is only in the context of the Marxist belief that human history constitutes both a part and an extension of natural history that this becomes clear.

The feudal relations of production that superseded slave society inevitably led to large scale acts of aggression. Bad treatment of the serfs led to revolts against the feudal lords in England, Germany and elsewhere. Within the feudal aristocracy there were frequent disputes, often settled by aggressive means, over questions such as land ownership and rights. Finally, the productivity of the serfs was so low that many feudal lords sought to augment their wealth by means of direct plunder, often under a religious cloak as in the Crusades. The Spanish looting of South America is another example.

The last form of class society, capitalism, could come into existence only through violence and aggression. The violent revolution of Cromwell in Britain and that which took place in France in 1789 were entirely necessary for capitalism to develop. Likewise the Industrial Revolution which made Britain 'the workshop of the world' could not have taken place without the violent and aggressive enforcement of the Enclosure Acts, which drove thousands of small farmers off the land to form the world's first large-scale proletariat.

From a Marxist standpoint, the widespread wars which are the inevitable concomitant of capitalism have to be seen as manifestations of rival economic and financial interests. The first world war, for example, resulted from the late capitalist development of Germany. Looking for sources of raw material and for outlets for the export both of manufactured goods and — more importantly — of surplus capital, the German capitalist class found themselves blocked by the previous division of the world by rival capitalist powers such as Britain and France. Their only way to avoid economic collapse was to smash their rivals by taking over the British and French empires. The second world war was essentially a continuation of the first.

The purpose of this brief historical digression is to emphasise the Marxist belief that wars are not to be understood in terms of aggressive tendencies inherent in the genes of all individuals. Rather, they are to be understood as manifestations of specific socio-economic formations (based on relations of production) which have been entirely necessary for the development of humanity's productive forces and hence for the survival of the species.

It is the belief of Marxists that the future socialist society — which can only be built on a world scale[3] — will represent a return to the co-operative nature of humanity's first form of society: primitive tribal communism. But on a higher level. There will be two important differences. First, the world socialist society will be built upon the basis of a very high level of productivity, using all the latest developments of electronics, biotechnology and other scientific advances. This will ensure an abundance of the necessities of life. Second, whereas many primitive tribes often had to defend their territories against rivals, the future world socialist society will imply a highly integrated economy which would preclude economic rivalries. The basis for wars would therefore be eliminated.

At this point it might be objected by some that at certain periods of history wars have occurred which did not directly reflect rival economic interests. This is of course quite true. Feudal noblemen, for example, often started wars simply for spite or for reasons of prestige. The point here, however, is this: only in a society in which war is endemic for reasons of economic necessity could wars be carried out for reasons other than economic ones. In all previous socio-economic systems the objective, economic basis for wars have existed. Therefore their ideological and social superstructures must have been such that warlike behaviour has been socially condoned and regarded as acceptable. The same could of course be said of capitalism. However, in a world socialist society, in which the relations of production are of a co-operative character, there will be no objective need for wars and hence the social sanction for war-like behaviour will not arise.

A further objection that might be raised is that, while it might well be possible to eliminate wars by moving forward to a higher stage of society, at least some children, in whatever society, would be brought up in such a way that they would exhibit aggressive tendencies. Here two points need to be made. The first is that the effects of early training in children can lead to far-reaching and relatively lasting psychological consequences. Perhaps the most obvious example is that of toilet training. Another is that of eating with cutlery rather than with fingers. There are few adults, adolescents or older children — at least in most cultures — who would feel happy about eliminating in public places when a lavatory is available or about eating food in a restaurant solely with their fingers. There is therefore no reason, in principle, why all children should not similarly be trained to refrain from consciously and wilfully inflicting harm on others. The second point to be made is that a future world society, based on a far higher level of productivity than exists under capitalism, would quickly resolve the problems of food, clothing and shelter. This in turn would lead to the possibility of a far higher proportion of human resources being devoted to the upbringing of children than is the case under capitalism. Under capitalism, of course, the upbringing of children is the responsibility of the biological parents. Since so many parents are unwilling or unable to give adequate love and guidance to their children (as recent cases of child abuse have shown), it is inevitable that a proportion of children should grow up with tendencies to inflict harm on others. It is only by ensuring that all children receive adequate love and guidance regardless of their biological parentage that the problem of aggressively anti-social children can be eliminated. And in a world society with immense human resources such a task can and will be undertaken.

What has been said in the preceding paragraph leads on to a consideration of the widespread view that monogamic marriage and the nuclear family are considered by many to reflect and arise from some sort of innate 'human nature'. This view is not only held by lay persons. It is also that of many psychologists. The present author recalls one of his former colleagues referring to marriage as a part of what he termed 'the physics of life'.

Just as a consideration of human aggression requires a knowledge of human history as an extension of natural history, so does that of the institution of the nuclear family.

The institution of the family represents, as does aggression, a particular expression of society in its historical development. It constitutes a superstructural aspect of those relations of production which in turn constitute the basis of every socio-economic formation. Far from being a manifestation of any innate 'human nature', the family as we know it today has a long history.

During the first few tens of thousands of years of humanity's existence the monogamous nuclear family did not exist. This fact can be deduced from a study of primitive hunter-gatherer tribes.[4]

It was only when primitive tribal communism had reached a relatively advanced stage of development that forms of the monogamic nuclear family began to appear. Marx's co-thinker and colleague Engels, in his well-known work *The Origin of the Family, Private Property and the State*[5], has shown an interesting dialectical relationship between the development of the family on the one hand and private property on the other.

The institution of monogamic marriage, which carries within it the responsibility of the husband for the upbringing of any children his wife may have (whether they are biologically his or not) is a product of class society, from slave society to capitalism. The principal reason for this is that, by and large, it absolves the state from any responsibility of bringing up children. In other words, class society functions better if the biological parents of a child are made responsible for his or her upbringing. This can be shown to be especially true in capitalist society. Here the cost of bringing up children in orphanages or in children's homes is relatively high. As a general rule, the cost of bringing up a child in an orphanage or home exceeds the income of many lower-paid workers. If on the other hand the state allows the biological parents of a child relief from income tax and other benefits, its duty to children — apart from providing a rudimentary educational system — is financially minimised. To make this point clearer, the capitalist state in Britain today is financially unable to maintain intact both the National Health Service and the educational facilities that have been built up since the second world war. It could not possibly afford to undertake the role now undertaken in the upbringing of children by their biological fathers.

Despite the fact that many children in capitalist society are quite happy to be brought up by their biological parents in a nuclear family, it is clear that the institution of monogamic marriage and the family suffers from severe deficiencies. There are two principal deficiencies which deserve mention. The first of these is that, if the upbringing of children is left in the hands of the biological parents, the death of one or both parents can leave a child without adequate love and guidance. Similarly the divorce of parents can also deprive children of adequate emotional security. The problems encountered by children of one-parent families are of course well known. The second principal deficiency of the monogamic family is that people who are quite incapable of giving children adequate love and guidance are legally quite entitled to bring them up. Within certain quite wide limits they can do whatever they like with them. Recent horrifying cases of the torture of children by their parents underline the fact that a certain percentage of parents are no more capable of giving adequate love and guidance than was Dracula.

Further difficulties associated with the monogamic family will be mentioned later in this chapter. Enough has so far been said, however, to indicate that it is impossible to maintain the existence of monogamic marriage and the nuclear family without at the same time depriving a certain proportion of children of adequate love and guidance.

As has already been indicated in the above discussion on aggression, an advanced world society based on the latest technology would be able to provide sufficient human resources to bring up all children without exception with love and adequate guidance. Just as happens today in primitive tribes, no child will need to feel emotionally insecure because of his or her biological parentage.

The question of the monogamic family is of course closely linked with that of the oppression of women. Generally speaking, women cannot obtain a livelihood by going out to work while they are having children. They therefore have to rely on financial support from their husbands. This is especially true of those women with large families. Thus there can be no real social equality between men and women as long as the latter remain in a position of financial dependence on the former.[6]

It is clear, therefore, that the institution of monogamic marriage and the family based upon it is by no means the product of any innate and unchanging 'human nature'. Rather, it is the product of historical development which, like capitalism, has become historically outmoded and destined to make way for more satisfactory methods of child rearing.

A further example of how an understanding of society is necessary for an understanding of human behaviour now has to be considered. This relates to the prevalence of commodity production under capitalism. In this context a commodity can be defined as something that is produced specifically for sale on the market.

Commodity production can perhaps be better understood when contrasted to natural production, which is production for direct use rather than for sale. Thus when people grow potatoes in their gardens for their own consumption they are engaging in natural production. If on the other hand they take them to the market in order to exchange them for money, the potatoes thereby become commodities. Capitalism represents a form of society in which commodity production predominates over natural production.[7]

In a society in which commodity production predominates, many aspects of the world take the form of commodities even though they may not, strictly speaking, be commodities as such. Examples are works of art, honour and the the bodies of prostitutes, all of which may be exchanged for money.

An inevitable feature of capitalism must be, not only the production of commodities, but also their exchange, which takes place in the market. (Here the term 'market' is used in a wide sense). Every exchange of commodities involves a confrontation between buyers (money is simply a commodity of a special kind) and sellers. Every owner of commodities will try to sell them, while every owner of money will seek to buy whatever commodities he or she needs or desires. Every confrontation between buyers and sellers necessarily involves, directly or indirectly, bargaining and deals. Sellers will consider how much money they are prepared to accept in exchange for their commodities. Buyers will consider how much money they are prepared to part with in exchange for the commodities they desire to possess.

This production and exchange of commodities find their reflection in virtually all aspects of interpersonal relationships in capitalist society. Individuals will consider first, what they desire from others and second, what they are prepared to do or to give up in order to get what they want. They will then sum up the pros and cons and decide what to do. Social relationships ranging from the saying of 'Good morning' to marriage partnerships are arrived at in this way.[8] In other words, the most significant aspects of social relationships under capitalism are those for which bargains have to be made.

From the standpoint of personality development in the young child this bargaining is of extreme importance. This is mainly because affection, which should be the birthright of every child, exists as a relationship which has to be bargained for. It can usually be obtained only in exchange for conformity. If the child conforms to its parents' demands it will in exchange receive affection. In other words affection, instead of being the right of children, becomes contingent upon conformity to parental wishes. It is no wonder that so many children grow up to regard the world as a hostile or potentially hostile place in which one has to take rather than to give. They will learn to operate the principle: 'I will do this for you only if you do that for me.'

It should be noted that parents themselves are not entirely to blame for this state of affairs. They are victims of the system the same as anyone else. A harassed housewife, with a husband out of work and with several children, might well find it extremely difficult to cope if she did not sometimes threaten withdrawal of affection in order to obtain conformity. All this is of course an additional reason for the replacement of the monogamic family by more satisfactory methods of child rearing. If sufficient social resources were available to assist women who wanted to have children, it would be possible to train the latter to conform to social norms while at the same time providing them with adequate and unconditional love and affection.

The bargaining and exchange that takes place under capitalism is clearly revealed in male/female relationships. The remark of George Bernard Shaw that marriage is only veiled prostitution is very apt. However, psychologists need to be more precise than was Shaw, mainly because sex constitutes only a part of the marriage contract. Most men want to enter into a marriage contract for a number of reasons. These include a desire for affection, sex, children, a permanent home kept clean and tidy by their wives, social status, companionship in old age and so forth. It is often the case that, for men, affection is regarded as being of more importance than sex (or at least sex with their own wives). If, for example, things go wrong at work for a man and he gets the blame, he likes to feel that, when he arrives home, his wife will treat him as if he were the most marvellous man in the world. The need for affection therefore represents a significant part of the desire to marry and remain married.

Most women, like men, want to enter into a marriage contract for a variety of reasons. As has been observed in preceding paragraphs, most women want to have children but find it impossible or at least difficult to do so without financial support from a husband. This need for financial support undoubtedly constitutes a major factor in the desire of women to get married. Companionship and financial security in old age is another factor. As with men, needs such as those for affection, sex, social status and so on undoubtedly enter into the equation.

A marriage contract therefore represents a bargain, an unspoken deal. Both men and women sum up what they want on the one hand and what they are prepared to do or give up on the other just as do the buyers and sellers of commodities.

Within the framework of the monogamic, nuclear family, it often happens that children become the objects of social manipulation. In other words they become pawns in bargaining procedures. Some single women will deliberately allow themselves to become pregnant so that their boy friends will marry them. The present author knows of a sixteen-year-old girl in care who deliberately became pregnant so that the local authority would provide her and her boyfriend with a flat. Her child thus became a means of bargaining with the local authority. The actual manipulation of children by their parents is in fact widespread. Thus it frequently happens that if parents disagree about how their children are to be brought up, the husband will defer to his wife's wishes in the expectation that, in exchange, he will receive more affection from her. The effect on the psychological development of children who are manipulated in these and similar ways can well be imagined.

It can therefore be concluded that, generally speaking, in capitalist society, affection can be obtained only if it is bargained for. Genuine affection between individuals is the exception rather than the rule. It would probably be true to say that in capitalist society most people are, in one degree or another, unhappy.

The fact that affection takes the form of commodity undoubtedly plays a significant part in this.

It is clear that no real understanding of social relationships under capitalism is possible unless and until the nature of capitalist commodity production is understood.

The fourth aspect of human behaviour to which attention should be drawn is that of religious activity. Reference to this question has already been made in Chapter Six. It needs, however, to be mentioned further.

Any explanations of religious behaviour — the performance of rituals, the singing of hymns and so on — must of course be the responsibility of any genuine psychology worthy of the name. Yet the empiricist methodology of contemporary psychologists is totally inadequate to provide a scientific explanation of the phenomenon.

Religious behaviour cannot be understood through the medium of the empirical observation of people praying or singing hymns. Neither can it be understood by asking churchgoers to fill in questionnaires and then making a statistical analysis of the answers. For it is only through abstract, theoretical, non-empirical thought that the basis of religious ideas and behaviour can be comprehended.

For Marxists, religion can only be comprehended from an historical standpoint. Its development has to be traced back from the primitive animism of the first forms of human society to the monotheism of feudalism and capitalism. Essentially religion represents an historically developed reflection, in the human mind, of those forces of nature and history over which humanity has no conscious control and about which there is inadequate knowledge. It can be easily understood that people living in the society of primitive tribal communism could understand thunder, lightning, wind and rain only in terms of spirits. It is perhaps less obvious that under capitalism a belief in a supreme supernatural being who can be influenced by prayer and ritual arises, not so much from natural forces but — principally and decisively — from the domination of humanity by the relationships between the commodities we produce. Marx writes that the producers 'own social action takes the form of the action of objects, which rule the producers instead of being ruled by them.'[9] To illustrate this, consider the relationship between gold and oil. Both of these are produced by human individuals working in co-operation. Yet the relationships between gold and oil, which directly affect the lives of millions of people, are quite independent of the wishes and intentions either of those who produce them or of anyone else. Our lives are dominated by the laws of the market, over which we have no control and which few people are able to comprehend. It is precisely these laws of the market, being responsible for economic crises, mass unemployment, poverty and — ultimately — war, which are personified in the imagination by a supernatural deity.

It follows from the above that in the future world society, in which the producers would have direct control of whatever they produce, religious beliefs will disappear. This is because relationships between producers would be plain for all to see. There would be no social forces to personify in the imagination as a supernatural being. Marx writes:

> The religious reflex of the real world can . . . only . . . finally vanish, when the practical relations of everyday life offer to man none but perfectly intelligible and reasonable relations with regard to his fellow man and to nature.'[10]

Of course, the question of why certain individuals are religious while others are not has to be answered by a concrete study of the life-activity of the individuals concerned. But such a study can only be effective if there is a theoretical understanding of religious beliefs as such.

To conclude these brief remarks about religious behaviour, it can be stated that few aspects of human behaviour and thinking reveal so clearly the inadequacy of empirical methods in psychology.

The fifth point to be made concerns the basic contradiction to be found in capitalist society, namely the conflict between the productive forces and the relations of production. It will be recalled that the term 'productive forces' refers to the overall ability of humanity to create its own conditions of life.

Under capitalism, the relations of production are those of capitalists and wage-workers. The former own the means of production such as factories, machinery and land. The latter own only their ability to work or labour-power which they have to sell on the market in exchange for wages. What above all characterises capitalism today is the fact that the productive forces cannot be fully and properly used to produce what is needed by humanity as a whole. The periodic wars that are inherent in capitalism lead to the widespread destruction of productive forces. Perhaps more importantly, the periodic economic crises that are just as endemic to capitalism as wars hold back the productive forces from producing worldwide abundance for all. The abundance has of course been in principle possible for many decades, but never more so than in the present era of computer technology.

The conflict between the productive forces and the relations of production is revealed with great clarity in formerly heavily industrialised countries such as Britain. Here capitalism has closed down industry on a massive scale while millions are unemployed. The unemployed, who represent part of the productive forces just as much as the industrial concerns that have been closed down, would in principle be quite capable of working in industry to produce in abundance what humanity requires. But the contemporary capitalist relations of production prevent this.

It is within the above context that much of the widespread demoralisation and frustration of today can be explained. Just as every element in a system must carry within it and reflect the system as a whole, so individuals, living in capitalist society must reflect the basic contradiction of the socio-economic system. For most people, the contradiction finds its reflection in their being prevented from doing what they are fully capable of doing. The fact must be faced that the upbringing of the great majority of the population provides them with skills and abilities which they find themselves unable — or at least partially unable — to use. The skilled worker whose factory closes down — as thousands of factories have — and who cannot find alternative employment is a case in point. So is the school-leaver who possesses the ability and willingness to work but who cannot find a job. On top of this there are countless millions throughout the world who are doing jobs in which their capacities and potentials are not being fully utilised. The frustrations and demoralisations, manifested in such anti-social behaviours as drug-taking, hooliganism and vandalism, can be at least partially explained as a direct reflection of the basic contradiction of capitalism. They certainly cannot be explained by any tendencies to 'adapt' or 'adjust' to the environment.

A further aspect of human thought and behaviour which cannot be understood unless human society in its historical development is understood is that of the alienation of thought which occurs under capitalism.

As has been stated in the previous chapter, the term 'alienation' has been — and still is — used very widely. In the Marxist sense the term, generally speaking, refers to the alienation of the producers from what they produce. This implies that, through the laws of the market, objects that are produced 'rule the producers instead of being ruled by them'.

It is in this general context that the alienation of thought has to be considered. The term 'alienation of thought' implies that the thought of individuals often prevents them from behaving appropriately in given situations. In other words, instead of using thought to analyse a situation and carry out necessary actions, individuals are dominated by their own thought. Extreme examples are the delusions of psychiatric patients and religious beliefs. The latter are, of course, extremely widespread. Many behaviours of individuals are dominated by a supernatural being the existence of whom depends solely on the imagination. In the past (even before capitalism in fact) people have allowed themselves to be burned at the stake because they have been dominated by their own thoughts and beliefs. The personality theorist Sullivan, briefly discussed in the previous chapter, has pointed out that a rigid self-concept, that is a person's ideas about himself or herself, represents a barrier to favourable changes in personality.[11] In other words many individuals tend to be dominated by the ideas they have about themselves rather than by objective situations requiring carefully considered action.

The question of the domination of individuals by their own thought is of course an important question for the discipline of psychology. Much research needs to be done. Although alienation, in the strict sense of the term, is characteristic of capitalism alone, the alienation of thought which occurs under capitalism was no doubt also a feature of the preceding feudal and slave societies. It can be related to the development of idealist philosophy from Plato onwards.

From the Marxist standpoint, idealist philosophy, which implies a belief that the objective, material world is simply a projection of thought, has a definite historical origin. This was the objective division of labour (characteristic of all forms of class society) between mental and manual labour. In slave society the slave owners or their representatives thought what the slaves should do and then made the slaves actually do it. In other words the slave owners or their representatives did the mental work while the slaves did the manual work. This division between mental and manual labour led to the illusion — still prevalent today — that, from the standpoint of the survival of the human species, thinking was more important than doing. From the materialist philosophical standpoint, of course, we exist by practical activity in a world which has objective existence independently of our consciousness or will. Furthermore, it is objective practical activity which leads to the development of thought. The history of the human race has primarily depended — and still primarily depends — on the actions of men and women rather than on their thought. Those who fail to realise this are always in danger of regarding their own ideas as more important than they actually are. They will thus allow themselves to be dominated by thought rather than allow their thought to guide their objective behaviour effectively in objective situations which force them to undertake practical activity.

The relation between the development of idealist philosophy and the degree of alienation of thought under capitalism is a topic for future research. A good starting point would be an essay by Marx on the subject.[12] However, it is already clear that the very posing of the question of the relationship between individuals and their own thought must involve a consideration of the relation of the development of thought to human history.

One extremely important aspect of human thought and behaviour of which brief mention now needs to be made is that of art, music and literature. The discipline of psychology has of course to answer the question of why people paint, listen to music, read literature and so on. This is an area in which the present author does not feel competent to make any really positive contribution. All that can be done here is to indicate how, from the Marxist standpoint, the question should be approached.[13]

There can of course be no understanding of music, art and literature unless and until human society and its historical development is understood. As has been pointed out in Chapter Two, the basis of human society is production and the relations of production. Upon this basis arises society's ideological, political and social superstructure. The function of this superstructure, from the standpoint of the survival of the species, is to maintain intact the relations of production when they enable the productive forces to develop. When the productive forces have developed to a point at which the existing relations of production become a barrier to their further development, the function of the superstructure is to replace the existing relations with those that enable the development of production to continue unhindered.

From the Marxist standpoint, art, music and literature form an inseparable part of the superstructural aspects of society. Their function is a part of that of the superstructure as a whole. However, it needs to be stressed that society's total superstructure has a certain relative independence from its base. The relations of production and their conflict with the development of the productive forces find their reflection only indirectly in the superstructure. This is especially true of art, music and literature. However, any psychological understanding of why humanity needs these forms of culture must take as its starting point an understanding of the nature of human society's historical development as a whole.

It is clear that the conventional empirical approach is quite inadequate. An understanding of the social role of art, music and literature cannot be reached by empirical observations of, say, people enjoying music or by questionnaires designed to investigate possible correlations between childhood deprivations and an appreciation of literature. It is only through the theoretical understanding that human history constitutes an extension of natural history that the problem can begin to be understood.

It is hoped that the above examples have shown how essential it is, from the standpoint of a genuinely scientific psychology, to take as a starting point an understanding of the development and history of the human race.

Further applications of the principles outlined in preceding chapters remain to be considered.

The first of these is that of the unity and integrity of life-activity. While this may not have been referred to directly in previous chapters it can certainly be inferred from Chapters Seven and Eight. Especially relevant is Piaget's conception of 'organisation' which implies a tendency for the mind to exist as an organised and integrated whole.

It is characteristic of many contemporary psychologists and psychiatrists that, when evaluating individuals, they take as a starting point the individual's ideas, values and feelings. They do not start from objective life-activity. And yet, as has been shown in Chapter Eight, there must exist a dialectical relationship between what individuals think and feel on the one hand and what practical activity they engage in on the other.

Any psychological evaluation must of course seriously consider the subjective states of those who have to be evaluated. Yet this by itself is inadequate for any really thorough understanding of the individuals concerned. For all subjective states must ultimately reflect those objective social situations which force individuals to undertake social actions.[14] Any serious evaluation must therefore include answers to the questions of what social situations the individuals concerned have had to confront.[15] Of exceptional importance is the question of how the individuals concerned obtain a livelihood. Here it is necessary to reiterate what should be obvious but which is often overlooked. This is that before people can enjoy sports or music, get married and raise children, engage in physical assaults on others or go mad they first of all have to obtain food and shelter. Further, owing to the essentially unified and integrated nature of life-activity the ways in which individuals are forced to act in order to obtain food and shelter will at least heavily influence — directly or indirectly — all other aspects of their lives.

There is, of course, a limited number of ways in which adults and adolescents who have left home can obtain a livelihood. They can obtain employment, be dependent on others (such as housewives who do not go out to work themselves), be dependent on the state (social security), live in institutions (prisons, hospitals, old people homes) and so on. All other aspects of life-activity have to be understood within the context of these various ways of obtaining a livelihood. Although what has just been said may appear to be a commonplace observation, it has to be recognised that many psychiatrists and psychologists conclude clinical interviews simply by stating that the interviewee 'suffers' from say, a 'personality disorder' or 'psychopathic tendencies'. The actions the person has to undertake in order to obtain a livelihood and the social situations that arise therefrom are not given the importance they deserve or, in some cases, are ignored altogether. It is important to realise, however, that without knowledge of how individuals obtain the bare necessities of life there can be no understanding of their life-activity and hence of their subjective states.

Any consideration of the unity and integrity of life-activity poses the vitally important psychological question of how and to what extent the personality characteristics (the term 'minds' can just as well be used) of individuals can be changed.

From the Marxist standpoint, any significant change brought about in individuals must primarily imply a change in life-activity. This is of course because the thoughts, feelings, motives and goals of individuals at any given time must represent moments, reflections and manifestations of their total life-activity — or at least of its most significant aspects. However, this is not understood by the majority of contemporary psychologists.

There are two contemporary approaches to the changing of personality characteristics. The first involves attempts to change individuals directly, that is without changing their life-activity. This implies a belief that changes in life-activity represent a result rather than a cause of changes in personality characteristics. In other words it is assumed that personality characteristics have to be changed before life-activity can change. The second approach is that which involves attempts to change individuals through the changing of their respective environments. It is necessary to consider these two approaches in turn.

The first approach includes direct medical intervention. This implies the changing of individuals by means of the administration of drugs, electro-convulsive therapy (ECT), brain surgery or other physical methods. Such methods do of course cause changes in personality. Usually, at least in the long run, they lead to personality deterioration.

Far more important, however, from the standpoint of the present discussion, are attempts to change individuals by means of verbal interactions. The most outstanding example of this is that of orthodox Freudian psychoanalytic treatment. This involves verbal interactions between patient and analyst. The task of the latter is to explain to the patient the nature of the Oedipus complex and to bring about an abreaction (a release of emotional feelings) about the complex. The patient is thereby alleged to be fundamentally changed psychologically. Psychotherapists other than Freudians also believe that their patients can be changed, either individually or in groups, simply by verbal interactions in a therapeutic situation.

There is no doubt that individuals can, at least to a certain extent, be changed through the medium of conventional individual or group psychotherapy. Simple misunderstandings that lead to problems can be cleared up. Feelings of guilt about sexual or other matters can be reduced through reassurance. There are, of course, relatively exceptional cases of some aspects of peoples' lives being radically changed through purely verbal means. Some alcoholics can be verbally persuaded to give up drink. Probably the most dramatic examples are those of religious conversion.

The importance of the effect of presenting individuals with new ideas by means of the spoken or written word cannot of course be ignored. The very fact that human thought is simultaneously individual and social must imply that the thought of individuals must — at least potentially — be constantly changing as they absorb new ideas from others. It would therefore be senseless to deny that at least some forms of psychotherapy do lead to positive results. But the real benefit from psychotherapy comes — it is hereby suggested — not from the therapy as such but from the practical suggestions that the therapist makes about actually changing the patient's life-activity.[16]

Very relevant to this discussion is the subject matter of Chapter Eight. Here the relationship between practical activity and personality characteristics, or between thinking and doing, was outlined. It was pointed out that, in the long run, it was practical activity rather than existing personality characteristics that was more important for the psychological development of individuals. Some examples would serve as a useful reminder. A child going to school for the first time will engage in such activity that will cause him or her to change and develop in various ways. This is especially true of only children. The personality characteristics of people going to prison for the first time will change, usually unfavourably, owing to the new forms of activity in which they have to engage in coping with their new surroundings. Women who become mothers for the first time will change and develop in all sorts of ways in coping with the new situation. Many further examples could be given.

Thus it becomes clear that, whatever merits psychotherapy may have — and it undoubtedly has some — there can be no real substitute for the changing of practical life-activity if the psychological characteristics of individuals are to be changed.

The second approach of contemporary psychology to the question of the changing of behaviour now has to be discussed. This involves attempts to change individuals through the manipulation of their respective environments. These attempts are exemplified by the work of Skinner and of Eysenck — both mentioned in the previous chapter. A whole series of techniques — collectively known as behaviour therapy — has been developed.

Broadly speaking, the above term implies the use of both operant (Skinner) and classical (Pavlov) conditioning. The rationale underlying it is the belief that many neurotic and other undesirable behaviours are due to one or other form of conditioning — or to a failure of the conditioning processes to occur.

There can be no doubt that conditioning does occur in human individuals. When hungry we salivate at the sound and sight of food being prepared just as did Pavlov's dogs. There can also be no doubt that a knowledge of conditioning can be used to bring about favourable changes in behaviour. As an example, consider an apparatus designed to stop bedwetting. This involves an electric circuit which rings a bell. Electrical contacts are separated by a sheet of gauze. When urine penetrates the gauze the electric circuit is completed. This causes the bell to be rung. Through classical conditioning the subject learns to associate feelings of bladder tension with waking up. In other words, bladder tension becomes a conditioned stimulus which evokes the conditioned response of waking up. A further example is a technique sometimes used by dentists to avert — or at least minimise — the fear of treatment often shown by young children. Before children are old enough to require treatment they are brought into the dental surgery, sat in the chair and given a toy to play with. When they are relaxed enough the dentist lets the children hear the sound of his drill. Through conditioning, the sound of the drill, the dentist himself and the surgery as a whole become associated with feelings of pleasure rather than of apprehension.

Although techniques such as those just described can certainly be successful, great caution should be used when evaluating some of the more extravagant claims made by certain behaviour therapists. These include the claim that severely neurotic behaviour is both caused and can be cured by processes of conditioning.[17] The view is expressed that, for example, the acquisition of phobias (unnatural fears) result solely from conditioning. Take as an example agoraphobia (a fear of open spaces), which often prevents sufferers from leaving their homes. This is held to result from an unpleasant event occurring in an open space. Such a view is of course totally mechanical. It starts from the basic premise that both individuals and their respective environments are objects which interact in a manner determined by their internal structures. It has to be rejected for two related reasons. First, human individuals are not the passive recipients of environmental pressures, but rather makers of history possessing the conscious ability to view their own activity objectively and to master their own destiny (of course within the limits of objective situations). Second, since human life-activity constitutes a coherent and integrated whole, any significant aspect of it like a severe phobia cannot but be a manifestation of the sufferers' present life-activity taken as a whole — or at least the most significant aspects of it. Although the actual form taken by a phobia may result from a conditioning situation (such as an unpleasant event in an open space), it is reasonable to suppose that phobias such as that given in the above example serve the purpose of preventing the sufferers from facing up to what to them represents an unendurable social situation. From the standpoint of the present author, phobias and other forms of 'mental illness' result from what are termed 'double-bind' situations in which individuals are forced to take action and in which all possible courses of action appear to lead to equally unpleasant consequences.[18]

Any consideration of phobias or of other forms of 'mental illness' must start from the assumption that human beings exist primarily by means of practical activity rather than by thinking and feeling. From the standpoint of the biological and historical evolution of the human species thinking and feeling are for doing rather than vice versa. Feelings such as phobias, therefore, have to be regarded not as mechanical imprints of the environment on the individual, but as manifestations of objective life-activity.

The mechanical view of human beings is further reflected in the attitude of some leading proponents of behaviour therapy that homosexuality can be explained in terms of operant (Skinnerian) conditioning. The former arises — it is asserted — because chance sexual encounters are reinforced by orgasm. It is also asserted the homosexuality can be 'cured' by what is termed 'aversion therapy' (a form of behaviour therapy). As an example, homosexual men are given an emetic. When they feel sick, they are shown photographs of other men who are naked. It is held that, through classical conditioning, the thought of naked men will be associated with feelings of nausea. Their homosexuality will thereby be 'cured'.[19] It needs to be remarked that it would be hard to find a better example of the way in which psychologists regard human individuals as machines.

It is not hard to understand that sexual behaviour is extremely difficult to separate from other social relationships which are not sexual. In fact, it is sexual relationships which demonstrate clearly that human life-activity is guided by the basic principle that 'the whole is greater than the sum of its parts'. Perhaps the clearest example is that of prostitution. The sexual relationships between a prostitute and her clients is inextricably linked to their financial relationships. The sexual relations between husbands and their wives cannot be separated from other, non-sexual relationships such as those involved in the rearing of children, financial arrangements, social status and so forth. Thus the sexual behaviour of individuals cannot be understood outside other aspects of their lives — or at least the main ones. Homosexuality is thus to be comprehended, not as a result of mechanical interactions, but in the context of numerous forms of social and hence historical relationships.[20]

It is of course possible that, on occasions, behaviour therapy can lead to beneficial results, just as can nearly all forms of psychotherapy. Before actually undergoing behaviour therapy, the patient usually discusses aspects of his or her life with the therapist. If this discussion should lead to actual changes in everyday live-activity, then the neurotic symptoms may disappear. However, it is important to note that, if beneficial changes do occur, this at least is mainly due to changes in life-activity rather than in the behaviour therapy as such.[21]

From the preceding few paragraphs, it becomes clear that any outlook that starts from the conception of the mechanical interactions of individuals with their respective environments is fundamentally false. For to change individuals — at least beyond a certain point — it is necessary to change their practical life-activity. This is the basic lesson to be learned from any scientific evaluation both of psychotherapy and behaviour therapy.

One final point remains to be made to conclude this section of the present chapter. This concerns the extent to which the personality characteristics of human individuals can be changed.

Generally speaking, there are three factors to be considered. First, there is the practical life-activity itself which must be changed if personality characteristics are to be changed. Second, there is the length of time during which the new life-activity takes place. Third, there is the age of the individual concerned.

In regard to this third point, it will be recalled from Chapter Seven that all biological matter contains two opposed properties — to undergo change in the course of and as a result of practical activity and to conserve intact its own functioning. As a general rule, the older one gets the more the tendency to conserve intact one's own functioning comes to predominate and consequently the ability to change decreases. It is therefore possible to produce a general formula for the changing of personality characteristics:

$$\frac{\text{Change in practical life-activity X Time}}{\text{Age}}$$

There are a number of good reasons why the above formula cannot be regarded as being as precise as those in some other disciplines, for example physics. The decline in the ability to change with age is probably not uniform and varies from individual to individual. Likewise the length of time during which changes take place in practical life-activity is unlikely to be reflected uniformly in changes in personality characteristics. Other objections could no doubt be made. However, as a general guide to the problem — but no more — the above formula is put forward for consideration.

The penultimate application of the principles outlined in previous chapters concerns what is termed the 'nature versus nurture' or 'heredity versus environment' controversy.

This is a controversy which has been fought, with great bitterness on both sides, for a number of decades. Participants on both sides of the dispute all take the standpoint of mechanics. As do most other contemporary psychologists, they conceive of behaviour as the result of the mechanical interaction of bodies. It is necessary to show, therefore, that the nature versus nurture controversy is just as meaningless as is the so-called mind-body problem. (see below).

Traditionally, the nature versus nurture controversy has centred on the question of intelligence. I.Q. score (the score obtained on intelligence tests) has been and still is held, by many influential figures, to be largely dependent on the genes. Thus Burt, who for many years was regarded as the father figure of British educational psychology and who has been one of the few psychologists to receive a knighthood, states categorically that: '. . . differences in intelligence . . . result from differences in genetic constitution (and) they are to a large and measurable extent transmitted from father to son.[22] As has already been noted in Chapter Four, a more modern psychologist, Jensen, expresses similar views: 'individual differences in intelligence — that is, I.Q. — are predominantly attributable to genetic differences. . . .'[23]

An I.Q. score can undoubtedly be used to estimate some of an individual's abilities and to predict future performance. Thus those with high I.Q. scores are more likely to be able to cope with an university degree course than are those with low scores. However, what an I.Q. score actually measures (apart from the ability and motivation to perform well on intelligence tests) is a matter of great uncertainty. Indeed, the very concept of 'intelligence' is extremely vague and it is doubtful if future psychologists will regard it as meaningful.[24] However, for the purpose of the present exposition it will be necessary to examine the question of how a child develops the ability to obtain an I.Q. score.

Very relevant to this question is the dialectical relationship between the individual and the social. All thought, it has been stressed previously, is simultaneously unique and individual on the one hand and social and historical on the other. There can never be, therefore, individual thought arising from an individual's genes. The rhetorical question has to be asked: if a baby born of parents both with high I.Q. scores was abandoned early in life to become a feral child, would he or she grow up possessing the ability to obtain a high I.Q. score? Or if he or she were to be born blind and deaf-mute and left untrained? To pose the question is to answer it. There is not, and there can never be, an inherited I.Q. score. All items on any intelligence tests are tests of skills learned through the means and media of historically developed social relationships. Quite apart from anything else, no intelligence test can be administered without the use of language, which is the product of history rather than of genes and brains.

There is, of course, an important distinction to be made between an innate ability to perform well on intelligence tests and an innate ability to learn to do so. Of course, children born with brains that are physically grossly defective are unlikely — at least under relatively normal conditions — to learn to perform well. If pressed, most psychologists who insist on the existence of an inherited I.Q. score would probably agree that at least a certain amount of environmental stimulation is necessary to develop innate potential. The principal argument in the 'nature versus nurture' controversy is therefore that of how much of an I.Q. score can be attributed to genetic and how much to environmental factors. As has been stated above, important figures in psychology like Burt and Jensen have maintained that I.Q. score is very largely attributable to genes.

It is necessary to re-emphasise that the above viewpoint is essentially that of mechanics. I.Q. score is conceptualised as the product of the mechanical interaction between two bodies. The form of this interaction is determined by the internal structure of the bodies themselves. In other words the child, largely dependent on the physical structure of his or her genetic constitution, acts on the environment. In turn the environment, dependent on its structure, acts on the child.[25]

It is also necessary to re-emphasise that human individuals are not machines. As has already been pointed out in Chapter Six, the behaviour of all machines — including the most sophisticated computers — is at least ultimately determined by fixed and rigid rules *which constitute a part of their internal structure* and hence determine their interaction with other mechanical objects (including their respective environments). In contrast to machines, human individuals, being the products of history, thereby possess the conscious ability to create, in the imagination, their own rules. It is these rules, derived from historically developed means and media (language, concepts, values etc.) which will determine at least the most significant aspects of their behaviour rather than any innate (genetic) structure. Further, it is through the conscious mastery of their respective environments that they became what they are. This is how the ability to perform intelligence tests — as well as other abilities and personality characteristics — develop.

The question that now has to be answered is that of how a child's I.Q. score can be raised to a maximum. Of course, to acquire a high I.Q. score it is necessary to possess a physically intact and well-functioning brain. It is also necessary to have favourable environmental conditions. No child will develop a high I.Q. if he or she is brought up in a grossly deprived environment. (Let it be recalled that there have been not a few instances of children being locked away in isolation by mentally deranged or sub-normal parents). But to make this a starting point is to avoid the really important issues.

The vitally necessary starting point in any consideration of the problem is that of individual life-activity. For it is only in and through life-activity that individuals became what they are. It is within this context that the effect of the environment has to be considered.

Human abilities do not represent passive responses to environmental pressures. This being so, the development of a child's ability to obtain an I.Q. score cannot arise from an environment as such. Rather, what is important is what the child actually does within the context of any given environment. The environment can be an objective factor in the development of abilities, therefore, only to the extent that it causes individuals to undertake practical activity.

Similarly, it is only within the context of life-activity that the relevance of genetic constitution can be understood. There are many anatomical and physiological factors of at least partial genetic origin[26] which influence the sort of activity which the young child is able to undertake. Examples are proneness to fatigue, lability of the autonomic nervous system, limitation of span of attention and hyperactivity. Numerous further examples could be given. Since each individual (with the exception of identical twins) possesses an unique genetic constitution it follows that there must be wide differences in the abilities of young children to carry out certain activities under definite conditions. Since abilities develop through activity this alone would account for differences in the ability to obtain high I.Q. scores.

The real question that has to be asked by psychologists is, therefore, not that of how much of an I.Q. score can be attributed to heredity and how much to environment. Rather, the question to be asked is that of: What type of activities should each (genetically unique) individual undertake in order to boost his or her I.Q. score to the maximum? For it is clear that there are all sorts of activities which might increase the I.Q. score of some children but not that of others. Further, if a child cannot effectively perform some of the activities carried out by most other children, this need not necessarily imply that he or she is incapable of carrying out other activities that would result in a growth of I.Q. The same principle of course applies to mental abilities other than those involved in intelligence tests.

The main 'evidence' put forward by the proponents of 'inherited I.Q. score' has involved a study of twins.[27] The most widely known of these studies involve a comparison of identical or monozygotic (MZ) twins (possessing identical genes) with same-sex fraternal or dizygotic (DZ) twins (possessing different genes). It has been found that MZ twins raised apart tend to resemble each other more closely in I.Q. score than do same-sex DZ twins raised together. This finding has been widely claimed to prove the existence of an 'inherited I.Q. score'. At first sight this claim might appear to have some validity. It therefore deserves brief comment.

Any interpretation of the above findings that concludes that there exists an 'inherited I.Q. score' involves a fundamentally false assumption. This is that any 'environment' (in which twins are 'raised apart' or 'raised together') will influence the psychological development of all individuals in a similar way. Yet, as has already been noted above, since individuals are not the passive products of environmental pressures, the development of abilities depends not so much on the environment as such. Rather it depends on what activities children undertake within the framework of the given environment. Further, what children do within the framework of a given environment will be partially determined by their own genetic constitution. The examples of genetically determined anatomical and physiological differences given above are very relevant here. If a MZ twin suffers from, say, genetically caused proneness to fatigue or hyperactivity, his or her twin, even if raised in a different environment, will encounter similar difficulties in undertaking various forms of activity. On the other hand, if a DZ twin suffers from proneness to fatigue or from hyperactivity, his or her same sex twin, who may be raised in what appears to be the same environment, need not necessarily suffer from the same manifestation of genetic factors. The two DZ twins may thus be unable to undertake the same forms of activity and thus their I.Q. scores may be different.

To look at the matter in another way, it is necessary to recall that individual life-activity takes place within the framework of social relationships. Further, the genetic constitution of individuals will, in part, determine the type of social relationships into which they enter. Take the case of genetically determined ugliness. The fact has to be faced that ugly children are, on the whole, socially disadvantaged. They do not make friends easily and are teased and bullied. In contrast children who, by virtue of their genes, are good-looking, enter into pleasant social relationships far more easily. In environments which superficially appear to be the same — like a school or a family setting — the life-activities of children who are ugly will differ from those of children who are good-looking.

This may well cause their learned abilities to differ. The relevance of this to twin studies becomes obvious. If one MZ twin is ugly, the other will be ugly. Even if they are raised apart, they are both likely to encounter the same sort of difficulties and hence their respective life-activities may in many respects be similar. Conversely, if one DZ twin is ugly his or her twin may well be good-looking. Even if they are raised together, their respective life-activities may in some respects be very different.[28]

All that twin studies have shown, therefore, is what could have already been worked out theoretically. This is that each individual needs to undertake specific forms of activity in order to boost his or her ability to obtain high I.Q. scores (or indeed any other ability). Furthermore, the necessary forms of activity to be undertaken may differ widely from one individual to another.

Of course, it may well be that individuals differ in their genetically determined potential to acquire certain mental abilities. However, it would be very rash indeed to maintain that psychologists are in any way near to showing the way to maximising the potential of children with physically intact and normally functiioning brains. Indeed, there are good reasons for believing that the mental potential of at least the great majority of children are far from being actualised. The training of blind deaf-mutes up to university post-graduate level is an indication that this is so.[29]

To conclude this section of the present chapter, it is clear that the nature versus nurture (or heredity versus environment) controversy is a meaningless one. It is a controversy only for those who think in terms of mechanical interaction of bodies. For mental abilities do not arise from a mechanical interaction between individuals and their respective environments, but rather from an objective life-activity taking place within the framework of historically developed means and media.[30]

Finally, a brief consideration of the so-called 'mind-body problem' is called for. From a Marxist standpoint, there is no problem at all. Rather it is a pseudo-problem, which can arise only in the minds of those who consider thought to result from the mechanical interaction of bodies.

The 'problem' was first raised in a clear and unambiguous way by René Descartes in the course of showing that thought could not be understood in terms of mechanics. In the form in which Descartes raised it, thought had to be either the product of the material brain or of a non-material soul. Some 300 years later, modern psychology is really no closer to a solution to the 'problem'. A contemporary theorist states: 'The mind-body problem remains unresolved at present'[31] and apparently holds out no hope of a solution. Further:

> Descartes brought cognitive processes into the realm of the sciences, and he planted the mechanistic seed that has blossomed so fully in contemporary models of cognition. . . . Yet Descartes did not go all the way in his mechanism. . . . The view that humans have both a mechanistic body and a rational non-physical soul is called mind-body dualism. . . . This dualistic outlook has had a strong impact on philosophy and theology and has worked its way into our legal and government institutions.[32]

As has already been pointed out in Chapter Six, the human mind represents a form taken by the world external to the brain. It is a form of the external world aspects of which are acted upon, experienced, thought about and remembered by the separate person. The activity of the brain can only represent a form taken by the mind. It can never be the mind itself. (Very relevant to this question is that of the relationship between subjective and objective. This has also been discussed in Chapter Six.) It has also pointed out in Chapter Six that the brain can never be the basis of thought (mind). Although the physical existence of the brain is absolutely necessary for thought, both the former and the latter are interdependent. For no truly human individual [33] can survive physically without thought. It follows that the basis both of thought and of the body (brain) is the life-activity of individuals — life-activity continually co-ordinated with that of others in historically developed social situations.

Once it is recognised that thought and the mind represent a manifestation of life-activity, the content of which is history, then it becomes clear that the 'mind-body problem' is a pseudo-problem. It is a problem only for those who think in terms of the mechanical interaction of bodies. The individual body (brain) is conceptualised as interacting with similar bodies, the forms of interaction being determined by the internal structure of the bodies. With such an outmoded and false outlook it is no wonder that modern psychologists consider that the mind-body 'problem' should 'remain unresolved at present.'

In conclusion, the purpose of this chapter has been to indicate some of the ways in which the principles outlined in preceding chapters can be used to achieve a better understanding of various aspects of human thought and behaviour. Some sections of the chapter may well require future elaboration and modification. Moreover, the list of topics mentioned above could well be significantly enlarged. (No doubt a subject for a future book). However, enough has been said to indicate how a Marxist approach can both enrich and develop the discipline of psychology.

NOTES TO CHAPTER ELEVEN

1. See Chapter 4, Note 15.
2. See Chapter 4, Note 24.
3. Any attempt to build socialist societies on a purely national basis are necessarily doomed to failure — witness the economic and social crises now developing in the former U.S.S.R. and China.
4. The anthropologist Eleanor Burke Leacock writes: 'The significant point . . . is that the household was communal . . . the economy did not involve the dependence of the wife and children on the husband . . . in hunter-gatherer societies (people) either shared large tepees or other such shelters in adverse climates, or might simply group together in separate wickiups or lean-tos in tropical or desert areas. The children in a real sense belonged to the group as a whole; an orphaned child suffered a personal loss, but was never without a family. Women did not have to put up with personal injuries from men in outbursts of personal anger for fear of economic privation for themselves or their children.' (Introduction to Engels, F. *The Origin of the Family, Private Property and the State*. Lawrence and Wishart, 1972, p. 33.)
5. See Note 4 above. Although some modern Marxists have reservations (discussion of which is outside the scope of this book) about certain aspects of this work, it still provides a good general guide to the question of the nature of the family.
6. It should perhaps be noted that, in an inverted and distorted manner, the principle of direct assistance being given to mothers is shown today in the lives of the rich. Nannies and nursemaids take over much of the mother's duties while as soon as they are old enough children are sent to boarding schools.

7. It was one of the achievements of Marx to show, in *Capital* and other works, that a further essential feature of capitalism was the transformation of labour-power, or the ability to work, into a commodity. Those who themselves lacked the ability to produce commodities, that is proletarians, had to sell their labour-power to an employer in return for money (wages).

8. This view of social relationships has in fact already been put forward by the social psychologists Thibaut and Kelly. See Kelly, H. and Thibaut, J. *Interpersonal Relations: A Theory of Interdependence.* Wiley, 1978. It is indeed a great pity that this work has not been developed further.

9. Marx *Capital* Vol.1. FLPH, 1959, p. 75.

10. *Ibid.* p. 75.

11. See Chapter 10, Note 8.

12. See Marx 'Critique of Hegelian Philosophy' in *Economic and Philosophical Manuscripts.* International Publishers, 1964.

13. Probably the greatest barrier to a genuine Marxist approach to art and literature has been the so-called 'socialist realism' imposed on writers and artists during the Stalin era. This and other factors have combined to hold back studies which are urgently needed. However, the following works can be recommended: Plekhanov, G. *Art and Social Life.* Lawrence and Wishart, 1974; Slaughter, C. *Marxism, Ideology and Literature.* Macmillan, 1980; Trotsky, L. *Literature and Revolution.* Bookmarks, 1991.

14. The term 'ultimately' is used here because, of course, objective physiological brain changes such as those induced by tumours or drug abuse can alter subjective states. It is important to note, however, that physiological changes can only alter the form taken by the content of thought. In turn, the content of thought can only but represent a form of the objective, material world as it is experienced and acted upon by the individual. See Chapter Seven.

15. It has been noted in Chapter Eight that although it is thought that guides and directs the most significant aspects of behaviour, it is those aspects of the situation which compel individuals to action that are decisive in psychological development and change.

16. It is the belief of the present author that all forms of psychotherapy, including Freudian and Jungian analysis, can lead to beneficial changes. This is first, because the therapist, despite his or her theoretical beliefs, may make useful suggestions about what the patient should actually do. Second, in the course of posing their own problems to the therapist, the patients in fact pose them more clearly to themselves and hence stand a better chance of resolving them in practice.

17. See, for example, Eysenck, H.J. and Rachman, S. *The Causes and Cures of Neurosis.* Routledge, 1965.

18. The view of 'mental illness' as a manifestation of 'double-bind' situations was first put forward by Bateson and his co-workers (See Bateson et al. 'Towards a Theory of Schizophrenia'. *Behavioural Science.* Vol.1, no. 251, 1956.) R.D. Laing put forward an almost identical view in some of his earlier works (See, for example, Laing, R.D. and Esterson, A. *Sanity, Madness and the Family.* Penguin, 1970.) Miller, Gallanter and Pribram, in their seminal work *Plans and the Structure of Behaviour.* (See Chapter Six, Note 11.) put forward a similar explanation. It needs to be remarked that few psychologists appreciate the implications of the sequence: Objective situation → need to act → thought to decide action → action. In other words they fail to see that the origin of thought lies, not in the head, but in objective situations which force individuals to take action.

19. See, for example, Eysenck and Rachman *op. cit.* Although these methods are now used less frequently in Britain than previously, they are still used in other parts of the world.

20. Homosexuality — like all complex behaviours — is undoubtedly multifactorial in origin. However — it is hereby suggested — the principal factor underlying homosexuality, at least in most cases, is that of difficulty in establishing satisfactory heterosexual relations. Both male and female homosexuals are those whose individual experience has led them to believe that heterosexual intercourse is associated with various undesirable aspects of life. For example, men who associate heterosexual intercourse with the responsibilities of marriage and child-rearing and who, for various reasons, want to avoid the latter, may opt out of these responsibilities by engaging in

homosexuality. (The proportion of male homosexuals who come from broken homes is very high. Clearly many of them will therefore feel that heterosexual relationships may be associated with undesirable consequences.) Similarly, many female homosexuals or lesbians are those whose experience has led them to regard heterosexual intercourse as something associated with various undesirable features of the marriage contract. (As with men, a high proportion of lesbians come from broken homes.) It needs to be re-emphasised that sexual relationships in general cannot be understood outside the context of other social and historically developed relationships. It follows that people who are dissatisfied or unhappy about their own homosexual feelings can best be helped by indirect means, that is by help to readjust the most important aspects of their life-activity so that normal heterosexual behaviour becomes possible.

21. The mechanical outlook of modern psychology is well exemplified by a book actually entitled *Changing Man's Behaviour*. (H.R. Beech. Penguin, 1969.) This work, which is about 100,000 words in length, never once mentions the need for individuals to change their life-activity if they are to change themselves.

22. Burt, C. 'The Evidence for the Concept of Intelligence' in Wiseman, S. (Ed.) *Intelligence and Ability*. Penguin, 1967, p. 279.

23. See Chapter Four, Note 20.

24. From a Marxist standpoint, the concept of intelligence, if meaningful at all, can only be used in a social and historical context. Thus members of primitive hunter-gatherer tribes, some of whom have to exist in extremely harsh environmental conditions (Arctic regions, Kalahari desert and other places) have evolved highly ingenious methods of survival. Within the context of their existence their survival techniques could well be termed the result of intelligent behaviour. Yet members of these tribes would no doubt obtain low scores on conventional tests of intelligence. Conversely, at least most of those in modern cultures who have high I.Q. scores would find it hard to survive if transported to regions such as those inhabited by these tribes.

25. Skinner's model (see Chapter Ten) is relevant here. The rat in a Skinner box, by virtue of its genetic constitution (structure), presses the bar. The environment, also dependent on its structure, rewards or reinforces the rat with food. What might be termed the rat's 'I.Q. score' will reflect the rat's ability to learn to press the bar when hungry.

26. It should be noted that the physical constitution with which we are born is not determined solely by the genes. Also important are inter-uterine factors such as position in the womb, the mother's diet, maternal infections and so on.

27. For a concise outline of these studies see, for example, Kamin, L. *The Science and Politics of I.Q.* Penguin, 1977, Chapters Three and Four.

28. It needs to be noted that analogous studies with twins have been used to support the view that schizophrenia is of genetic origin. It has been shown that if one MZ twin develops schizophrenia the other twin is far more likely to become schizophrenic than would a DZ twin of the same sex. (See, for example, Gottesman, I. and Shields, J. 'Contributions of Twin Studies to Perspectives on Schizophrenia.' in Maher, B. (Ed.) *Progress in Experimental Personality Research*. Academic Press, Vol.1.) But such twin studies no more demonstrate the existence of 'inherited schizophrenia' than they do 'inherited I.Q. score'. All they demonstrate is that people possessing certain genes should avoid stressful social situations. In view of what has already been said about I.Q. scores readers can work out for themselves why this should be so.

29. See Chapter Four, Note 27.

30. An interesting point here is one concerning the actual merit of conventional tests of mental ability. All these tests, of course, tend to be administered just once, the resulting score being held to measure the ability to perform the test. The Russian psychologist Vygotsky, however, proposed that a better way of testing abilities was to test children twice. The first time was in the conventional manner of testing the child alone. After this the child received help to master the ability from an adult or an older child. The test was then administered a second time. The change in the test score thus represented a measurement, not simply of the child's ability to perform the test, but of his or her ability to develop abilities with the help of adults or of older children. (See, for

example, Luria, A.R. *The Role of Speech in the Regulation of Normal and Abnormal Behaviour*. Pergamon Press, 1961, pp. 15-20.) In view of the fact that mental abilities develop within the framework of historically developed social relationships, together with their means and media, this proposal certainly deserves serious consideration.   ·

31. Wessells, M.G. *Cognitive Psychology*. Harper and Row, 1982, p. 11.

32. *Ibid*. p. 11.

33. As compared with, say, those individuals whose brains are so damaged or deformed that they have constantly to be cared for by others.

12

FOUNDATIONS FOR A PSYCHOLOGY OF EVERYDAY LIFE

One of the principal criticisms that can be made of modern psychology is that it has proved unable to provide a set of principles by means of which ordinary men, women and adolescents can at least begin to understand their own behaviour and thinking, together with that of others.

In preceding chapters the criticisms of the main aspects of modern psychology that have been made have been intertwined with alternative approaches. It is now possible to present these alternative approaches in the form of a set of sixteen principles. Together, these principles can form the foundations for what can be referred to as a Psychology of Everyday Life. They are set out below.

(1) Human individuals are a part of society and of its history. Since 'the whole is greater than the sum of its parts', it follows that, for human individuals to be understood, society and its history has to be understood.

(2) Society and its history is the mode of existence of the human race. The human race constitutes a part of nature the material existence of which rests on historically developed culture. In turn, human culture rests primarily on production, that is by the making and use of tools to wrest the necessities of life from nature.

(3) Since the skills of production (together with other necessary skills such as those of child-rearing) are too complex and varied to be transmitted genetically, nature (of which we are a part) had to find a new way to transmit (and to develop) the necessary skills and knowledge from generation to generation. This transmission and development of skills and knowledge takes place through historically developed social relationships, together with their means and media.

(4) Human beings, like all biological organisms, change themselves during and as a result of their own activity. The concept of 'life-activity' (all that an individual actually does) is therefore essential for the development of a genuine psychology of everyday life.

(5) The most significant aspects of an individual's life-activity are forced on him or her by historically developed social relationships (family, school, employment and so on) which have objective existence independently of the individual's consciousness or will.

(6) It is through the life-activity which is forced on individuals that they acquire the necessary skills and knowledge which in turn enables them to recreate and develop the social relations and their means and media which form the basis for the life-activity of succeeding generations.

(7) The basis of each new individual's subjective life or personality — his or her goals, plans, values, attitudes etc. — is not to be found in any innate ability to adapt to the 'social environment' or to 'process information'. Rather it is to be found in his or her own life-activity. In turn, the basis of an individual's life-activity is to be found in his or her social relationships, together with their means and media.

(8) An essential aspect of the human individual's subjective life is consciousness. This implies the ability to look at one's life-activity objectively, from the side, as it were. This ability arises from the co-ordination of the child's activity with that of others. The term also implies the ability to perceive the world in terms of what it could become with human intervention. Just as the term 'life-activity' is essential for the development of a genuine psychology of everyday life, so is that of 'consciousness'.

(9) The possession of consciousness (as defined above) enables human individuals to recreate (and develop) existing social relationships and their means and media. Thus they represent not only the products of history. They are also the makers of history. It follows that history is not made simply by a few individuals. Everyone possessing consciousness participates in the making of history.

(10) It is necessary to distinguish between individual members of the species *Homo sapiens* and those individuals that are truly human. Although every newborn baby represents a member of the species, it is only to the extent that individuals acquire consciousness that they become truly human, that is the products and hence the makers of history. The truly human individual is thus the historical individual, not just a biological organism.

(11) The human individual and society in its historical development represent a dialectical unity of opposites. One is not the other, yet society (social

relations and their means and media) and its history are inseparable from the life-activity of individuals. The content of their thought, feelings, values and so on are simultaneously both unique and individual on the one hand and social and historical on the other. Thus it can be said that the individual is the social and the social is the individual.

(12)While the life-activity of all human individuals constitute a definite part of (the universal of) society and history, the thought, goals, values, etc. of all individuals (i.e., their subjective lives) differ from those of all others because their respective life-activities represent not history as such but the various particular shades and aspects of it which they experience, act upon and think about.

(13)In every individual there exists a dialectical interpenetration of biological and social factors. The most important of these is that of the content and the form of thought. The content of an individual's thought arises from a life-activity which constitutes a part of history. It represents a form taken by the objective world existing outside the individual's brain. In contrast, the form which thought takes is the activity of the brain, or at least of parts of it. It needs to be re-emphasised that, although the brain is essential for thought, the latter can never be produced by the brain as such.

(14)There exists a dialectical relationship between thinking and doing, between abstract thought and practical activity. What individuals can do is limited by the content of their thought. Conversely, the extent to which individuals understand various concepts and categories of thought is limited by their practical activity. Since individuals frequently find themselves in objective situations which require new forms of practical activity, from the standpoint of psychological development it is practical activity which is more important than is thought itself.

(15)It is necessary to reject the 'adaptation' or 'adjustment' model of modern psychology. For two reasons: Firstly, because the possession of consciousness enables individuals to master their environments consciously rather than 'adapt' or 'adjust' to them. Secondly, because the 'social environment' to which individuals are alleged to 'adapt' or 'adjust' can only meaningfully imply society. And society is relationships. Furthermore, relationships cannot be seperated from individuals. This is so because the internal needs, abilities, values etc. of individuals represent an essential aspect of the means and media of all relationships. In other words individuals themselves constitute a definite aspect of any relationships into which they enter. They cannot and never will be able to 'adapt' or 'adjust' to themselves. Likewise, the 'interaction' (with the 'social environment') model must also be rejected. Just as one cannot adapt or adjust to oneself so one cannot interact with oneself.

(16) It is necessary to reject the current mechanical approach to human individuals. This includes the belief that the workings of the human mind resembles those of a computer. The workings of any machine — including the most sophisticated computer — ultimately depends on fixed and rigid sets of rules. In contrast to this, the thought which guides the most significant aspects of human behaviour is governed by mental goals and plans to achieve them. These plans are governed by 'rules' which individuals themselves make up mentally and which they are able, also mentally, to change at will. Computers — however sophisticated — lack the ability to criticise their own programmes. In contrast to this human individuals — possessing consciousness — can view their own life-activity objectively and self-critically. In other words, humans possess the ability to make choices, whereas whatever a computer does is predetermined both by its initial programme and by subsequent input. A related difference is that computers cannot create their own goals. They can only, at best, change their goals in response to predetermined input. In contrast to computers, however, humans can use that creative ability which represents an essential aspect of consciousness to create, in their imaginations, entirely fresh goals.

The above sixteen principles collectively represent an outline of a Marxist attempt to get to grips with the question of individual behaviour and thought. It may well be that they will require future modification and/or addition. But at least it can be said that together they are infinitely superior to the view of modern psychology that the 'mind is a bodily process' and that it arises as a result of separate bodies mechanically adapting to or interacting with similar bodies (the so-called 'social environment').

13

CONCLUSION

The present author is aware that a significant proportion of readers will have had little or no previous acquaintance with the writings of Marx. Although they may agree with many of the author's views about psychology, they may possibly find it difficult fully to appreciate the significance of Marx's world outlook for an understanding of human individuals. It would therefore be appropriate to use this concluding chapter to re-affirm the author's belief that, in order to understand the content of people's lives, to understand 'what a man makes of his life and what life makes of him' it is first of all necessary to understand precisely that which constitutes what is referred to as 'human nature'. Further, it is also necessary to understand why it is that it is precisely Marx who, together with his co-thinkers, has at least laid the scientific basis for such an understanding.

Leaving aside theories of divine creation, it can be said that essentially, for the discipline of psychology, there are two basic and opposed fundamental standpoints. These are first, that of Darwinian (or neo-Darwinian) functionalism and, second, that of Marxism. A brief recapitulation of key aspects of each of these standpoints is necessary.

Darwinian functionalism implies that there is no *qualitative* difference between humans and other higher animals and that 'the difference in mind between man and the higher mammals, great as it is, certainly is one of a degree and not of kind.'[1]

Clearly the above words reflect Darwin's conviction that the human race exists primarily by means of the adaptation of its individual members to their respective environments. Furthermore, they imply that human minds come into existence as adaptive mechanisms. Carrying on this basic assumption, at least the great majority of modern psychologists start from theoretical assumptions involving 'a biological survival model . . . which borrows much from Darwin' and a belief that 'individuals must adapt to the world around them'.[2] From this fundamental standpoint, society can be no more than a 'social environment' to which individuals have to adapt. Further, 'human nature' can be understood simply as the sum total of innate biological needs plus the ability to adapt to this 'social environment'.

In contrast to this, Marxists start from the assumption, now verified by many anthropologists,[3] that the human race *created itself* from an ape-like creature through the making and use of tools. Further, the basis of human life (as distinct from that of other species) is our ability purposefully to create the social conditions of our own existence, primarily through the making and use of tools. The development of this ability constitutes the ultimate basis of human history.

From a Marxist standpoint, the human species is qualitatively different from all other species not only because its existence depends on the making and use of tools. For what is implied by the making and use of tools (a social process) is that, since the skills involved are frequently complex and, moreover, in a relatively continual state of development, they cannot be fixed genetically. The same is true of other essential human activities such as those involved in child-rearing. Therefore nature (of which we are a part) has had — so to speak — to find a way of transmitting such skills from generation to generation in a way which does not involve genetic fixation. Such transmission from generation to generation can take place only through the life-activity of individuals. As has been explained previously, the basis of the life-activity of human individuals is precisely those social relationships into which they have been forced to enter. In turn the life-activities of individuals, by creating and re-creating social relationships, lay the basis for the life-activities of future generations. (The term 'social relationships' of course refers to the ways in which and the means by which individuals co-ordinate their activities with those of others). A further point about which a reminder needs to be made is that the transmission of both skills and social relationships from generation to generation is impossible without the possession of consciousness and creativity as previously defined.[4] For without the ability to think of one's own activity objectively and to view the world with historically developed knowledge of what it could become with human intervention, individuals cannot create the conditions for the life-activities of those in the next generation. This is why, for Marxists, new-born babies of the biological species *Homo sapiens* are not truly human individuals. They only become such to the extent to which they acquire consciousness and creativity.

From the Marxist standpoint, therefore, 'human nature' can never be, as modern psychologists tend to believe, innate biological needs plus the ability to adapt to the 'social environment'. Rather, human nature is the sum total of those social relationships that form the basis of the life-activity of individuals. As Marx himself wrote: 'the human essence is no abstraction inherent in each single individual. . . . In its reality it is the ensemble of the social relations.'[5]

It might of course be objected that the above definition of human nature leaves aside the question of innate biological needs. However, it is necessary to point out that the most significant aspects of the behaviour of individuals are guided by thought. And thought is produced, not by biological activity as such, but the ways in which and the means by which human activities are co-ordinated. Further, it is impossible for human individuals to exist physically outside social relations and their means and media. Individual members of the species who might appear to contradict this general rule, such as feral children or those with grossly deformed or damaged brains, cannot, for reasons already stated, be considered as genuinely human.

What has been said above makes it easier to understand that only a Marxist approach can reveal the true basis of human minds. The two approaches to the human mind must of necessity reflect fundamental differences in theoretical assumptions about the nature of the human race. On the one hand there is the Darwinian, functionalist, anti-Marxist assumption that the human race survives — like other species — primarily through the adaptation of individuals to their respective environments. From this standpoint the basis of the mind is no more than biological adaptation. On the other hand there is the Marxist assumption that the human race survives — as distinct from other species — primarily through historically developed culture based on production and that therefore human history represents an extension of natural history. From this second standpoint the basis of the mind is the ways in which and the means by which human individuals have to co-ordinate their own activity with that of others.

It is thus clear that the anti-Marxist, Darwinian, functionalist approach condemns the discipline of psychology to be no more than a 'collection of specialisms'. Moreover, such an approach renders impossible the elucidation of a set of principles by means of which ordinary men, women and adolescents can at least begin to understand their own thinking and behaviour together with that of others.

From what has been said above — and in preceding chapters — it becomes clear that there are irreconcilable differences between the approach of modern psychology to the thinking and behaviour of individuals and that of Marxists. What is less clear, however, is that these two approaches reflect a far wider difference. This is the difference in approach to what may be termed 'the world as a whole'. The world outlook of Marxism was built — at least in part — on the achievements of German classical philosophy, which culminated in Hegel. It was precisely Hegel who showed that the world (the term 'universe' could just as well be used) constituted an integrated and coherent whole, a whole that exists as much more than the sum of its parts. Furthermore, the world can only exist in a continuous state of development and change. This conception of the world now finds its expression in at least most of the natural sciences. Biologists, for instance, conceptualise species as existing not statically, but as a definite part of evolutionary time. In other words, each species is seen in terms of a definite continuity. Each species has arisen from an earlier and different one. And each species will — at least potentially — form the basis for the origin of others. In addition, the existence of each species is always considered to be dependent upon its relationship with other species existing within a given ecological habitat. What has just been said does not of course imply that biologists and other scientists are necessarily Hegelians or Marxists. But the important point here is that Hegel's basic idea that the world has to be seen as a totality in a constant state of development and change receives continual verification from the findings of modern natural science.

In contrast to this basic outlook stands that of at least most modern psychologists. To understand this it is necessary to return to the question of the objective alienation of individuals under capitalism which has been mentioned in previous chapters. The prevalent view that society is no more than a 'social environment' standing separate and apart from individuals implies a corollary. This is that society itself exists simply as a collection of individuals. Further, it is these individuals who are seen solely as biological organisms which interact with each other. It is believed that, as a result of such interactions, sensory input impinges on the organisms, the brains of which receive 'information' which is 'processed' by the internal structure of their brains. It is in this way that each human mind is allegedly formed as a 'bodily process' constituting one part of 'a human being' who is conceptualised as no more than 'a transmission device for receiving input signals, coding them, and processing them for output'. Here it should be noted that the rejection by psychologists of Hegel's view of the world as an integrated and changing whole is no accident. Like their current assumption that humans should be thought of as machines, their rejection represents the objective alienation of individuals under capitalism.

To return to the philosophical categories of the universal, the individual and the particular, it is clear that the modern anti-Marxist approach renders impossible the essential understanding that the life-activity of each particular individual represents the expression and manifestation of the universal of history — a history which must be understood if the contents of people's lives are to be understood.

It may be concluded that the above difference in world outlook must be reflected in the choice which psychologists have to make: EITHER their subject matter is a collection of 'transmission devices' all mechanically interacting with each other in a manner determined by their internal structure. OR their subject matter is the life-activity of individuals the content of which constitutes a one-sided expression of the total and integrated yet many-faceted historical development of the human race.

It is necessary to reiterate a point made in the introductory chapter. This is that, despite the fact that modern psychology represents no more than a 'collection of specialisms', a number of positive advances have been made. No Marxist, least of all the present author, would wish to deny that this is so. However, it needs to be understood that, since human thought is simultaneously individual and social,[6] the view of modern psychologists that their discipline 'has its roots in biology' condemns it to be one-sided and hence very limited. Quite apart from anything else, the above prevalent view renders impossible any understanding of the real content of people's lives.

It is of course necessary that psychologists should possess a knowledge of human biology. The effects of brain damage on thinking, the role of the endocrine glands in emotion and a host of similar aspects of human biology have to be understood by psychologists. But such factors cannot by themselves form the basis for an understanding of the content of people's lives. It has been one of the principal aims of this book to show that the content of people's lives has to be understood at least primarily in terms of social relationships and their means and media. And these are historical phenomena rather than biological.

It needs to be said that the current view that 'psychology has its roots in biology' does have a further positive aspect. It at least recognises that *human individuals constitute a definite part of nature.* Yet it fails to recognise that — as Marx showed — *human history represents an extension of natural history.* And that therefore the laws of history are natural laws just as are the laws of human biology. It must therefore follow that the content of the life-activity of each and every human individual, which must represent a one-sided aspect of human history, has to be seen as a natural process. It may be concluded that the discipline of psychology needs to have its roots not purely in biology, but equally in history.

This book has been written on the basis of the assumption that a genuinely scientific psychology has to confront two major but closely related tasks. The first of these is to provide an understanding of what constitutes 'human nature'. The second is to establish a set of principles by means of which the content of individual lives can at least begin to be understood. As the title of this book indicates, these tasks cannot be undertaken until the question of the relationship between the individual and society has been clarified. That this is possible is due to the work of Karl Marx. This is the contribution that the Marxist world outlook can make to the discipline of psychology.

NOTES TO CHAPTER THIRTEEN

1. See Chapter 3, Note 1.
2. See Chapter 5, Note 1.
3. See Chapter 2, Notes 5 and 6.
4. See Chapter 4.
5. See Chapter 2, Note 19.
6. See Chapter 5.

Name Index

Subject Index